A FUTURE FOR PEACEKEEPING?

Also by Edward Moxon-Browne

EUROPEAN TERRORISM (*editor*)

NATION, CLASS AND CREED IN NORTHERN IRELAND

POLITICAL CHANGE IN SPAIN

A Future for Peacekeeping?

Edited by

Edward Moxon-Browne
Jean Monnet Chair of European Integration
University of Limerick
Ireland

First published in Great Britain 1998 by
MACMILLAN PRESS LTD
Houndmills, Basingstoke, Hampshire RG21 6XS and London
Companies and representatives throughout the world

A catalogue record for this book is available from the British Library.

ISBN 0–333–71158–0

First published in the United States of America 1998 by
ST. MARTIN'S PRESS, INC.,
Scholarly and Reference Division,
175 Fifth Avenue, New York, N.Y. 10010

ISBN 0–312–17593–0

Library of Congress Cataloging-in-Publication Data
A future for peacekeeping? / edited by Edward Moxon-Browne.
p.   cm.
Includes bibliographical references and index.
ISBN 0–312–17593–0 (cloth)
1. United Nations—Armed Forces.   2. Security, International.
I. Moxon-Browne, Edward.
JX1981.P7F84 1997
341.5'84—dc21   97–8444
                                                   CIP

This book is printed on paper suitable for recycling and made from fully managed and sustained forest sources.

10   9   8   7   6   5   4   3   2   1
07   06   05   04   03   02   01   00   99   98

Printed in Great Britain by
The Ipswich Book Company Ltd
Ipswich, Suffolk

For A.E.A.

Contents

List of Tables

Preface

The origins of this book go back to a conference held at the University of Limerick in June 1995. The conference was entitled 'Peacekeeping in the 1990s' and brought together academic, military, police and civilian experts in the field of UN peacekeeping. The conference marked an important milestone in the evolution of a two-year research project, coordinated by the Initiative on Conflict Resolution and Ethnicity (INCORE) at the University of Ulster, whose principal focus was the training and preparation of both civilian and military peacekeepers in the late 1990s. Earlier in the year, the research team had met in Paris and had benefited from an intensive day of interaction with, among others, Mats Berdal (from the International Institute for Strategic Studies) and Michael Harbottle, a former UN force commander in Cyprus. The chapters by Ryan, Macdonald, Bullion and Fetherston originate in the Limerick conference. The chapter by Heje is a substantially revised version of his contribution to the Final Report of the INCORE project; and the chapters by Adibe, Whitworth and Hammond are revised versions of papers presented at the International Studies Association conference held at San Diego in April 1996. The concluding chapter, by the editor, was prepared for this book.

The rationale for this collection of papers on peacekeeping is the ongoing debate surrounding the appropriate training and preparation for peacekeepers in the post-Cold War era. The debate centres on a number of distinct but related themes, all of which are touched on in this volume: the extent to which the traditional concept of 'peacekeeping' has been replaced by the newer concepts of peace enforcement and peacebuilding; the increase in civilian participation in peacekeeping tasks; the shift away from inter-state towards intra-state conflicts; the increasingly multidimensional and complex character of contemporary peacekeeping operations; and most fundamentally, perhaps, the well-worn question of whether soldiers make the best peacekeepers or are simply the only people who can do the job. The successive chapters of this book form a natural progression that takes the reader from conceptual definitions, through the practical and positive achievements of peacekeeping towards the problems thrown up by negative experiences, and culminating in a more radical critique of the peacekeeping ethos in Chapters 7 and 8.

A basic dichotomy – that between peacekeeping and peace enforcement – is introduced by Heje at the start of the book in a discussion that goes a long way towards clearing some of the semantic undergrowth that so often impedes a lucid analysis. Heje traces the evolution of peace enforcement from its relegation as a species of peacekeeping in *Agenda for Peace* through Berdal's insistence that the term should be kept analytically and operationally distinct from peacekeeping, to the British Army's elaboration of the distinction in the newly coined concept of *Wider Peacekeeping*. This analytical distinction between types of response to discrete levels of 'conflict' is echoed by Ryan in the second chapter where the intrinsically dynamic and evolutionary character of conflict is illustrated in Fisher's 'contingency model' as part of a broader argument in favour of more interchange between conflict studies and the academic literature on peacekeeping. From a practical perspective, both Heje and Ryan posit a more flexible approach to the management of conflict: soldiers have a role to play at certain junctures, but civilians, police units, election supervisors and health workers exemplify the multifaceted approach to maintaining peace that both writers advocate.

Macdonald and Bullion discuss the Irish and Indian contributions to peacekeeping. The two countries have much in common: the experience of being colonized; a neutral stance in foreign policy; and a substantial participation in peacekeeping. Both Irish and Indian troops are viewed as reinforcing the legitimacy of any UN operation because neither country is perceived as having an 'axe to grind' in world affairs. This can cut two ways, however, as Bullion points out with reference to India. While, on the one hand, Indian troops acquitted themselves well in the difficult circumstances of Somalia, there was also a perception that the United States had reneged on its responsibilities and that 'India and other participants were left to pick up the pieces'. Although, and perhaps because, Ireland's participation in UN peacekeeping operations is well known, Macdonald highlights the success of non-UN operations, such as the EC in Russia and the OSCE in Georgia. These novel instruments of regional assistance provide a theme which is taken up later in the book, since the success of these initiatives is predicated on the classic virtues of traditional peacekeeping: impartiality, international cooperation, good organization and a clearly defined mandate.

In the next two chapters, by contrast, Adibe and Hammond look at two of the less successful arenas for peacekeeping: the Lebanon and Somalia. In both cases, the United States was a key player, raising the question once again of whether, and if so to what extent, 'lead-nation' operations can be successful in essentially Third World settings. Although drawing on different sets of evidence, and making no distinction between UN and non-UN operations, both writers see 'lessons to be learnt' in future operations of this kind: external actors should not presume that they know what is best in complex ethnic and religious situations; impartiality should never be compromised and if impartiality cannot be maintained the involvement should be terminated; peacekeepers need special training; not all soldiers make good peacekeepers; soldiers who abuse human rights at home should not be deployed to build a law-based and peaceful society in another country.

In the chapters by Fetherston and Whitworth, we move into a new paradigm: the discussion is no longer about how to make peacekeeping, as it is currently conceived, more effective, but whether the military context of peacekeeping in particular presents us with an insoluble problematic. Inevitably, perhaps, both writers are more concerned with 'host' populations affected by peacekeeping than the 'efficiency' or otherwise of the peacekeeping operation itself. For the first time, the 'gendered' construction of peacekeeping enters the debate. These two writers traverse some of the same territory – the impact of UNTAC on Cambodian society and the murder committed by a Canadian unit in Somalia – but while these two case studies form the focus for Whitworth they are part of a much broader canvas in Fetherston's argument. Both writers arrive at a similar destination, effectively providing the denouement for this volume. Fetherston wonders whether peacekeeping activities can provide a moral antidote to war, or if they simply add to the prestige of armed forces, in their traditional mould, by adding 'peacemaking' to 'warmaking' or, worse still, blurring the distinction between the two. Whitworth concludes in similar vein: 'We need to rethink the automatic response found in most quarters that soldiers make the best peacemakers.'

By way of conclusion, the editor delineates areas of debate that may need to be pursued if some of the questions raised in the earlier chapters are to be answered. This book is intended to take the reader on an intellectual journey starting from the comfortable landscapes of mainstream interpretation, moving towards the rocky terrain of failure and doubt, and ending the journey amid innovative, and sometimes disquieting, analysis that raises questions about the journey itself. Was it worthwhile? Where do we go from here?

List of Contributors

Clement E. Adibe obtained his PhD in political science from Queens University at Kingston, Ontario, Canada, and is currently Assistant Professor of Political Science at DePaul University, Chicago. He was formerly Killam Post-Doctoral Fellow and Assistant Professor at Dalhousie University in Halifax, Nova Scotia, and an International Institutions Fellow at the Center for International Affairs, Harvard, Cambridge, Massachusetts. Dr Adibe recently worked as a researcher for the United Nations Institute for Disarmament Research in Geneva, Switzerland. His publications include *Managing Arms in Peace Processes: Somalia* (Geneva, 1995); 'Weak states and the emerging taxonomy of security in world politics', *Futures*, Vol. 26, No. 5, 1994; 'Africa and global developments in the twenty-first century' (with Timothy M. Shaw), *International Journal*, Vol. 51, No. 1, 1995/96.

A. Betts Fetherston obtained her PhD in Peace Studies from the University of Bradford in England where she is currently a Lecturer in Peace Studies. She was formerly a Visiting Fellow at the Kroc Institute for International Peace Studies at the University of Notre Dame, South Bend, Indiana and a Post-Doctoral Fellow at the Peace Research Center at the Australian National University in Canberra. Dr Fetherston has recently worked as a consultant for the US-based National Research Council's project on Evaluating Peacekeeping Missions. Her publications include *Towards A Theory of United Nations Peacekeeping*, London/New York: Macmillan/St. Martins Press, 1994; 'Overcoming *habitus* in conflict management: UN peacekeeping and warzone ethnography' (with Carolyn Nordstrom), *Peace and Change*, Vol. 20, No. 1, 1995; 'Peacekeeping as peacebuilding: towards a transformative agenda', in L.-A. Broadhead (ed.), *Issues in Peace Research 1995–6*, Bradford: Bradford University Press, 1996.

Alan Bullion is an Associate Lecturer in Politics and European Studies for the Open University in the UK. He is author of *India, Sri Lanka and the Tamil Crisis 1976–1994: An International Perspective*, London: Pinter, 1995, and has recently published articles on South Asian politics in *International Peacekeeping*, *The World Today*, *New Statesman* and *New Times*.

Grant T. Hammond is Professor of International Relations in the Department of Strategy Doctrine and Airpower at the Air War College, the senior service school of the US Air Force at the Air University, Maxwell Air Force Base, Alabama. Prior to his current post, he taught at Rhodes College and was Executive Officer at the Center for International Affairs at Harvard University. His interests lie in recent military history, strategy, airpower and peacekeeping operations. His publications include *Countertrade, Offsets, and Barter in International Political Economy*, London: Pinter, 1990 and 1993, and *Plowshares into Swords: Arms Races in International Politics 1840–1991*, Columbia University of South Carolina Press, 1993, as well as numerous contributions to US Air Force special studies and to edited volumes and journals in the US and UK. He is completing work on a forthcoming book entitled *On Winning and Losing: John Boyd and American Security*.

Claus Heje completed his MA by research from the University of Limerick in 1996. A Danish national, he has also studied in Austria, France and Spain. In 1994–95 he was the Principal Research Assistant at the Irish Peace Institute Research Centre, and carried out much of the research for the military side of the *INCORE Report on the Training and Preparation of Military and Civilian Peacekeepers*. In 1997, he is completing a postgraduate degree in political science at the University of Copenhagen.

Lt-Col. Oliver A.K. Macdonald is Executive Officer and Chief Instructor at the United Nations Training School, Ireland (UNTSI), in the Military College. An Infantry Officer, he served two tours of duty with UNFICYP in Cyprus. He was Operations Officer of the Irish Battalion in UNIFIL in Lebanon. He served with UNTAG in Namibia where he was Military Coordinator for the election operation and was appointed to the Tripartite Integration Commission. He was a member of the EC Task Force in Russia in 1992 and was Chief of Staff of the CSCE Mission to Georgia in 1994. In 1995, he visited UNIFIL, UNTSO and UNDOF in the Middle East and attended the International Peace Academy in Vienna (IPA). He attended the Ecole Supérieure de Guerre Interarmées in Paris and holds a BA (Mod) and MA degree from the University of Dublin (Trinity College).

Edward Moxon-Browne was educated at the University of St Andrews, and then at the University of Pennsylvania where he was a

Thouron Scholar. He has been Jean Monnet Professor of European Integration at the University of Limerick since 1992 and, before that, Reader in Politics at the Queens University of Belfast. He is author of *Nation, Class and Creed in Northern Ireland*, Aldershot: Gower, 1983, and *Political Change in Spain*, Routledge, 1989; and co-author of *The Police, Public Order and the State*, 2nd edn, London: Macmillan, 1993. He has contributed articles to a variety of journals including *Regional Politics and Policy*, *Revista de Estudios Politicos*, *Revue française de civilisation britannique*, *Journal of Political Science*, *Conflict Studies*, *The World Today* and *Administration*. In 1996, he was appointed Fulbright Scholar-in-Residence at Hollins College, Virginia.

Stephen Ryan is Senior Lecturer in Peace and Conflict Studies at the University of Ulster. He is author of *Ethnic Conflict and International Relations*, 2nd edn, 1995, Aldershot: Dartmouth, and has also written numerous articles on ethnic conflict.

Sandra Whitworth is an Associate Professor of Political Science and a Research Associate at the Center for International Security Studies, York University, Canada. She has published articles in *Review of International Studies*, *Millennium* and *Studies in Political Economy* as well as a number of chapters in edited anthologies, and is past-Chair of the Feminist Theory and Gender Studies Section of the International Studies Association. She is the author of *Feminism and International Relations*, London: Macmillan, 1994.

List of Abbreviations

ADF	Arab Deterrent Force
AHG	Ad Hoc Group on Cooperation in Peacekeeping
AIDS	Acquired Immune Deficiency Syndrome
ASPR	Austrian Study Centre for Peace and Conflict Resolution
BTL	Battalion Landing Team
CIVPOL	Civilian Police
CIS	Commonwealth of Independent States
CMO	Chief Military Officer
CSCE	Conference on Security and Cooperation in Europe
DOMREP	Representative of the Secretary-General in the Dominican Republic
EC	European Community
ECMM	European Community Monitoring Mission
ECOMOG	ECOWAS Ceasefire Monitoring Group
ECOWAS	Economic Community of West African States
ECTF	European Community Task Force
EU	European Union
EUNELSA	European Union Election Unit in South Africa
FYROM	Former Yugoslav Republic of Macedonia
HIV	Human Immunodeficiency Virus
ICRC	International Committee of the Red Cross
IDF	Israeli Defence Forces
IFOR	Implementation Force
INCORE	Initiative on Conflict Resolution and Ethnicity
IPA	International Peace Academy
IPKF	Indian Peacekeeping Force
IRSG	International Rwandan Support Group
LAF	Lebanese Armed Forces
JCC	Joint Control Commission
JPKF	Joint Peacekeeping Force
KKK	Ku Klux Klan
MAU	Marine Amphibious Unit
MEF	Marine Expeditionary Force
MINURSO	Mission for the Referendum in Western Sahara
MOOTW	Military Operations Other Than War
NAM	Non-Aligned Movement

NATO	North Atlantic Treaty Organization
NGO	Non-Governmental Organization
NNRC	Neutral Nations Repatriation Commission
NORDSAMFN	Joint Nordic Committee for UN Cooperation
NUF	National United Front
NUPI	Norwegian Foreign Policy Institute
OAS	Organization of American States
OAU	Organization of African Unity
ONUC	United Nations Operation in the Congo
ONUCA	United Nations Observer Group in Central America
ONUMOZ	United Nations Operation in Mozambique
ONUSAL	United Nations Operation in El Salvador
ONUVEH	United Nations Verification of Elections in Haiti
ONUVEN	United Nations Verification of Elections in Nicaragua
OSCE	Organisation for Security and Cooperation in Europe
ORH	Operation Restore Hope
OSGAP	Office of the Secretary General for Afghanistan and Pakistan
PFLP	Popular Front for the Liberation of Palestine
PFP	Partnership for Peace
PKO	Peacekeeping Operation
PLAN	Peoples Liberation Army of Namibia
PLO	Palestine Liberation Organization
PVO	Private Voluntary Organization
ROE	Rules of Engagement
RUSI	Royal United Services Institute
SNM	Somali National Movement
SRSG	Special Representative of the Secretary-General
SWAPO	South West African Peoples Organization
SWEDBATT	Swedish Battalion
UN	United Nations
UNAMIC	United Nations Advance Mission in Cambodia
UNAMIR	United Nations Assistance Mission for Rwanda
UNASOG	United Nations Aouzou Strip Observer Group
UNAVEM	United Nations Angola Verification Group
UNBRO	United Nations Border Relief Organization
UNCC	United Nations Consular Commission
UNCOK	United Nations Commission on Korea

UNCRO	United Nations Confidence Restoration Operation in Croatia
UNDOF	United Nations Disengagement Observer Force
UNEF	United Nations Emergency Force
UNICEF	United Nations Childrens Emergency Fund
UNFICYP	United Nations Force in Cyprus
UNGOMAP	United Nations Good Offices Mission in Afghanistan
UNHCR	United Nations High Commissioner for Refugees
UNIFIL	United Nations Interim Force in the Lebanon
UNIKOM	United Nations Iraq-Kuwait Observer Mission
UNIMOG	United Nations Iran-Iraq Military Observer Group
UNIPOM	United Nations India-Pakistan Observer Mission
UNITAF	Unified Task Force
UNITAR	United Nations Institute for Training and Research
UNMIBH	United Nations Mission In Bosnia-Hercegovina
UNMIH	United Nations Mission in Haiti
UNMLO	United Nations Military Liaison Office
UNMOGIP	United Nations Military Observer Group in India and Pakistan
UNMOP	United Nations Mission of Observers in Prevlaka
UNMOT	United Nations Mission of Observers in Tadjikistan
UNNY	United Nations New York
UNOGIL	United Nations Observer Group in the Lebanon
UNOMIG	United Nations Observer Mission in Georgia
UNOMIL	United Nations Observer Mission in Liberia
UNOMUR	United Nations Observer Mission in Uganda-Rwanda
UNOSOM	United Nations Operation in Somalia
UNPREDEP	United Nations Preventive Deployment Force
UNPROFOR	United Nations Protection Force
UNSCOB	United Nations Special Commission on the Balkans
UNSCOP	United Nations Special Committee on Palestine
UNSMIH	United Nations Support Mission in Haiti
UNTAC	United Nations Transitional Authority in Cambodia
UNTAES	United Nations Transitional Administration for Eastern Slavonia

UNTAG	United Nations Transition Assistance Group
UNTCOK	United Nations Temporary Commission on Korea
UNTEA	United Nations Temporary Executive Authority
UNTSI	United Nations Training School Ireland
UNTSO	United Nations Truce Supervision Organization
UNYOM	United Nations Yemen Observation Mission
USC	United Somali Congress
USCENTCOM	United States Central Command
USLO	United States Liaison Office
USMC	United States Marine Corps
WHO	World Health Organization

1 United Nations Peacekeeping – An Introduction[1]

Claus Heje

Peacekeeping, whether by the United Nations or another organization or state, has never been adequately defined. The practice of United Nations peacekeeping has fluctuated, adapting itself to the tasks and the situations it has faced. Some might even argue that this ability to adapt is one of the important strengths of United Nations peacekeeping. Peacekeeping was not invented by the United Nations, and the United Nations has never had a monopoly on peacekeeping. Before the creation of the United Nations, the League of Nations had experimented with operations which had some of the characteristics of modern-day peacekeeping. In the lifetime of the United Nations, other international organisations, multilateral coalitions, and individual states have practised what they have termed peacekeeping, and indeed, some non-United Nations operations have been successful in pursuing their objectives. Nevertheless, it is United Nations peacekeeping operations around the world which have created some of the characteristics that today are seen as the basics of peacekeeping. Through the United Nations, peacekeeping has proven itself to be a useful instrument for the settlement of conflicts that have affected international society. At the end of the day, it is international society which decides how this instrument is applied, though there is a tendency to forget this, and this leads to wishful thinking – peacekeeping by the United Nations can only be practised in the ways that the member states of the United Nations are willing to let it be practised.

The Cold War served to limit both the scope and the number of United Nations peacekeeping operations. The operations initiated prior to 1988 are nowadays known as 'traditional peacekeeping'. The end of the Cold War has given rise to a revitalization of United Nations peacekeeping, with many new missions differing significantly from the traditional peacekeeping operations. The new operations have often been large in size, and have been charged with far-reaching objectives, hence being termed 'multidimensional'. The reasons for initiating a peacekeeping operation are less transparent than in the time of the Cold War, and the peacekeeping operations are increasingly required to take a holistic approach to conflicts, and need to contain pre- and post-conflict elements. Nevertheless, these larger and more complex operations have also accentuated some of the problems associated with the practice of peacekeeping, and there seems to be a need to clarify the concept of peacekeeping.

The first operations, officially starting with UNTSO in 1948, were the military observer missions. This type of mission consists of a small number of officers who are normally unarmed. UNEF, in 1956 was the first United Nations peacekeeping force. A peacekeeping force is composed of lightly armed national military contingents. In 1964, civilian police (CIVPOLs) were deployed for the first time with the creation of UNFICYP. Although even early operations such as ONUC could be considered multidimensional, the first multicomponent operation was UNTAG in 1989. Civilian peacekeepers began to play an increasing role in United Nations peacekeeping operations from this stage onwards.

This chapter seeks to establish the core principles of peacekeeping, describe and discuss the concepts and functions of peacekeeping. Afterwards, it discusses the challenges facing contemporary peacekeeping, before briefly examining some recent trends in peacekeeping.

THE PRINCIPLES OF PEACEKEEPING

In the absence of a definition of peacekeeping, concrete rules for the conduct of United Nations peacekeeping have never been formally set out. Instead, with accumulated experience, a code of practice has been developed over time:

> As the United Nations practice has evolved over the years, a peacekeeping operation has come to be defined as an operation involving military personnel, but without enforcement powers, undertaken by the United Nations to help maintain or restore international peace and security in areas of conflict.[2]

Before 1988 the so called 'UNEF II rules'[3] were perhaps the closest the United Nations peacekeeping came to being codified. United Nations peacekeeping operations since 1988 have not all followed the same model, although precedent from most United Nations peacekeeping operations does allow us to identify certain key peacekeeping principles:

- consent;
- impartiality;
- the non-use of force;
- mandate;
- a United Nations multinational deployment;
- the 'willingness' of the member-states;
- the non-interference in the sovereignty of states.

It should be emphasized that none of these principles represent fixed rules; they have all been deviated from at certain times. They do, however, form a base for the conduct of peacekeeping by the United Nations.

Consent

The consent of the conflicting parties to 'the establishment of the operation, to its mandate, to its composition and to its appointed commanding officer'[4] is essential at the initiation of a peacekeeping operation, and, ideally, it is important that the consent of all sides is maintained throughout the operation.[5] The consent of the parties involved is one of the most basic principles for any kind of peacekeeping and it raises some important issues in the conduct of peacekeeping. The consent of the parties involved implies that some kind of successful interaction precedes the peacekeeping operation, i.e. peacemaking efforts. It also requires an understanding of who are considered parties to the conflict. This may be a problem, if, for instance, a representative of a party is not acknowledged as such by all within the party or if a party is ignored altogether. Defining all the parties to the conflict was perhaps one of the major problems in the early stages of UNPROFOR. Furthermore, if there has been no contact between the parties and/or if not all parties are acknowledged, a peacekeeping operation will commence in an environment of continued fighting. According to Mackinlay, 'Unless the mandate for intervention has the unqualified consent of every armed gang in the involved state, a local UN commander or official is likely to face subversion, and therefore confrontation, of some kind.'[6]

Defining the parties to a conflict becomes more difficult when the area of a conflict is within the borders of a dissolved/dissolving state. Problems can also arise if the consent of one party is withdrawn during the peacekeeping operation; this caused the termination of UNEF in 1967. On the other hand, UNTAC was continued despite some resumed fighting. While the matter of consent was vital to a traditional peacekeeping operation, if the peacekeeping is undertaken as assistance to and protection of humanitarian aid (as was the case in UNOSOM and UNPROFOR in Bosnia-Hercegovina), the entire foundation of the operation may be different.

Impartiality

A very important principle in peacekeeping is that the peacekeepers 'must be impartial between the parties'.[7] Impartiality is essential for the legitimacy of a United Nations peacekeeping operation, although it remains difficult to achieve. The United Nations has often been the best, if not the only, 'choice' for an impartial third party in international society. Yet, already the impartiality of ONUC was repeatedly questioned: the peacekeepers were more heavily armed than on previous missions and were seen to conduct military operations against one party. In the case of UNIFIL, almost all parties have at some point more or less soundly claimed that the UNIFIL force was partial.[8]

A distinction between the macro and the micro levels of peacekeeping may be useful in understanding the principle of impartiality as it applies to peacekeeping.[9] UNIKOM could then represent a partial peacekeeping operation at the macro level;

> UNIKOM is not a traditional peacekeeping operation because it is backed by the guarantee of uncompromising force. Such 'battleship diplomacy' emphasises that UNIKOM was not intended to be impartial.[10]

The same may be the case in operations where special international sanctions are sought and implemented against one of the parties, as has been the case in, for instance, UNPROFOR and UNOSOM.

The problem of the micro level relates both to the duties of the individual peacekeepers and their socialization. Peacekeepers often find it difficult to remain impartial when they experience one party as more aggressive than the other or when one group of civilians is hostile. Many peacekeepers deployed in former Yugoslavia noticed the hatred against UNPROFOR among the Croats.[11] Problems may also arise with the deployment of contingents which have historical links and/or sympathies for one party in the conflict. For example, in the case of UNPROFOR, Russian troops may have favoured the Serbs or the Turkish the Muslims.

The non-use of force

Peacekeepers are not deployed to take part in the armed fighting – on the contrary, a central objective of any peacekeeping operation is to ensure a cessation of violence. It is for this reason that efforts have been made to make the non-use of force a trademark of peacekeeping: 'Non-use of force except in the last resort in self-defence – self-defence, however, including resistance to attempts by forceful means to prevent the peace-keepers from discharging their duties.'[12] Persuasion and negotiation are regarded as the foremost weapons in the peacekeeper's armoury. When armed, peacekeepers have normally only been equipped with light weapons. In the past, ONUC has been an exception. More recently, implementing the mandate(s) of, for instance, UNPROFOR in Bosnia-Hercegovina has again raised the armament of the peacekeepers. Arguments for heavier weapons include:

> UN forces do not necessarily enjoy the support of all the local parties in the conflict, and consequently will have to take more rigorous steps to reach a standard of military effectiveness that can achieve the objectives of the mandate without jeopardizing the personal safety of the UN troops involved.[13]

More generally, it is contended that 'The characteristics of forces must be matched to the environment and circumstances of the area to which they are assigned.'[14]

Mandate

Since 1962, all peacekeeping operations have been authorized by the Security Council, and the continued support by the Security Council is considered a precondition for any United Nations peacekeeping operation. Urquhart notes that 'a clear and practicable mandate' is one of the essentials to a peacekeeping operation.[15] However, the clarity of the mandates in some of the present operations seems to fluctuate. In UNPROFOR, the mandate was evolved through a number of amended resolutions, which meant that it was difficult to implement any of the recognized objectives of the deployment. Yet, operations like UNIFIL and UNFICYP have been able to lower the level of violence without being able to pursue their respective mandates.

A United Nations multinational deployment

United Nations peacekeeping operations have to be responsible to the United Nations Security Council with the operational command and control vested in the Secretary-General. Against these criteria, the 1991 Gulf War multinational force cannot be properly considered a United Nations operations because troops remained under national control.

With relation to troop contributing countries, the parties involved in the conflict cannot contribute to the peacekeeping force. Until 1988, the Permanent Five member-states normally did not contribute with troops on the ground for peacekeeping operations.[16] The Secretary-General requests member-states for the contribution of military and police personnel. The contributing states are selected in consultation with the Security Council and the parties involved. The consultation of the parties involved is important. For instance, when UNTAG was formed in 1989, South Africa refused the deployment of a Swedish military contingent. Another example is the deployment of Argentinians in UNFICYP in 1993, side by side with their foes from the Falklands/Malvinas war, the British. Though this composition could have been a small 'powder keg', all reports so far indicate that the combination has not caused additional antagonisms in the Cyprus conflict. Civilian personnel traditionally came from within the United Nations or were locally recruited. Selection methods have changed recently given the increased civilian involvement in recent peacekeeping operations.

The large and multinational nature of operations such as UNTAC, UNPROFOR, UNIKOM and UNOSOM have raised problems of command and communication structures. Crucially, questions of peacekeeper loyalty have arisen: 'Suspicions that peacekeepers were acting as instruments of their government's policy, rather than of the collective will of the international community, could be fatal for the credibility of an operation.'[17] The principle that 'troops must not receive orders from their national governments'[18] seems essential.

The 'willingness' of the member-states

The growth in the size of many recent United Nations peacekeeping operations has resulted in both quality and quantity problems. There are limits to the number of troops and material which member-states can and will contribute. Furthermore, the training and equipment of peacekeepers from contributors varies significantly. It is therefore essential that the member-states are willing to provide financial and logistical support, as well as troops, for a peacekeeping operation. In the late 1980s, Sweden and later on Denmark withdrew their troops from UNFICYP partly because they were unhappy with the financial arrangements of the operation.[19] Another concern is that not all countries are able to provide the necessary logistical equipment, and it was therefore a precedent before 1988 that the Permanent Five provided transportation of troops in most cases. The willingness of member-states to provide troops is crucial for any peacekeeping operation. States may not approve of the character of the operation, may object to the mandate, or not have any particular interest in the operation. The difficulty of finding countries willing to contribute troops for the 1994 operation in Rwanda provides a striking example, and similar problems have occurred in UNPROFOR.

The non-interference in the sovereignty of states

The peacekeeping operation, in order to be effective, may not interfere in internal affairs of the host country. Sovereignty is enshrined in the United Nations Charter,[20] and is often referred to in United Nations pronouncements.[21] Nevertheless, many past and present peacekeeping operations have operated within the territory of one state. But often they represent cases where the authority of the state within the territory has more or less ceased or where the state is on its way to dissolve into several new states. Since at least ONUC, peacekeepers have also operated within internal borders. The principle of sovereignty may therefore be interpreted as interference only on the request and consent of the state concerned.

THE CONCEPTUAL FRAMEWORK OF PEACEKEEPING OPERATIONS

The changing nature of United Nations peacekeeping and the environment in which the peacekeeping operations operate have resulted in problems of conceptualization. As already noted, a satisfactory definition of peacekeeping was never established. A 1984 working definition from the International Peace Academy came close:

The prevention, containment, moderation and termination of hostilities between or within states through the medium of third party intervention organized and directed internationally using multinational military, police and civilian personnel to restore and maintain peace.[22]

This definition, however, goes on to note that peacekeeping does not operate in a vacuum, and is only one activity among others directed at peace and conflict resolution. If such terms as 'peacemaking', 'peacebuilding', 'preventive diplomacy', 'peace enforcement' and 'humanitarian assistance' are to be included in the conceptualization it can be seen that a holistic approach is required. Peacekeeping practitioners themselves need to conceptualize their own activities, yet given the changing nature of peacekeeping itself, they face difficulties in this task. The United Nations Secretary-General, Boutros Boutros-Ghali, in many ways set the agenda for the discussion of the concept of peacekeeping with his 1992 *An Agenda for Peace*. In it he sought to define the United Nations peace efforts. He outlined four main activities:

- preventive diplomacy;
- peacekeeping;
- peacemaking;
- post-conflict peacebuilding.

These headings serve as the basis for the discussion of peacekeeping concepts below, although it is worth noting that peace operations, and the terminology associated with them, have changed since the publication of *An Agenda for Peace*.

Preventive diplomacy

The starting point of the *Agenda for Peace* is the need for tools to resolve disputes and conflict, where disputes are considered non-violent, and conflicts violent. Preventive diplomacy is then considered 'action to prevent disputes from arising between parties, to prevent existing disputes from escalating into conflicts and to limit the spread of the latter when they occur'.[23] The proposed measures include 'measures to build confidence', 'fact-finding', 'early warning', 'preventive deployment' of troops, and the establishment of 'demilitarized zones'.[24]

Preventive diplomacy, however, is only conceptualized in strictly military terms, and does not fully appreciate the complexity of conflicts. Disputes themselves are not the problem, and it is unlikely that they ever can be prevented. The real problem lies with attempts to resolve disputes by violent means. The concept of preventive diplomacy may be valuable, but one should not forget its questionable features. The chief criticism is that it is largely untried; the preventive deployment of UNPREDEP ranks as the only example and attempts to perform peacekeeping-type activities prior to the stage where a conflict has reached a phase of armed violence.

Peacemaking

According to the *Agenda for Peace*, a dispute that becomes violent can be met by mechanisms of dispute resolution. This may take the form of mediation and negotiation conducted by assigned individuals (for example, through the Secretary-General's Good Offices) or intervention from the International Court of Justice. Other measures may include assistance to displaced persons or the implementation of economic and other sanctions.

The *Agenda for Peace* defines peacemaking as 'action to bring hostile parties to agreement, essentially through such peaceful means as those foreseen in Chapter VI of the Charter of the United Nations.'[25] The *Agenda for Peace* also includes the use of military force or 'peace enforcement' in 'peacemaking'. Peace enforcement is defined as military activities under Chapter VII of the United Nations Charter. It is worth noting that the Secretary-General has since made attempts to more clearly separate peace enforcement from peacemaking.[26] However unpalatable the combination of peace enforcement and peacemaking, the fact remains that military force can be an attractive policy option in otherwise uncontrollable conflict situations. The use of force came to be regarded as something of a norm in UNOSOM and UNPROFOR in Bosnia-Hercegovina with the result that they could be considered as entirely or partially enforcement operations. Strictly speaking, peace enforcement operations do not conform to the core principles of peacekeeping (consent, impartiality and the non-use of force). The use of NATO for the implementation aspects of UNPROFOR, and the transition of UNPROFOR into IFOR, which is explicitly based on a doctrine of disproportionate force, is revealing. With organizations such as NATO willing to assume enforcement roles, the United Nations may be able to distance itself from enforcement.

Peacekeeping

Slightly reformulated from the original definition, the Secretary-General now sees peacekeeping as 'a United Nations presence in the field (normally including military and civilian personnel), with the consent of the parties, to implement or monitor the implementation of arrangements relating to the control of conflicts (ceasefires, separation of forces, etc.) and their resolution (partial or comprehensive settlements), and/or to protect the delivery of humanitarian relief.'[27]

It is worth underlining that peacekeeping is only one measure among others that a third party can take in order to resolve a conflict. Peacekeeping alone does not settle a conflict, it only keeps a conflict from re-emerging into armed violence. If no other action is taken it is quite possible that a conflict will not de-escalate further; UNFICYP is, rightly or wrongly, an example of this.

Post-conflict peacebuilding

In the *Agenda for Peace*, peacebuilding is defined exclusively as post-conflict action, 'comprehensive efforts to identify and support structures which will tend to consolidate peace and advance a sense of confidence and well being among people.'[28] These efforts 'may include disarming the previously warring parties and the restoration of order, the custody and possible destruction of weapons, repatriating refugees, advisory and training support for security personnel, monitoring elections, advancing efforts to protect human rights, reforming and strengthening government institutions and promoting formal and informal processes of political participation.'[29] Yet, peacebuilding should not be wholly restricted to the post-conflict phase of a conflict and perhaps can be viewed in the general category of 'civilian peacekeeping activities'.

It is important to acknowledge that these activities can be performed both on a macro and a micro level. For instance, when a peacekeeper succeeds in negotiating with local leaders on certain issues, it is peacebuilding at the micro level.

Finally, humanitarian assistance is another activity which recently has been part of some peacekeeping operations (UNOSOM and UNPROFOR). Though similar to peacebuilding, humanitarian assistance is different from other actions in peacekeeping operations through its intention of bringing relief immediately, primarily to

sustain life in the short term, and not necessarily with any consideration of the long-term perspectives.[30]

FUNCTIONS AND PERSONNEL

The main objective of 'traditional' peacekeeping operations was
usually to keep the belligerents apart. The International Peace Academy once summarized the functions of the peacekeepers thus:

- internal ceasefire management to prevent a renewal of fighting;
- maintaining a 'buffer force': patrolling and observation of a buffer
  zone;
- border patrol: patrol, report, interpose if deemed necessary;
- observation from observation posts of armistice or ceasefire
  lines.[31]

The major techniques and skills involved in the conduct of these
duties were seen as:

- observation;
- surveillance and supervision;
- interposition;
- patrolling and reporting;
- investigation of complaints;
- negotiation and mediation;
- information gathering.[32]

All of these functions and skills were to be performed by military
personnel, and before the end of the Cold War, United Nations
peacekeeping operations were predominantly defined by the military
in task and composition, with civilian personnel often limited to
administrative roles.

The two important exceptions in the Cold War period were ONUC
and UNFICYP. In ONUC, military peacekeepers were involved in
the transport of food and medicine,[33] but there were also some 2,000
civilians attached to ONUC. The civilian personnel served as technical personnel and assisted in the administration of Congo. Similar
functions were performed in UNTEA, but in that operation all the
personnel were military.

In UNFICYP, non-military tasks and responsibilities are carried
out by military peacekeepers as part of or incidental to the mandate.
Furthermore, UNFICYP added a new aspect to peacekeeping by

the deployment of civilian police. The non-military tasks became more apparent after the change in the situation on Cyprus in 1974, after which UNFICYP was reorganized, and a so-called 'Humanitarian Branch' was established. However, even before that, an important part of the work of the military peacekeepers in UNFICYP was to 'negotiate the restoration of public services and ensure that they operate efficiently, and establish clinics and stock them with medical supplies.'[34] Also in UNIFIL the military peacekeepers directly assist the civilian population in the deployment area.[35] It has therefore not been unusual for military personnel to carry out a wide range of functions which could feasibly be termed as 'peace-building'.

Since 1988, the functions of the peacekeepers have been modified and broadened in various ways. Military peacekeepers have undertaken many new tasks, and civilian peacekeepers have taken a more prominent role. Some of the United Nations peacekeeping operations after the end of the Cold War have been organized in several components, and the number of functions of peacekeepers have increased significantly. Goulding anticipates six different types of United Nations peacekeeping operations for the present and the future:

1. preventive deployment of United Nations troops before a conflict has reached a stage of armed conflict (such as UNPREDEP);
2. traditional peacekeeping: unarmed observer missions (MINURSO), peacekeeping forces (UNFICYP, and UNPROFOR in Croatia), or as a force deployed as an adjunct to an enforcement operation (UNIKOM);
3. support to the implementation of a comprehensive settlement (UNTAG, ONUSAL, UNAVEM, UNTAC and ONUMOZ);
4. protection of the delivery of humanitarian relief supplies (UNOSOM and UNPROFOR in Bosnia-Hercegovina);
5. deployment of a United Nations force in a country where the institutions of state have largely collapsed (such as ONUC and UNOSOM);
6. ceasefire enforcement against any party which violated the ceasefire (such as UNPROFOR in Bosnia-Hercegovina?).[36]

It is questionable whether 5 and 6 are really peacekeeping operations, and not peace enforcement. However, this question entirely depends on where one draws the line. In the outline of these six different types of peacekeeping operations, there seems to be an almost complete neglect of the enhanced involvement of civilian peace-keepers. Beyond the functions of traditional peacekeeping, peace-keepers have become involved in several different new tasks: electoral monitoring, repatriation, observing human rights and so on. Though these functions sometimes are carried out by military personnel, it seems obvious that these functions should be predominantly carried out by civilians who may have a professional background in these areas. It should be emphasized that any 'clear-cut' definition of what civilian and what military personnel can and should do is not poss-ible. What is essential is that the assignments of the various personnel groups in a particular peacekeeping operation be clearly stated.

THE PRESENT CHALLENGES TO PEACEKEEPING

Despite the many new functions brought into United Nations peace-keeping operations, the United Nations have in recent years, once again, been criticized for not being able to take action or not being able to take the 'right' action in armed conflicts. However, there often seems to be an expectation of the United Nations and peace-keeping being able to deal with any situation. Though some of the difficulties in the practice of United Nations peacekeeping have roots back to the birth of United Nations peacekeeping, the new and larger peacekeeping operations with many functions and impacts have not made it easier for the United Nations to succeed. As Alan James points out, there is a limit to what United Nations peacekeeping operations can achieve: 'In appropriate circumstances peacekeeping can make a valuable contribution to peace – but only if and to the extent to which disputants choose to take advantage of it.'[37] United Nations peacekeeping faces ever more complex chal-lenges[38] which contemporary conflicts raise. These challenges may be listed as:

- the framework of peacekeeping operations;
- the limits to peacekeeping;
- the ripeness for intervention;
- juxtaposing military and civilian operations;
- organization and management of peacekeeping operations;
- impacts on the contributing countries;
- the impact on the recipients of peacekeeping;
- preparation of the peacekeepers.

The framework of peacekeeping operations

Peacekeeping operations are mandated by the Security Council. The process whereby the mandate is drawn up varies enormously and often involves a good deal of politics. Mandating countries may have differing motives (national interest, security or humanitarian assistance), may think along different timeframes, or may consider different problems with different degrees of urgency. A further problem arises when the mandate is modified during the conflict. For instance, by 1993, 'In the former Yugoslavia, 42 resolutions and no less than 15 mandate enhancements have been adopted since the Vance Plan was approved by Security Council Resolution 743 on 21 February 1992'.[39] This results in the complication of the mandate and the confusion of the mission objectives. Crucially, it diminishes the chances of peacekeepers successfully completing their task. According to Berdal:

> Resorting to peacekeeping and the ambiguity of mandates also reflects a larger failure on the part of member-states, especially the permanent five of the Security Council, to examine the role of the UN with regard to internal conflict. Short-term objectives – be they humanitarian relief operations, transitional assistance or preventive deployments – cannot be a substitute for addressing the root cause of internal conflict. The decision to deploy peacekeeping forces cannot, as in the case of the former Yugoslavia, be divorced from considerations of the long-term political and administrative arrangements which UN involvement is designed to promote within fractured societies.[40]

Importantly, despite the efforts of formulating a clearer concept of peacekeeping, it appears that the United Nations still lacks a clearly formulated policy for conflict management.

The limits to peacekeeping

Different problems demand different responses, with some arguing for a greater enforcement element in United Nations peacekeeping operations (often with reference to Chapter VII in the United Nations Charter), and others calling for an increased emphasis on humanitarian assistance. Recent peacekeeping operations, such as UNOSOM and UNPROFOR, have involved a certain degree of experimentation with the use of force and the degree of consent.

There is, however, a limit to how far peacekeeping can be moved away from its basic ideas of consent impartiality and non-use of force and still be called peacekeeping. For the purpose of conflict resolution, experimentation with the use of force and the degree of consent seem less fruitful than operations where new functions in terms of, for instance, human rights monitoring and election assistance have been implemented. Therefore, 'the basic distinction between peacekeeping and enforcement action must be upheld. Increasingly the distinction has been blurred, both in practice and theory'.[41]

The ripeness for intervention

The enhanced role of the United Nations means that states are inclined to call for United Nations intervention as a first recourse; that is, before a ceasefire agreement has been reached. This is hardly surprising, as 'De-escalating efforts are especially likely when a conflict has rapidly escalated and violence has broken out.'[42] But peacekeeping *per se* may not always be the most effective form of third-party intervention, and a conflict may not always be 'ripe' for peacekeeping. Indeed, 'One major problem occurs in the timing of referral of conflicts to the United Nations for consideration.'[43] However, 'It is not enough to send a force into the field with a vague notion that they should be impartial and help facilitate settlement.'[44] Instead, consideration should be given to the precise role of any peacekeeping operation, and the 'ripeness' for intervention. Peacekeeping as an effort to de-escalate a conflict is related to the presence of some favourable conditions for such de-escalation, the real challenge is not to wait for these conditions to appear but to create these conditions. Therefore, it is imperative to understand that peacekeeping is not enough to resolve a conflict, but peacekeeping is closely related to other efforts which will suit different stages in a conflict.

Juxtaposing military and civilian operations

In traditional peacekeeping, 'Infantry battalions have been the basic operational unit in all peacekeeping forces with the exception of small-scale observer missions,'[45] and civilians have been used 'sparingly'.[46] In the past, civilian aspects of peacekeeping have often been ignored. New, larger peacekeeping operations have resulted in many new tasks, which often are qualitatively different from tasks traditionally carried out by the military. Civilian personnel have therefore come to play a more significant role in many peacekeeping operations. This development is clearly justifiable if a peacekeeping operation is to have a role in a larger framework aimed at resolving a conflict. It is important that the larger role assigned to civilian personnel is not merely seen as an extension of military operations. However, 'juxtaposing military and civilian operations, although interrelated and mutually supportive, results in major command, control and co-ordination problems.'[47] More flexible mechanisms for coordinating the civilian and military aspects of peacekeeping operations are required, as is a greater mutual understanding of the problems both groups face.

Organization and management of peacekeeping operations

Many academics and practitioners have pointed out the problems in the organization and management of United Nations peacekeeping operations. Mats Berdal summarizes many of these problems in the following list:

> The insufficient attention given to the formulation of clear and achievable mandates ... The limited logistical capabilities available ... The failure to establish time-sensitive and secure communications between the UN headquarters and the field mission ... The failure to establish an efficient command-and-control system in the field ... The inadequate training of units from other than the traditional troop-contributing countries ... The paucity of UN joint doctrine ... the lack of tactical mobility of operation and insufficient attention to the requirements of force protection ... The insufficient delegation of financial and administrative authority ... A general lack of air assets to carry out transport ... The failure to exploit fully advances in technology ...[48]

Among the most pressing problems is the lack of financial resources. This has been compounded by the increasing demand for larger and more complex peacekeeping operations. The national balance of peacekeepers in key positions has also become more sensitive. While more states show an interest in contributing to peacekeeping operations, not all governments are in a position to offer properly equipped or trained personnel. Organizational problems also stem from recent United Nations operations which have been carried out in conjunction with other regional and international organizations.

Most notably, this is illustrated by NATO's taking charge in Bosnia-Hercegovina. Again methods of mission handover have yet to be established, and coordination between the United Nations and other international organizations seems to have an *ad hoc* basis.

Impacts on the contributing countries

While United Nations peacekeeping is dependent on the willingness of the member-states to pay and the willingness to train personnel for peacekeeping operations, the countries contributing with troops to peacekeeping operations may also make financial gains from the deployment. However, the impact of contributing to United Nations peacekeeping has other aspects, both in relation to foreign and domestic politics and the interests of military establishments. Countries can view the participation in United Nations peacekeeping as an opportunity to further their own foreign policy.[49] This is not only the case among the greater powers; also the smaller states of the world may have foreign policy interests in participating in United Nations peacekeeping. In the case of Norway, Holst notes that 'Peacekeeping is likely to become an essential element in the maintenance of minimum world order. Norwegian security depends on that order.'[50] Also countries with a fragile political system may see an advantage in their armies committing themselves to peacekeeping, or countries may see participation in peacekeeping as a way to gain more political acceptability internationally. In a study of Argentina, Norden writes:

> Argentina's relative geographical isolation, the military's lack of professional experience, the constrained economic conditions and the armed forces' pressing need to improve their image all contribute to a higher level of receptivity to international peacekeeping.[51]

There is also the possibility of the military establishment of a particular country having a vested interest in a peacekeeping operation.[52] Officers and soldiers may benefit from the experience they obtain during a peacekeeping deployment.[53] Holst notes that a peacekeeping force 'has to cope with different challenges from those presented to ordinary military units during peacetime conditions at home. Leadership is tested in a more direct way than is possible in any peacetime army.'[54]

The changing nature of peacekeeping operations also has implications for the contributing countries. For example, the trend towards peace enforcement and the associated possibility of higher death tolls may cause some member-states to reassess both the size of their contributions and the type of mission on which they send their troops. Among the Nordic countries, 'there is an uneasiness emerging concerning the expansion of the concept of peace-keeping'.[55]

The impact on the recipients of peacekeeping

Peacekeeping is not an exact science, and it is extremely difficult to foresee the impact of a peacekeeping operation on a particular conflict, society or locality. According to Fetherston, 'we do not have enough information to begin to understand the effect of UN interventions – peacekeeping especially – on a conflict situation...'[56] Inevitably peacekeeping operations, especially those with more farreaching objectives, for instance UNTAG and UNTAC, will have an impact on the recipient country both during and after the operation. Peacekeeping operations, and especially peacekeeping forces, can have unfortunate effects on the local population of the host country. In the case of the UNTAC operation:

> Once the cantonment process had collapsed in the summer of 1992, several infantry battalions were left with little to do and appeared in the eyes of ordinary Cambodians to be spending most of their time in bars and brothels or to be driving recklessly in UN vehicles.[57]

The relationship between peacekeepers and the local population is an understudied issue, and, as Heiberg writes, 'It can be convincingly argued that the nature of the relationship a peacekeeping force achieves with the local population within its area of control is a decisive element determining the operation's success or failure.'[58]

Preparation of the peacekeepers

According to Maj. Gen. Lewis Mackenzie, former UNPROFOR commander:

> As surprising as it may seem and, dare I say it, shocking for some academics, the last thing that a peacekeeper wants to know is the history of the region he is going into. It complicates the task of mediation, and obscures the immediate task, which may well be to deliver food or medicine.[59]

Nevertheless, training does seem vital to the overall performance of a peacekeeping force. This is particularly the case given the complexity of modern peacekeeping operations and the delicacy of the situation many peacekeepers find themselves in. According to Berdal, 'It is estimated that 90% of the training for peacekeeping is training for a general combat capability,'[60] but, as Blechman and Vacarro point out, 'Specialized peacekeeping training is needed to teach modifications in some tasks that *are* stressed in traditional military training.'[61] Therefore, a more sophisticated approach to the preparation in general is needed. Peacekeepers themselves frequently call for greater attention to be paid to training,[62] and civilian peacekeepers rarely receive any preparation at all.

SOME RECENT TRENDS IN UNITED NATIONS PEACE-KEEPING

It is often claimed that the larger and more complex United Nations peacekeeping operations have broken new ground. More correctly, however, it can be argued that recent developments in peacekeeping are merely emphasizing features which have always been there, rather than changing its nature entirely.[63] Some changes can be identified: United Nations peacekeeping forces are increasingly deployed for humanitarian purposes, and United Nations peacekeeping operations have often been deployed to assist in the implementation of comprehensive settlements. Finally, it is more frequently anticipated that peacekeepers shall perform peacebuilding tasks.

However, recent trends in peacekeeping operations have also involved a blurring of the lines between peacekeeping and coercive actions. This has been illustrated by the changed application of the three core principles in some operations, where it is questionable whether the peacekeepers are impartial in preventive deployment and operations involving enforcement. Similarly, the consent of the parties has several times been downgraded, and there has been an apparent readiness to use force in some operations. The question remains, how far can peacekeeping be extended and still be considered peacekeeping?

A major problem in identifying the limits to peacekeeping can be found in the paucity of a joint doctrine for peacekeeping, operational as well as conceptual. It has become a major deficiency because it prevents an efficient pursuance of the objectives in the field, and it makes it difficult to determine what a peacekeeping operation may and may not be able to do.

To comply with this deficiency, traditional contributors to peace-keeping, particularly national armies, have been keen to formulate new peacekeeping doctrines. The new doctrine attempts to come to terms with the changing nature of peacekeeping, particularly the trend towards peace enforcement operations, and may have important implications for the performance of the peacekeepers on the ground. This is particularly the case if there is a divergence of the terminology[64] used, or more fundamentally, there is a different emphasis on the core elements of what peacekeeping is perceived to be. New manuals which describe peacekeeping routines have been drawn up, adding to the two most well known, the International Peace Academy's *Peacekeeper's Handbook*[65] and the manuals of NORD-SAMFN.[66] Many national armies, especially larger armies new to United Nations peacekeeping, have developed their own briefs and manuals for participation in peacekeeping operations.[67] Indeed, in the case of the US forces, different branches have developed their own doctrines. However, when national armies develop new briefs and manuals, there is a tendency not to appreciate peacekeeping operations as something beyond traditional combat activity.[68] This may be encouraged by events in recent years, where, for instance, a peacekeeping operation has been converted into a more peace enforcement-type operation under the command of NATO in Bosnia-Hercegovina. But if this trend is more commonly applied, important and useful knowledge may be lost. Even though peacekeeping is not the 'pill for all illness', peacekeepers have accumulated experiences which could be useful in the future. A further problem may arise if there are too many manuals and doctrines. Modern large-scale peacekeeping operations are inherently complicated and could well do without the added complication of differing interpretations of what peacekeeping is meant to be.

Some of the more visionary doctrines for international operations for peace have been named 'peace-support operations',[69] 'enlarged peacekeeping'[70] or 'wider peacekeeping'.[71] All of these to a different extent accept international operations without the consent of all the parties involved, more partial and more forceful intervention, and emphasize thus the military aspects of third-party intervention without fully appreciating the political, social, ethnic and cultural dimensions of conflict. The most interesting and differentiated doctrine is that of 'wider peacekeeping', which has been developed by the British

Army. In a more holistic approach, 'wider peacekeeping' suggests different types of (military) action depending on the particular assignment. The issue of consent is kept central, and is seen to operate on two levels: operational and tactical (which could be considered similar to the previously mentioned macro and micro levels). As long as consent is maintained on one of these two levels, it is still possible to keep a situation stable, and it is only if there is no consent on either level that the border to peace enforcement is crossed.[72]

Again this marks a development from traditional interpretations of peacekeeping, although due to the diminishing role of consent, and the seemingly ready progression to the use of force, it is important that some sort of distinction is maintained between peace enforcement and peacekeeping – primarily not to compromise the image of peacekeeping and thus its future use. There is also a recognition that while peacekeeping must rest on its pillars of consent, impartiality and the non-use of force, it must also be flexible enough to encompass new activities demanded by contemporary peacekeeping operations. Recent examples have shown it is not difficult to cross the Rubicon towards peace enforcement. Yet this confusion about what actually constitutes peacekeeping can only add to the problems that peacekeepers face in the field.

NOTES

1. This chapter was first written in the spring of 1994 as a working paper for the INCORE project on the training and preparation of United Nations peacekeepers. A later version can be found in the final report from the project, Andrea Haberl-Zemljic, Claus Heje, Edward Moxon-Browne, Stephen Ryan and Arno Truger, *Final Report. The Training and Preparation of Military and Civilian Peacekeepers*, Derry: INCORE, 1996, pp. 17–38. The author would like to thank all who have been involved in the project and have given comments to the paper. Especially Professor Edward Moxon-Browne and Roger Mac-Ginty should be thanked for their comments and help. The author would also like to thank Dr Luke Ashworth, Matt 'Balls' Cannon, Samantha Crouse, Elizabeth De Boer Ashworth, Lt-Col Colm Doyle, Lewina Farrell, Sandra Heje, Terry McErlane, Kate Lanigan, Andrew Sherriff and Brian Synnott for their help.
2. United Nations, *The Blue Helmets. A Review of United Nations Peacekeeping*, 2nd edn, New York: UN Department of Public Information, 1990, p. 4.

3. The 'UNEF II rules' were the principles for the setup of UNEF II as the Secretary-General presented them to the Security Council in a report on the implementation of the UNEF II peacekeeping force. In this report, principles such as the non-use of force and the impartiality of the peacekeeping force are emphasized. UN document S/11052/ REV. 1.

4. Brian Urquhart, 'Beyond the "Sheriff's posse"', *Survival*, Vol. 32, No. 3, 1990, p. 198.

5. Jesper Jacobsen and Henning Lund, *FN's fredsbevarende aktioner*, København: Akademisk Forlag, 1990, p. 41.

6. John Mackinlay, 'Successful intervention', *Internationale Spectator*, Vol. 47, No. 11, 1993, p. 660.

7. Marrack Goulding 'The evolution of United Nations Peacekeeping', *International Affairs*, Vol. 69, No. 3, 1993, p. 454.

8. James Parker, 'UNIFIL and peacekeeping. The defence forces experience', *Irish Studies in International Affairs*, Vol. 2, No. 2, 1986.

9. The distinction between the macro and micro level is, among others, suggested by Fetherston in A.B. Fetherston, *Towards a Theory of United Nations Peacekeeping*, New York: St. Martin's Press, 1994.

10. Richard Connaughton, 'Military intervention and UN peacekeeping', in Nigel Rodley (ed.), *To Loose the Bands of Wickedness*, Oxford: Brassey's, 1992, p. 185.

11. See the case studies in Haberl-Zemljic et al., pp. 38–128.

12. Urquhart, op. cit., p. 198.

13. John Mackinlay and Jarat Chopra, *A Draft Concept of Second Generation Multinational Operations 1993*, Providence, RI: Watson Institute, 1993, p. 4.

14. Connaughton, op. cit., p. 195.

15. Urquhart, op. cit., p. 198.

16. The only exceptions before 1987 were UNTSO, UNFICYP and UNIFIL.

17. Goulding, op. cit., p. 454.

18. NORDSAMFN, *Nordic UN Stand-by Forces*, Helsingfors: NORD-SAMFN, 1993, p. 19.

19. For a further discussion of Swedish participation in UNFICYP, see Sune Persson, 'Svensk Militär På Cypern: SWEDBAT och UNFICYP 1964, 1974 och 1987', *FOA Rapport GEMS 5*, Sundbyberg: Försvarets Forskningsanstalt, 1991.

20. Jacobsen and Lund, op. cit., and Boutros Boutros-Ghali, *An Agenda for Peace*, New York: United Nations, 1992.

21. 'The foundation-stone of this work is and must remain the State. Respect for its fundamental sovereignty and integrity are crucial to any common international progress' and 'If every ethnic, religious or linguistic group claimed statehood, there would be no limit to fragmentation, and peace, security and economic well-being for all would become ever more difficult to achieve.' Boutros-Ghali, op. cit., p. 9.

22. International Peace Academy, *The Peacekeeper's Handbook*, New York: Pergamon Press, 1984, p. 7.

23. Boutros-Ghali, op. cit., p. 11.

24.   Ibid., pp. 13–19.
25.   Ibid., p. 11.
26.   See *Improving the Capacity of the United Nations for Peace-keeping. Report of the Secretary General,* 14 March 1994, S/26450, 2.
27.   Ibid.
28.   Boutros-Ghali, op. cit., p. 32.
29.   Ibid., p. 32.
30.   For further discussion of humanitarian assistance and United Nations peacekeeping, see Andrew Sherriff and Claus Heje, *Bedfellows?... Humanitarian Assistance and United Nations Peacekeeping Operations,* paper presented at the BISA Conference, Southhampton, 20 December 1995.
31.   International Peace Academy, op. cit., pp. 31–2.
32.   Ibid., pp. 83–154.
33.   Robin Hay, 'Civilian aspects of United Nations peacekeeping', *Background Paper 38,* Ottawa: Canadian Institute for International Peace and Security, 1991, p. 2.
34.   Ibid., p. 3.
35.   Parker, op. cit.
36.   Goulding, op. cit., pp. 458–64.
37.   Alan James, *Peacekeeping in International Politics,* London: Macmillan, 1990, p. 1.
38.   Mats R. Berdal, 'Whither UN peacekeeping?' *Adelphi Papers 281,* London: HSS/Brassey's, 1993.
39.   Ibid., p. 31.
40.   Ibid., p. 32.
41.   Ibid., p. 76.
42.   Jeffrey Z. Rubin, 'The timing of ripeness and the ripeness of timing', in Louis Kriesberg and Stuart J. Thorson (eds), *Timing the De-Escalation of International Conflict,* Syracuse, NY: Syracuse University Press, 1991, p. 245.
43.   A. Betts Fetherston, 'Toward a theory of United Nations peacekeeping', *Peace Research Report No. 31,* Bradford: Department of Peace Studies, University of Bradford, 1993, p. 33.
44.   Ibid., p. 40.
45.   Berdal, op. cit., p. 7.
46.   Hay, op. cit., p. 1.
47.   Berdal, op. cit., p. 11.
48.   Ibid., pp. 49–50.
49.   This narrow view was reflected by President Clinton's National Security Adviser, Anthony Lake, who regarded 'the primary purpose of our military forces is to fight and win wars.' In 'New US isolationism turns its back on UN peacekeeping', *The Irish Times,* 9 May 1994.
50.   Johan Jorgen Holst, 'Support and limitations: peacekeeping from the point of view of troop-contributors', in Indar Jit Rikhye and Kjell Skjelsbaeck (eds), *The United Nations and Peacekeeping,* London: Macmillan, 1990, pp. 113–14.
51.   Deborah L. Norden, 'Keeping the peace, outside and in: Argentina's UN missions', *International Peacekeeping,* Vol. 2, No. 3, 1995, p. 240.

52. Åge Eknes 'Prepared for peace-keeping: the Nordic countries and participation in U.N. military operations,' in Winrich Kühne, *Blauhelme in einer turbuleten Welt*, Baden Baden: Nemus, 1993, p. 511.

53. There might be a distinction here between countries with a professional army and countries with conscription. A professional army often expects that the soldiers, through peacekeeping, will both be 'kept busy' and remain 'fit for fighting'. Yet the United States in particular has questioned the command structures of multilateral peacekeeping operations, where the contributing country might lose command of its own forces.

54. Holst, op. cit., p. 122.

55. Eknes, op. cit., p. 518.

56. Fetherston, op. cit., p. 73.

57. Berdal, op. cit., p. 46.

58. Marianne Heiberg, 'Peacekeepers and local populations: some comments on UNIFIL', *NUPI Rapport, No. 142*, Oslo: NUPI, 1990, p. 3.

59. Lewis Mackenzie, 'Military reality of UN peacekeeping operations', *RUSI Journal*, February 1993, p. 21.

60. Berdal, op. cit., pp. 45–6.

61. Barry M. Blechman and J. Matthew Vacarro, 'Training for peacekeeping: the United Nations' role', *Report No. 12*, Washington, DC: The Henry L. Stimson Center, 1994, p. 4.

62. Haberl-Zemljic et al., op. cit.

63. Alan James, 'A review of UN peacekeeping', *Internationale Spectator*, Vol. 47, No. 11, 1993, p. 622.

64. For example, modern peacekeeping operations may be described as 'multifunctional' or 'multidimensional'. They may also be described as 'second generation' or even 'third generation peacekeeping'. The last term is used by Kühne in Winrich Kühne, 'Fragmenting states and the need for enlarged peacekeeping – Deutsche Kurzfassung: Zerfallende Staaten und erweitertes Peacekeeping', *SWP-KA 2869 Oktober 1994*, Ebenhausen/Isartal: Stiftung Wissenschaft und Politik, 1994, p. 23.

65. International Peace Academy, op. cit.

66. NORDSAMFN, *Nordic UN Tactical Manual. Volumes I and II*, Jyväskylä: NORDSAMFN, 1992.

67. Two examples of such briefs are from the French and the Spanish armies. See d'Astorg, *Doctrine militaire française des operations de maintien de la paix*, Exposé au Seminaire OTAN, le 5 octobre 1994, and Arturo Garcia-Vaquero y Pradal and Fernando Alejandre Martinez, *Operaciones de Interposición de Fuerzas (OIF)*, Madrid, 1993.

68. A quotation like the following, taken from d'Astorg, op. cit., p. 5, is illustrative of this approach: 'La meilleure armée de maintien de la paix nous paraît être la meilleure armée tout court. Plus une armée sera entraînée au combat, plus elle aura de chance d'être une bonne armée de maintien de la paix' and 'En matière de formation générale, il faut avant tout privilégier la formation au combat et ensuite seulement assurer l'acquisition des techniques spécifiques de maintien de la paix.'

69. Jim Whitman and Ian Bartholomew, 'Collective control of UN peace support operations', *Security Dialogue*, Vol. 25, No. 1, 1994, pp. 77–92.
70. Kühne, op. cit.
71. HMSO, *The Army Field Manual. Volume 5. Operations Other than War. Part 2. Wider Peacekeeping*. London: HMSO, 1994.
72. Ibid.

2 The Theory of Conflict Resolution and the Practice of Peacekeeping

Stephen Ryan

If we accept conventional genealogies the practice of peacekeeping and the academic area of study known as peace and conflict research began about the same time in the mid-1950s. In this sense both are offspring of the Cold War. Peacekeeping was the brainchild of the Canadian politician Lester Pearson and an initially skeptical UN Secretary-General Dag Hammarskjold (Urquhart, 1987, p. 133). It was first used at the end of the Suez crisis in November 1956 when the United Nations Emergency Force was deployed between the Israeli and Egyptian armies in the Sinai Peninsula. Of course there were 'peacekeeping' forces established before this by the League (James, 1990) and by the UN (e.g. UNMOGIP and UNTSO), but UNEF was the 'real debut' of peacekeeping (Rikhye, 1984, p. 4).

At about the same time peace and conflict research was emerging in two separate areas of the world. In the US, and especially in a sub-group of the Center for Advanced Study in the Behavioral Sciences at Stanford University, American academics were 'creating' conflict research by applying scientific analysis to the causes of violence (see, for example, Kelman, 1991). As a result of collaboration between researchers such as Rapaport, Boulding and Kelman the most visible form of the emergence of this new area of study, the *Journal of Conflict Resolution*, appeared in 1957. Meanwhile, the embryo of what was to become peace research was developing in Scandinavia. This became a research centre in Oslo in 1958.

A HISTORY OF MUTUAL NEGLECT

However, despite their obvious overlapping concerns the relationship between peacekeeping and peace and conflict research has not been a very fruitful one. Indeed the nature of the contact between academic peace and conflict researchers and peacekeeping practitioners may best be characterized as mutual neglect. To explain why this has been the case we need to look at the attitudes that each has towards the other.

Of course, it would be wrong to suggest that peace and conflict research has not addressed peacekeeping. Not surprisingly, this interest has been strongest in countries which are 'traditional' contributors to UN peacekeeping missions. So, for example, influential studies have been produced by Galtung (Norway) (1976) in his classic and persuasive analysis of the relationships between peacekeeping, peacemaking and peacebuilding, and by Fisher (Canada) (1990, ch. 9) on how peacekeeping fits into his 'contingency model'. These ideas have also influenced others. Harbottle (1979) has developed Galtung's approach and Fetherston (1994) has recently taken up Fisher's ideas in her study of peacekeeping and conflict theory. It should also be pointed out that there has been a growing interest in peacekeeping in some important peace and conflict journals.

However, any analysis of the output of peace and conflict research over the past 40 years in the search for guidance about peacekeeping would be bound to disappoint. This is partly because of the way that agendas are created. Many conflict analysts, for example, seem to have been more concerned about the causes of violence than its resolution. Those conflict researchers who have concentrated their work on resolution have often tended to be dismissive of peacekeeping in conflict situations. This is usually because they regard peacekeeping as a form of conflict management, producing what George Sherry called a 'controlled impasse' (Skjelsbaek, 1990, p. 54) rather than conflict resolution and therefore never addresses the underlying causes of violence. Cordovez (1987, p. 173) has noted that if peacekeeping missions are not coordinated with peacemaking 'they may provide a false sense of security and perpetuate de facto situations without removing smouldering potential causes for renewed violence.'

Perhaps this is a reason why the work of John Burton (1979, 1982), one the most important conflict researchers of the last generation, hardly makes any reference to peacekeeping in several of his most significant contributions. When he does touch on peacekeeping issues it is only in the most cursory manner. In a recent analysis he argues that although peacekeeping has been used by the UN as means of containment, these means 'may make even more difficult a final resolution in the particular instance' (1990, p. 244). Banks (1984, p. 20) identifies peacekeeping with other 'forcible conflict suppressing devices' such as power balancing and hostile intervention, that need to be 'replaced with other procedures which would not only control symptoms' (1984, p. 20). Mitchell (1981, p. 264) examines peacekeeping under the heading of conflict suppression. He points out that it can prevent the continuation of overt conflict behaviour but that 'this may not be an unambiguous gain' since underlying attitudes and perceptions are unaffected and the situation remains unresolved (1981, p. 265).[1]

Another concern about peacekeeping in the conflict resolution literature is that when missions are successful in keeping the parties apart they may just be legitimizing separation and preventing opportunities for constructive interaction. This may be a problem with peacekeeping, but it is an avoidable one if, as Galtung (1976) pointed out over 20 years ago, peacekeeping work is coordinated with peacemaking and peacebuilding.

I have argued elsewhere that the 'conflict management *or* conflict resolution' approach is unhelpful and instead we should reject such uncompromising dualism and think about 'conflict management *and* conflict resolution' (Ryan, 1990). In other words, as Galtung and Harbottle have pointed out, we should think of how peacekeeping can be fitted into a more comprehensive peace strategy. Furthermore the image of peacekeeping presented by some conflict researchers is now rather dated. They ignore the 'remarkable period of development in function, scope and application' (Wiseman, 1990, p. 49) that peacekeeping has experienced in the past decade.

The practitioners' neglect of theory was perhaps most clearly revealed in *An Agenda for Peace*. In Boutros-Ghali's influential statement about the role of the UN in the new world order there is very little to suggest that conflict theory had had an impact on the organization at all. It was therefore criticized for being too legalistic, too militaristic and too unimaginative.

A major reason for the practitioners' neglect of peace and conflict theory appears to be their belief in pragmatism which is an approach suspicious of generalizations. So Urquhart (1990, p. 18) has warned us that 'care should be taken in attempting to generalize excessively about peacekeeping and to improve upon what has been part of the recipe of success, namely improvisation... one of the strengths of previous operations has been the creative and spontaneous adaptation of general principles to a specific situation.'

The practitioners' neglect of conflict theory is also mirrored in the academic studies of peacekeeping, which rarely dip their toes into peace and conflict research. For example, the excellent study by

Diehl (1993), which is 'designed to fill some of the theoretical and policy gaps that exist in our understanding of international peace-keeping operations' (p. 3) contains no references to contemporary peace and conflict research and restricts itself mainly to the existing literature on peacekeeping. A similar gap is found in Rikhye's study *The Theory and Practice of Peacekeeping* (1984).

PRAGMATISM AND THE CHANGING CONTEXT OF PEACE-KEEPING

Pragmatism has a lot going for it. It rejects a priorism, it is flexible and sensitive, practical, robust and concrete and allows knowledge to be accumulated in an evolutionary manner after being tested by the court of experience (Gellner, 1979). Ad hocery has its drawbacks, however. Apart from being too reactive, it is doubtful if pragmatism can cope with periods when the accepted rules of the game change in a fundamental way. Pragmatism, as Gellner notes, is a progressive and optimistic philosophy. It may have fitted in with the rosy assessments of international politics that emerged at the end of the 1980s as the Cold War was ending, but seems out of place in the more troubled and confused 1990s where the dreams of a new world have been shattered in places like Sarajevo and Mogadishu – two cities, by the way, where the UN Secretary-General had to be protected from angry locals furious about the failure of the UN to offer them peace and security.

The question is, has the world that the UN faces now changed in ways that make pure pragmatism an unhelpful response? We do seem to have moved from a situation where we can calmly think about the UN moving in to help resolve specific problems to a situation where commentators are talking about a crisis at the UN and a crisis in peacekeeping. Once again we can seek assistance from the assessment of pragmatism by Gellner (1979b). He notes:

> . . . a problem is a difficulty which may well be serious and the solution of which may call for the utmost exertions, and which may be prolonged and arduous, but which, for all that, does not count for a revaluation of the very criteria of what is to count as a solution, for any overall reassessment of all the criteria of solution themselves.
>
> (Gellner, 1979b, p. 242)

He then goes on to say:

> It seems to me that pragmatism is indefensible, because radical cata-
> clysms do occur. When they do, cheerfulness, in the sense defined –
> a happy reliance on the existing stock of tools and ideas, without
> any effort at prior philosophy – simply is not a workable strategy.

Of course any claim that a 'radical cataclysm' is occurring in international politics may seem unduly alarmist. But there does seem to be a
feeling that some fundamental changes are taking place which require
deeper reflection in Gellner's sense of 'prior philosophy'. If this is the
case, can conflict theory offer us any help?

However, before we do this should we examine what global developments are challenging accepted ideas of peacekeeping? These are
well known and have been identified by many analysts. One of the
most frequently cited features of contemporary politics is the growth
of internal conflicts. Most protracted violent conflicts in the world
now occur within states, not between them. Many of these are at
least partly linked to ethnic differences. Such conflicts present many
challenges to the UN. We can note four. The first is that ethnic conflicts are notoriously difficult to resolve. Miall (1992, p. 185) has calculated that only three of the 28 conflicts involving minorities that he
examined were peacefully resolved, and Mitchell (1992) has produced
a good analysis of some of the reasons why ethnic conflicts can be so
hard to manage or resolve (see also Zartman, 1993, pp. 24–7). Even
where peace agreements are signed they can be difficult to implement
(see especially de Silva and Samarasinghe, 1993). The UN, for example, has repeatedly had to return to the situation in Angola
because of the failure of peace initiatives. Therefore it seems likely
that a peacekeeping commitment in a situation of protracted ethnic
conflict will be a long and testing one. This has certainly been the
experience of the operations in Cyprus (since 1964) and Lebanon
(since 1978) and it may be the fate of UNPROFOR.

The second challenge is that modern ethnic conflicts create enormous humanitarian problems. Recent research suggests that 80 per
cent of the casualties in such conflicts are civilians since as someone
has pointed out the aim of the military in such wars is to attack the
civilians on the other side. This reduces the chances that they will be
killed or injured and allows them to purge areas of members of the
other communities. Those who do not become casualties usually
become refugees or displaced persons. The UN has recently found it
impossible to resist international pressure to do something about

those cases which come under the spotlight of the global media. So in Bosnia and Somalia, despite the Charter restrictions on intervention in the internal affairs of member-states, the organization has been dragged into situations that involve its going beyond 'traditional peacekeeping'. Global news agencies like CNN now have an important impact on public opinion and by offering images of suffering and distress can appeal to the public and create a powerful constituency demanding that something be done in specific situations. Of course such media attention is notoriously short-lived – who cares about the Kurds or the Rwandans now? But over a brief period a strong influence can be exerted on governments and international organizations. In such circumstances there will be a great temptation on governments to 'dump' the problem with the UN in order to appear that they are doing something constructive.

Once on the ground the peacekeepers then face the third challenge posed by internal conflicts. This is the type of work peacekeepers are expected to do on missions. Inevitably the growing involvement of the UN in internal conflicts has moved the organization away from border zone monitoring and the protection of buffer zones towards a greater law and order role.

It also brings the UN into situations where the control of armed groups and the lack of effective central authority is a real problem. In extreme situations the UN, as in Somalia or Liberia or Lebanon, may be called in where there is no effective government and the warlord has re-emerged as a significant actor. Ignatieff (1993, p. 28) has noted the return of these figures who tend to dominate war zones in Bosnia, Lebanon, Georgia, Cambodia and Somalia, describing them as follows:

> Their vehicle of choice is a four-wheel drive Cherokee Chief.... They pack a pistol but they don't wave it about. They leave vulgar intimidation to the bodyguards in the back of the jeep, the ones with the shades, designer jeans and Zastava machine pistols. They themselves dress in leather jackets, floral ties and pressed corduroy trousers favoured by German television producers.

These 'technicians in violence... provide the two commodities everybody... craves: security and vengeance' (p. 30).

The changing nature of peacekeeping and the move away from 'traditional' roles towards a multiplicity of functions has been noted by several commentators. Wiseman (1990, p. 35) has pointed out how these can be roughly grouped under three headings. First are military functions: observation and monitoring, supervision of withdrawal of forces, maintenance of buffer zones, regulation of disposition and movement of military forces, prevention of infiltration and prevention of civil war. Second are governmental/political functions: maintenance of territorial integrity, provision of law and order, ensuring political independence, assisting in the establishment of a viable government, security of the population, management of communal strife, coping with non-governmental entities, assumption of temporary governmental authority and administration, and election monitoring. Third are civil functions: humanitarian assistance, monitoring and regulation of the flow of refugees, the management of local disputes. Rikhye (1990, p. 184) has identified other possible future roles in combating terrorism, drug interdiction and naval peacekeeping. Finally, a report by the US Institute for Peace (1994, p. 8) points out that peacekeeping tasks now include 'civil functions, disarming militias, providing security to the population, rescuing "failed" countries, organizing elections, launching preventive deployment, encouraging peace settlement, providing humanitarian assistance, or security for delivery of humanitarian assistance'.

The changing international context and the wide variety of roles that UN peacekeepers now have to play raises certain questions about the accepted guidelines of peacekeeping. If the UN is going to play a stronger role in conflict prevention does this mean that contributions from great powers should not be welcomed? Or should US troops be used in a tripwire function as they are in the UNPROFOR mission in Macedonia? (Evidence of this is that the presence of British forces with UNFICYP in 1974 caused the Turkish invasion forces to halt attacks in certain parts of Cyprus, most notably at the Nicosia International Airport). How relevant is Article 2(7) in a world of global communications where the 'concept of non-intervention in internal affairs is crumbling and conflicts within and between states get inextricably linked' (Rupesinghe, 1990, p. 1)? How can one obtain the consent of a host state where all central authority has collapsed? Can one rely on moral authority rather than power when faced with warlords or by others who treat the UN with contempt and prevent it from helping the victims of violence?

INSIGHTS FROM CONFLICT RESEARCH?

Perhaps the most significant development in conflict research in recent years has been the trend towards viewing conflict as a dynamic phenomenon that moves through different stages. As a result successful and constructive intervention strategies have to take note of what stage a conflict is at and devise a strategy appropriate to that phase. There are several examples of this sort of thinking. Rupesinghe (1992), for example, has developed a model based on the matching of peace strategies to stages in a conflict. There are conflict formation (early warning), conflict escalation (crisis intervention), conflict endurance (empowerment and mediation), conflict improvement (negotiation and problem-solving) and conflict transformation (new institutions and projects). The place for peacekeeping is usually thought of as stage two – crisis intervention. However, is there any reason why peacekeeping cannot play a role at other stages?

The best known of the writers emphasizing the 'stages of conflict' approach is Ron Fisher. He believes:

> A co-ordinated plan of interventions requires that key elements in the conflict be identified and appropriate strategies then selected on the basis of their focus on and effectiveness in dealing with one or more of these elements.
>
> (Keashly and Fisher, 1990, p. 424)

His 'contingency model' is based on four stages: discussion, consultation, polarization, and segregation and destruction, and peacekeeping is associated with the last of these. Here, according to Keashly and Fisher (1990, p. 439), a 'power intervention by a third party which forcefully separates the parties would seem necessary'.

It is interesting to note, however, that Fisher's definition of peacekeeping seems rather dated. Also, according to experts on peacekeeping, the optimum time to deploy a mission is not when the conflict moves from the segregation to the destruction phase, but when the parties agree to end the overt violence through a negotiated ceasefire which the UN can monitor. When Fisher describes peacekeeping, he often seems to be proposing peace enforcement, which is a much more problematic strategy for the organization to adopt.

Another weakness with Fisher's approach, and one he shares with all writers who propose a 'stages of conflict' strategy, is that they tend to limit peacekeeping to a particular point in a conflict situation and may be underestimating the contributions that peacekeeping missions can make at other times. We have already noted the multiplicity of functions that UN forces are expected to perform. Many of these are applicable at several stages of a conflict. One of my particular interests at the moment is the idea of preventive peacekeeping, which is something neither Fisher nor Rupesinghe mention in their respective systems of classification.

One of the attractions of prevention is that it deals with the causes rather than the symptoms of conflict. Here a medical analogy is often used. All medicine tries to prevent illness, but there is a difference between the 'clinical' and 'public health' approaches. Although complementary, the former emphasizes the treatment of people when they become sick whereas the later tries to prevent the onset of illness by dealing with the environmental causes of it. Conventional peacekeeping can be viewed as the clinical approach, preventive peacekeeping as part of the public health or environmental approach.

Many writers have suggested that the UN needs to concentrate more on conflict prevention and *An Agenda for Peace* in paragraphs 28–32 refer to the preventive deployment of UN contingents in interstate and intra-state conflicts. So far the only large-scale example of preventive peacekeeping is in Macedonia, where UNPROFOR deployed about 1,000 troops in December 1992 following a request from the Macedonian government, supported by the EU and UN mediators in the former Yugoslavia. Here they are engaged in monitoring work. However, it is also possible that UN peacekeeping forces could play an even more constructive role. As Durch (1993, p. 10) has noted, the UN has already been asked to become 'the midwife of political transition'. For example, missions have assisted in the creation of a viable civil society through human rights monitoring (as in El Salvador), election supervision (Namibia and Cambodia), disarmament of the warring factions, and police monitoring and training. Peacekeepers can also provide assistance and protection for peacebuilding work.

Yet despite these doubts about the Fisher approach, it offers an intriguing framework for future research and Fetherston has begun to examine its implications for peacekeeping. There is no doubt that the conflict stages approach has important implications for peacekeeping operations even if experts may disagree on how to characterize the stages and what the appropriate strategies should be at each point. Flexibility should, therefore, be a feature of such missions.

Sadly, however, a striking feature of peacekeeping is the way that the pragmatic trial-and-error approach shown in the creation of missions is much more difficult to implement once a particular force is deployed in a conflict area. Here missions can become trapped inside a mandate that is inappropriate to begin with or which may become outdated as the dynamic of the conflict produces changes in the political context.

The case of the UN force in Cyprus (UNFICYP), which is the longest running peacekeeping force in UN peacekeeping history, shows the need to adjust peacekeeping policies in the light of a changing environment. Within four years of its deployment in 1964 UNFICYP, in combination with a series of other factors, was contributing effectively to the management of the inter-communal conflict on the island. There are some who believe that at this point the force should have redefined its role to include more active peacebuilding work in order to move from the creation of negative to positive peace.[1] This, of course, did not happen and the force muddled through on the basis of its original mandate. The incident reveals how difficult it can be to introduce flexibility into UN operations.

But where can the required flexibility come from? Galtung (1994) has recently proposed several things that could improve the capacity of peacekeeping to lower the level of violence: police training, non-violence training, conflict mediation techniques and having at least 50 per cent of the peacekeepers women. To this could be added a mechanism for mandate revision and greater cooperation with non-UN bodies – regional organizations, e.g. NATO etc., or non-governmental organizations (NGOs). But I want to concentrate on the personnel used on missions, and especially the role of civilian police.

There is a famous comment by Hammarskjold that 'peace-keeping is not a job for soldiers, but only a soldier can do it'. In fact the UN has always regarded peacekeeping as primarily a military activity. James (1990, p. 2) claims that 'peacekeeping is overwhelmingly, and distinctively, a military responsibility' and Rikhye (1984, p. 204) has noted that:

> UN peacekeeping operations have often been referred to as 'keeping the peace' or 'policing'. These terms can be misleading... While civilian police forces have been successfully employed in these operations, they have been so only within the limitations of their characteristics, and within the framework of their employment in their own countries. By virtue of their background and training, military personnel have proved better suited than policemen to meet the conditions likely to arise in the conduct of peacekeeping operations.... It is neither possible nor practical to employ police in military situations.

However, Rikhye (p. 204) goes on to qualify this statement by saying that this was true 'except where large-scale contact with civilians is needed'.

However, I think it is clear from what has already been said that many of the existing peacekeeping missions, especially those in 'internal conflicts', do involve large-scale contact with civilians. In these circumstances the need for what Fetherston (1994) has called contact skills is most apparent. But it is these skills which the military seem to lack and opportunities to acquire them do not seem to exist in many UN training courses (Fetherston, 1994, Ch. 7).

From the research undertaken for the INCORE project it seems clear that civilian police have a role to play in UN missions between the military and civilian contingents. The Irish police I have talked to who have been on missions, although they share the discipline and training qualities of soldiers, are very keen that they should not be 'militarized'. This, of course, has already been recognized by the UN and, beginning with UNFICYP in Cyprus, many missions have included a CIVPOL element. The tasks they undertake are varied and include: monitoring local police forces and potential trouble spots, providing guidance and training to local police, the control and assistance of movement, humanitarian relief and social welfare work, the investigation of criminal activity with an inter-communal aspect, the location of missing persons, securing the release of hostages, liaison between police forces representing the warring parties, the control or monitoring of checkpoints, joint patrolling.

Of course there are problems with providing a stronger police element. Their presence may not be appropriate for some missions (Bosnia?). It can be difficult to find sufficient numbers of well trained officers since police officers are fully employed in their normal duties, unlike soldiers who when not on active service are on stand by. So the Irish Minister of Justice has put a limit of 60 on the number of Garda who can serve on peacekeeping missions. Another problem is that the CIVPOL on some missions have not been up to the standard expected by the UN. The Secretariat is now attempting to remedy this situation and has introduced some basic criteria for selection of police: at least seven years' active service and at least 35 years of age, possession of a full driving licence and a certain standard of physical fitness. There is also a language requirement, usually English, and the UN has produced a comprehensive English language course for UN civilian police covering topics such as making contact, map reading, briefings, describing situations and people, 'persuasion and dissuading' and incident reports. The Department of Peacekeeping Operations has also produced in draft *Peace-keeping Training: United Nations Civilian Police Course* (UN Doc. 222/TP/CIP094), and the UN office in Vienna has written *United Nations Criminal Justice Standards for Peace-Keeping Police.* Furthermore, the recent CIV-POL operation in Haiti has been assisted by the drawing up of a comprehensive *Notes for Guidance of UNCIVPOL on Assignment* (September 1994). One hopes that this good practice will continue.

However, a point made very forcefully to me by Irish CIVPOL is that the problem is not so much the setting of standards for selection for UN peacekeeping. The real difficulty is enforcing these standards. But on this issue the UN is silent, at least in public. As Skjelsbaek (1990, p. 62) notes:

> In my experience officers who have served in peacekeeping forces are also reluctant to talk about them. Disclosures of large varia-tions in competence among national contingents could cause very serious political problems and could easily jeopardize an opera-tion. I know of no systematic and independent research in this field... However, the problem exists, and a discussion of possible remedies is called for.

To conclude, it seems that the UN is now operating in an interna-tional system which is presenting new challenges to the organization. These require a rethink of the role and purposes of peacekeeping, especially in internal conflicts. The pragmatic approach used in the past may not be satisfactory because the basic assumptions upon which this approach was based may no longer be adequate. Conflict peace and theory, although too dismissive (with exceptions) of peace-keeping in the past, should be able to help with this proposed reassess-ment, especially through the development and refinement of the 'stages of conflict' approach. One consequence of this approach may be that instead of attempting to work out which stage of a conflict peacekeeping should be matched to, we should be asking how we can alter peacekeeping to make it applicable at many stages, including the prevention stage. More flexibility is therefore needed on UN mis-sions, and one way to promote this could be through greater use of civilian police, who may have the contact skills necessary to deal with the sort of tasks expected on UN service today. Because there are so many unanswered questions this is a confusing but also an exciting time for peacekeeping. Fisher (1990, p. 247) is surely right that what we need is a 'more effective blending of theory, research, and practice toward the de-escalation and resolution of intergroup and international conflict.'

NOTES

1. This was an observation made by Michael Harbottle, a former UNFI-CYP chief of staff, at a workshop organized by the INCORE peacekeeping project in Paris in January 1995.

BIBLIOGRAPHY

Banks, M., 'The evolution of international relations theory', in M. Banks (ed.), *Conflict in World Society*, Brighton: Wheatsheaf Books, 1984.

Burton, J.W., *Deviance, Terrorism and War*, Oxford: Martin Robertson, 1979.

Burton, J.W., *Dear Survivors...*, London: London, 1982.

Burton, J.W., *Conflict: Resolution and Prevention*, London: Macmillan, 1990.

Cordovez, D., 'Strengthening UN diplomacy for peace: the role of the Secretary-General', in UNITAR, *The United Nations and the Maintenance of International Peace and Security*, Dordrecht: Nijhoff, 1987.

Diehl, P.F., *International Peace-keeping*, Baltimore, Md.: Johns Hopkins University Press, 1993.

Durch, W.J. (ed.), *The Evolution of UN Peacekeeping*, New York: St. Martins Press, 1993.

Fetherston, A.B., *Towards a Theory of United Nations Peacekeeping*, London: Macmillan, 1994.

Fisher, R.J., *The Social Psychology of Intergroup and International Conflict Resolution*, New York: Springer-Verlag, 1990.

Galtung, J., 'Three approaches to peace: peacekeeping, peacemaking, and peacebuilding', in *Peace, War and Defence: Essays in Peace Research, Volume II*, Copenhagen: Christian Ejlers, 1976.

Galtung, J., '*Peace and Conflict Research in the Age of Cholera: Ten Pointers to the Future*, Keynote address to IPRA's XV Conference, Malta, 31 October 1994.

Gellner, E., 'The last pragmatist, or the behaviourist Platonist', in *Spectacles and Predicaments*, Cambridge University Press, 1979a.

Gellner, E., 'Pragmatism and the importance of being earnest', in *Spectacles and Predicaments*, Cambridge University Press, 1979b.

Harbottle, M., 'The strategy, of third party intervention in conflict resolution', *International Journal*, Vol. 25, No. 1.

Ignatieff, M. *Blood and Belonging: Journeys into the New Internationalism*, London: Chatto & Windus, 1993.

James, A., *Peacekeeping in International Politics*, London: Macmillan, 1990.

Keashly, L. and Fisher, R.J., 'Towards a contingency approach to third party intervention in regional conflict: a Cyprus illustration', *International Journal*, XLV, pp. 424–53.

Kelman, H.C., 'On the history and development of peace research: personal reflections', in Jaap Nobel (ed.), *The Coming of Age of Peace Research*, Groningen: Styx Publications, 1991.

Licklider, R. (ed.), *Stopping the Killing: How Civil Wars End*, New York: New York University Press, 1993.

Miall, H., *The Peacekeepers: Peaceful Settlement of Disputes since 1945*, London: Macmillan, 1992.

Mitchell, C.R., *The Structure of International Conflict*, London: Macmillan, 1981.

Mitchell, C.R., 'External peacemaking initiatives and intra-national conflict', in M. Midlarski (ed.), The Internationalisation of Communal strife, London: Routledge, 1992.

Rikhye, I.J., *The Theory and Practice of Peacekeeping*, London: Hurst, 1984.

Rupesinghe, K., *The Disappearing Boundaries between Internal and External Conflicts*, paper presented to IPRA Conference, Groningen.

Rupesinghe, K., 'Conflict transformation in multi-ethnic societies', *Estudios Internacionales Revista del IRIPAZ*, Vol. 3, No. 6.

Ryan, S., 'Conflict management and conflict resolution', *Terrorism and Political Violence*, Vol. 2, No. 1, pp. 54–71.

Ryan, S., 'Preventive diplomacy, ethnic conflict and United Nations peacekeeping', in D. Carment and P. James (eds), *The International Dimensions of Ethnic Conflict*, forthcoming.

de Silva, K.M. and Samarasinghe, S.W.R. de A. (eds), *Peace Accords and Ethnic Conflict*, London: Pinter, 1993.

Skjelsbaek, K., 'UN peacekeeping: expectations, limitations and results: forty years of mixed experience', in I.J. Rikhye and K. Skjelsbaek (eds), *The United Nations and Peacekeeping: Results, Limitations and Prospects*, London: Macmillan, 1990.

Urquhart, B., *A Life in Peace and War*, London: Weidenfeld & Nicolson, 1987.

Urquhart, B., 'Reflections by the Chairman', in I.J. Rikhye and K. Skjelsbaek (eds), *The United Nations and Peacekeeping: Results, Limitiations and Prospects*, London: Macmillan, 1990.

US Institute for Peace, *The Professionalization of Peacekeeping: A Study Group Project*, Washington: Institute for Peace, 1994.

Wiseman, H., 'Peacekeeping in the international political context', in I.J. Rikhye and K. Skjelsbaek (eds), *The United Nations and Peacekeeping: Results, Limitations and Prospects*, London: Macmillan, 1990.

Zartman, I.W., 'The unfinished agenda: negotiating internal conflicts', in Licklider, R. (ed.), *Stopping the Killing: How Civil Wars End*, New York: New York University Press, 1993.

3 Recent Developments in Peacekeeping – The Irish Military Experience

Oliver A.K. Macdonald

INTRODUCTION

Peacekeeping is an activity most frequently associated with the United Nations as they pursue the primary purpose of that organization. This, according to the Charter, is:

> to maintain international peace and security, and to that end: to take effective collective measures for the prevention and removal of threats to the peace, and for the suppression of acts of aggression or other breaches of the peace and to bring about by peaceful means, and in conformity with the principles of justice and international law, adjustment or settlement of international disputes or situations which might lead to a breach of the peace.[1]

Primary responsibility for the maintenance of peace and security is vested in the Security Council (Ch. V, Art. 24) and the specific powers for the discharge of these duties are laid down as follows: in Chapter VI, which deals with the 'Pacific Settlement of Disputes'; in Chapter VII, which deals with 'Action with Respect to Threats to the Peace, Breaches of the Peace and Acts of Aggression'; in Chapter VIII, which deals with 'Regional Arrangements'; and in Chapter XII, which deals with the 'International Trusteeship System'.[2] As we celebrate the fiftieth anniversary of the signing of the Charter of the United Nations it seems to be particularly appropriate that peacekeeping should be very much in our minds. Yet in the context of the Charter peacekeeping is paradoxical, as the word *peacekeeping* does not appear anywhere in the text. Indeed, it was probably an unknown concept when the founding fathers drafted their plans for new collective security in the aftermath of two world wars in less than 30 years. However deeply the genesis of peacekeeping may be clouded in obscurity, the collective shivers of the Cold War made it abundantly clear from the very early days of the United Nations as an organization that the collective security intentions and the consequent enforcement action envisaged in Article 42 would be unworkable.

There must be strong support for the view that classic peacekeeping evolved in the creative mind of Dag Hammarskjold and that it was shaped into reality by Hammarskjold and Brian Urquhart. There is general consensus now that the first UN peacekeeping force was UNEF (Suez 1956).[3] There were earlier missions. UNTSO (1948 to present) is considered to be the first full military observer mission. However, the first UN mission was UNSCOB which was established by the General Assembly in response to Greek allegations of Communist border infiltrations from neighbouring countries. UNSCOB established observer groups with military observers and even produced a handbook for observers.[4] UNSCOB has a particular relevance today. It was an exercise in successful preventive diplomacy which has certain echoes in the effective preventive deployment today in Macedonia (FYROM).

UNEF was a development of enormous significance. The Blue Helmets (Les Casques Bleus) were adopted as a pragmatic response to the problem of providing a common identifying item of uniform for UN troops.[5] The blue helmet and the blue beret have become enduring symbols of UN troops and observers throughout the world. Of infinitely greater significance is the contribution of Hammarskjold's skill and tact which enabled the Anglo-French forces to withdraw in an orderly manner and with a minimal loss of face.[6] These pointed the way to the establishment of peacekeeping principles and negotiating practices which have retained a remarkable validity to the present time.

Chapter 6 1/2 was born and enjoyed a fairly stable existence for over 30 years, even if its role was considered to be somewhat in the margins of conflict resolution (or non-resolution) when measured in terms of superpowers and their military alliances.

The changes were rung in 1987. Symbolically, the turning point was the publication of Mikhail Gorbachev's *Perestroika – New Thinking for Our Country and for Our World.*[7] Inexorably, the wheel turned and the tundra of Communism melted in the warming dawn of democracy. Thoughts of war and its conduct yielded to problems of peace and its management. By the beginning of the 1990s peace was the cut diamond of international relations. As such it was multifaceted and deposited by a somewhat confused world for safe keeping in the vault of the United Nations.

Peacekeeping was rediscovered. It became an instrument or tool of conflict management of unprecedented popularity. It did so in a period of what might be called blurred focus following the ending of the Cold War and its concomitant balance of power. The peace spectrum was rapidly enlarged. Peacekeeping was given greatly increased horizons as new roles were being sought for large armed forces which had been focused primarily on the conduct of war between superpower alliances. Definitions became blurred and indeed some remain so. For example, for many years peacekeeping operations have included a humanitarian dimension. Now humanitarian operations have assumed a military dimension. This has led to confusion between peacekeeping and humanitarian operations with fairly dire consequences in terms of expectations of results from missions, and to uncomfortable overlapping of areas of authority and responsibility. In this environment the following definitions may be helpful:[8]

- *Preventive diplomacy*: action to prevent disputes from arising between parties, to prevent existing disputes from escalating into conflicts and to limit the spread of the latter when they occur.
- *Preventive deployment*: a military UN presence in the field, at the request of the party or parties concerned or with their consent, in order to defuse threats or discourage hostilities.
- *Peacemaking*: diplomatic action to bring hostile parties to a negotiated agreement through such peaceful means as those foreseen under Chapter VI of the UN Charter.
- *Peacekeeping*: a UN presence in the field (normally including military and civilian personnel), with the consent of the parties, to implement or monitor the implementation of arrangements relating to the control of conflicts (ceasefires, separation of forces, limitation of forces, etc.), to the resolution of conflicts (partial or comprehensive settlements), and (more recently) to protect the delivery of humanitarian relief in situations of conflict.
- *Peace enforcement*: may be needed when peaceful means fail. It consists of action under Chapter VII of the Charter, including the use of armed force, to maintain or restore international peace and security in situations where the Security Council has determined the existence of a threat to the peace, breach of the peace or act of aggression.
- *Peacebuilding*: is critical in the aftermath of conflict. It means identifying and supporting measures and structures which will

solidify peace and build trust and interaction among former enemies, in order to avoid a relapse into conflict.

AN OVERVIEW OF THE IRISH MILITARY EXPERIENCE IN PEACEKEEPING

The involvement of Ireland and the Defence Forces in United
Nations peacekeeping has been continuous since June 1958 when the
first group of officers went to Lebanon as observers with UNOGIL.
In the intervening 37 years Irish military personnel have completed
over 42,000 tours of duty, mostly of six months' duration, in 29 United Nations missions.[9] These can be seen in Table 3.1. The chronological spread of missions is quite uneven. As can be seen from Table
3.1, about half of the missions occurred in the 30 years to 1988. The
other half have arisen since then. This is significant for a number of
reasons. Firstly, the chronological spread reflects the dramatic
increase in demand for UN intervention in conflict areas since 1988.
This in turn accounts for the enormously increased demand on the
relatively little changed peacekeeping structures of the United
Nations Secretariat at the end of the decade. Thirdly, it has created a
huge demand for the human and the very limited material resources
necessary to establish and maintain peacekeeping missions in the
field.

There have also been other demands which have stretched concepts
of peacekeeping to previously unimagined limits, and perhaps beyond
them, as the tasks and situations facing peacekeepers have grown
more complex and demanding. Additionally other bodies such as
regional organizations (EC, OSCE, OAU, OAS) have had to become
actively interested in the management of peace since the ending of
the Cold War and all that has implied for the maintenance of international peace and security.

Referring again to Table 3.1, it can be said that from a military
standpoint the fundamental difference arising in the type of missions
listed is between peacekeeping forces on one hand, and missions
without troops on the other. It can be noted from Table 3.1 that over
40,000 of the approximate total of the 42,000 tours of duty have been
completed in the three major force missions to which Ireland has
contributed: ONUC in the Congo, UNFICYP in Cyprus and UNI-
FIL in Lebanon. The other missions in the table have been observer
or military adviser missions with two notable exceptions. The first of

Table 3.1 Participation in overseas missions: UN missions (as of 01/06/95)

Mission	Officers	NCOs	PTEs	Total	Remarks	From	To
UNOGIL	50			50	Closed	28/6/58	18/12/58
UNTSO	365			365	*Ongoing*	18/12/58	
ONUC	501	1,808	3,882	6,191	Closed	28/07/60	30/6/64
UNTEA	2			2	Closed	21/08/62	04/10/62
UNFICYP	879	3,275	5,300	9,454	*Ongoing*	27/03/64	
UNIPOM	14			14	Closed	23/09/65	22/03/66
UNEF II	49	194	330	573	Closed	30/10/73	06/09/74[1]
UNDOF		*From UNTSO*			*Ongoing*	03/06/74	
UNIFIL	2,231	8,201	14,352	24,784	*Ongoing*	13/05/78	
UNNY	8			8	*Ongoing*	27/11/78	
UNIT	9			9	Closed	24/06/84	31/07/88
UNMOGIP	2			2	Closed	28/09/87	26/06/92
UNRWA	2			2	Closed	01/02/88	30/06/92
UNGOMAP	8			8	Closed	25/04/88	15/03/90
OSGAP	5			5	*Ongoing*	15/03/90	
UNIMOG	44	133		177	Closed	14/08/88	10/03/91
UNTAG	20			20	Closed	16/03/89	07/04/90
ONUCA	57			57	Closed	03/12/89	27/01/92
ONUSAL	6			6	Closed	21/01/92	31/05/94
UNIKOM	27			27	*Ongoing*	18/04/91	
UNAVEM II	18			18	Closed	03/07/91	09/09/93
MINURSO	46			46	*Ongoing*	20/09/91	
UNAMIC	2			2	Closed	16/11/91	15/03/92
UNTAC	35	1		36	Closed	15/03/92	15/11/93
UNMLO-Y	7			7	Closed	12/01/92	05/04/92
UNPROFOR	29			29	*Ongoing*	28/03/92	
UNHCR (Y)	4			4	Closed	20/12/92	18/03/93
UNOSOM II	20	54	103	177	Closed	08/08/93	15/01/95[2]
UNMIH	4			4	*Ongoing*	21/09/94	
Totals	*4,444*	*13,666*	*23,967*	*42,077*			

1. Main body dep. 22/05/74.
2. Main body dep. 20/09/94.

these was the two infantry groups which served in the Sinai as part of UNEF II in 1973–74. The first group left Ireland to serve in Cyprus with UNFICYP in October 1973, and was transferred to UNEF from there. The second group was recalled from the Middle East by the government in May 1974 in response to increasing demands for troops for operations in aid of the civil power at home. The other exception is the deployment of two transport units to UNOSOM II in 1993–94. In the case of UNOSOM special legislation was passed to allow participation in a mission with a mandate which included peace enforcement as envisaged under Chapter VII of the Charter.

In addition to the 29 missions with the United Nations the Defence Forces have had overseas commitments to missions conducted by the European Union and the OSCE. Personnel have also been committed to humanitarian work in relief of some of the appalling suffering endured by the peoples of Somalia and Rwanda (see Table 3.2). These contributions are small, but so too are the missions to which the contributions of personnel and their expertise have been made.

There are many observations which could be made about these statistics. Of these it is intended to select just two. The first is that Ireland has given generously to international peacekeeping missions (see Table 3.3). This is obvious if contributions are calculated in terms of the size of the Defence Forces and the national population. We are also mindful that 74 of our comrades have lost their lives while on duty abroad in the service of peace (see Table 3.4). Thirty-five of

Table 3.2   Participation in overseas missions: Non-UN missions (as of 01/06/95)

Mission	Officers	NCOs	PTEs	Total	Remarks	From	To
OSCE	8			8	*Ongoing*	16/06/58	18/12/58
ECMM (Yug)	41	8		49	*Ongoing*	16/07/91	
ECTF (Rus)	3			3	Closed	29/01/92	31/12/92
ECTF (Yug)	10			10	*Ongoing*	25/02/93	
GOAL (Som)	3			3	Closed	14/04/93	03/04/94
EUNELSA	2			2	Closed	24/01/94	31/05/94
GEORGIA	2			2	*Ongoing*	13/04/94	
NGOs (Rwa)	20	7		27	*Ongoing*	21/07/94	
IRSG (Rwa)	4	18	17	39	Closed	11/08/94	05/12/94
Totals	*95*	*33*	*17*	*145*			

Table 3.3   Total contributions to international peacekeeping missions

	Officers	NCOs	PTEs	Total
Total UN mission	4,444	13,666	23,969	42,077
Total non-UN mission	95	33	17	145
Grand total	4,539	13,699	23,984	42,222

Table 3.4 Casualties

UNTSO	2
ONUC	26
UNFICYP	9
UNIFIL	37
Total	*74*

these casualties resulted from hostile action. The remainder are due to accidental or natural causes.

The second observation is that the Defence Forces have acquired a wide range of experience[10] both in classical, or traditional, peacekeeping and in other missions, which have been established to increase security or to relieve the acute human suffering which is an almost inevitable by-product of armed conflict wherever it occurs. This last is a particularly disturbing aspect of the intra-state conflicts which beset the search for world peace at the present time.

A study of some of these non-UN missions may show significant indicators of possible directions in the development of peacekeeping and related activities. They can have an importance which transcends the specific function of any one mission. For example, the four missions sponsored by the EU (or the EC in earlier times) may tell us something about the capacity and the future potential of the EU to act independently in the interests of international security. Equally, the conversion of the CSCE into the OSCE must surely encourage the prospect of an expanded capacity to implement operations which would be understood as regional arrangements as foreseen and understood by Chapter VIII of the Charter. The CSCE flagged a developing peacekeeping role for the participating state in the Helsinki Document of 1992, *The Challenges of Change*.[11] In the following year, the Rome Decisions (December 1993)[12] include a number of important principles and guidelines for the conduct of PKOs. These are sufficient to allow the formulation of elementary peacekeeping doctrine with a broad basis of application.

At the same time, the prospects for managing existing peace were further strengthened by the Vienna Document 1994 on confidence and security – building measures 'so as to give effect and expression to the duty of states to refrain from the threat or use of force in their mutual relations as well as in their international relations in general'.[13] At the United Nations, the *Agenda for Peace* (1992) and the *Supplement* (1995)[14] present important guidelines to the broader spectrum of operations which the UN is being required to undertake in this new world.

The Irish Defence Forces have amassed a wide range of skills and experiences in peacekeeping since 1958. They are equally anxious to remain abreast of developments. To this end a special military school was established in 1993. In November 1994 it was renamed the United Nations Training School, Ireland (UNTSI). It is a constituent school of the Military College and conducts courses for all missions abroad. At the time of writing (1995) UNTSI is conducting the first course for UN military observers and staff officers to be attended by foreign officers.

The Defence Forces have learnt many valuable lessons from their experiences – their implementation is standing us in good stead, in Lebanon and elsewhere. There are a number of what we would consider to be now well-established principles which form the basis of a peacekeeping operation. These principles are standing up well to the test of time. If these are ignored it is unlikely that a mission will (or can) succeed as a peacekeeping operation. The most fundamental is that peace is a prerequisite of peacekeeping. Secondly it can only be carried out with the consent of the parties to the conflict. Thirdly, peacekeepers must be totally impartial in the exercise of their duties. The non-use of force except in self-defence is also fundamental to the exercise of successful peacekeeping operations. One would therefore caution against the general application of peacekeeping as the panacea for all ills. Peacekeeping can only apply successfully in particular circumstances and under certain conditions. If these are absent the conflict situation may well deteriorate rather than improve, and peacekeeping itself becomes a victim of abuse. As the Secretary-General indicated in his *Supplement* to *An Agenda for Peace*, 'the last few years have confirmed that respect for certain basic principles of peacekeeping are essential to its success'.[15] In the same context he also made the two following observations: 'The logic of peacekeeping flows from political and military premises that are quite distinct from those of enforcement'[16] and 'To blur the distinction between the two (peacekeeping and enforcement) can undermine the viability of the peacekeeping operation and endangers its personnel'.[17] The messages in these statements are self-evident. Some missions in the first half of the 1990s have demonstrated just how carefully and precisely they should be heeded.

In order to illustrate the practitioner's perspective of the developments in peacekeeping three missions have been selected. The choice

may seem to be arbitrary. It is in the sense that they are the ones of
which I have personal experience. Each of them represents a new
departure, and hence is an addition to the Defence Forces' range of
experiences. In making the choice, missions in which Ireland was
responding to requests from the UN, the EC and the CSCE (as they
were at the time) respectively have been chosen. All are very different
but significant in their own right.

UNTAG – NAMIBIA

The United Nations Transition Assistance Group (UNTAG)[18] was
the first of the new UN field missions. The essential function of the
mission was to ensure the conduct of free and fair elections to a constituent assembly which would then draw up a constitution under
which Namibia would become an independent, sovereign state. As
such, it was a *political* mission. However, there was also a long background of war between South African forces and those of the South
West African People's Organization (SWAPO). There was the larger
military dimension in relation to Angola and the long conflict there.
As there was a ceasefire, there were forces to be monitored, withdrawn, disbanded, disarmed and eventually new forces would have to
be established. So UNTAG was a *peacekeeping* (military) mission.
Additionally there were many law and order problems centred on the
history of the acceptability of elements of the police force which had
to be monitored by the UN during the transition process. Therefore
it was a *civilian police* (CIVPOL) mission. As a result of the conflict
there were tens of thousands of refugees to be repatriated. So
UNTAG was a *humanitarian* mission (UNHCR). Elections would
have to be devised, conducted and monitored. So it was a mission for
the UN *electoral* division. There are even further dimensions: for
example, information and administration which could be added to
give public information and bureaucratic dimensions to the description of UNTAG as a UN operation. In short, UNTAG was very
much a multidimensional mission. As such it was a new experience
for most of its elements, military and civilian alike.

UNTAG's mandate which stems from UN Security Council Resolution No. 435 of 1978 finally began on 1 April 1989 and ended on
21 March 1990 when Namibia celebrated its independence. The
military component of UNTAG consisted of three infantry battalions, with four others in reserve in their home countries: air,

engineer, signals, administrative and logistics units and 300 observers and monitors from 14 different countries. The Irish contribution to this component was 20 military observers. Uniquely among the contingents, all the Irish officers had previously served with other UN missions. Indeed some had served with the Force Commander, Lt-Gen. D. Prem Chand in the Congo in the 1960s and in Cyprus in the 1970s.

It is obviously impossible in the present context to present even a summarized account of UNTAG and the preceding 70 years of efforts by the international community to secure independence for Namibia. An excellent conspectus is given in the 1990 edition of *The Blue Helmets*, a United Nations publication which reviews UN peacekeeping.

The tasks of the observer group were spread throughout Namibia and extended into Angola. About 200 of the group were classed as monitors. Most of these were operating in the general area of the Namibian–Angolan border. They were responsible for monitoring the ceasefire, the confinement of South African and South West African Territorial Forces to their bases and the dismantlement of the forces according to an agreed programme. A special group was set up in Angola, based at Lubango, to monitor the concentration and demilitarization of the SWAPO forces prior to their return to Namibia under amnesty as part of the agreed process. The remainder of the group were deployed as observers in the southern region of Namibia and along the border of the South African enclave of Walvis Bay. Subsequently some 200 of the observer group played a key role as team members in the electoral supervision operation and the arrangements for independence.

The Irish military role was quite significant. The commander of the Monitor Group in Angola was a very experienced Irish colonel.[19] The UNTAG liaison officer in Luanda throughout the mission was an Irish officer who had previously served as Assistant Military Adviser to the Secretary-General at UN Headquarters in New York.[20] In Namibia, the whole southern sector was placed under Irish control[21] with 80 observers of five nationalities deployed in the sector. The military coordinator for the election operation in October–November 1989 was an Irish officer, and an Irish officer was one of the three UN officers appointed to the tripartite military integration committee which was responsible for creating the nucleus of the new Namibian armed forces through the integration of South West African Territorial Forces and SWAPO/PLAN fighters.

UNTAG was a particularly interesting mission because of the multidimensional nature of the operation. It had another special significance for Ireland, apart from Irish UN Secretariat personnel deployed to the mission. It was the first occasion on which the Garda Siochana took part in a UN mission. Needless to say they made an outstanding contribution.[22]

EC TASK FORCE RUSSIA

The second mission I wish to highlight is the European Community Food Aid Task Force to Russia in 1992. This mission arose from a Maastricht decision in December 1991 that the EC would give a food aid package worth 200 million ecus to Russia on grounds of both humanitarian need and as assistance towards economic stability in the wake of the collapse of the Soviet regime. The project was conducted by a number of contracted agencies, who were responsible for moving the goods from EC countries to Russia; for arranging the controlled distribution and sale of the goods to the public; and for managing the counterpart fund which was created from the sale of the goods in shops and which gave the money generated by the sales to the most needy as identified jointly by the Russian authorities and the EC representatives.

Because of the difficulties obtaining in Russia at the time it was obvious that external coordinating controls and monitoring systems would be required in the country to assist the implementation of the aid programme. To these ends a military task force was formed in support of the contracted agencies. It had a small headquarters in Moscow and two subgroups of monitors, one in Moscow and one in St Petersburg. The initial plan was to confine the programme to these two great cities where the populations had been identified as suffering the greatest hardships resulting from food shortages during the long, hard Russian winter of 1991–92. Much of the food aid came from the huge EC intervention stocks, including large quantities of beef and butter from Ireland.

The concept of the aid programme including the counterpart funding was brilliantly imaginative in its response to the requirements of the situation in Russia as the problem was not a result of famine or drought which threatened the lives of multitudes through starvation. The problems of the changed order were manifold, but included the inability to link basic food resources with the consumer. This was due to the failure of the infrastructure once the centralized system had broken down.

The implementation of the programme posed many practical problems which are almost unknown in western market economies and developed societies where so much of the system is taken for granted. Thus there were no modern fleets of juggernauts to whisk the goods along expressways to modern, automated, hyper-warehouses. There were no chains of supermarkets through which the goods could be retailed rapidly. There were no sophisticated bulk-breaking and packaging systems. There were no computerized stock control or accountancy systems. There was no advertising, no quality control, no display counters and no modern hygiene regulations. There was not even a continuous railway system from west to east (wheels had to be changed because of the different railway track gauges).

The function of the Task Force was quite straightforward: to oversee the creation of a workable logistics chain from the sources of supply to the individual consumer, and to monitor the created system at all stages in order to ensure its efficient operation and at the same time to prevent fraud, theft or other breaches of agreed controls such as rationed quantities of food and fixed prices to the consumer.

This may seem to be an unlikely task for military personnel, but in the circumstances, it was probably only military officers who could have performed the Task Force duties as a cohesive international unit. Their knowledge of field administration and logistics, their training as observers and monitors combined with the practice of self-sufficiency make the military particularly suitable for these missions in difficult environments.

There were three Irish officers in the Task Force. All were assigned to Moscow where the Task Force group was commanded by a French general. He had two deputies, one French and one Irish, who controlled and developed the operations of the Task Force in Moscow. There were seven teams of monitors from France, Germany, Ireland, the Netherlands and the UK. Their common military background allowed the immediate creation of an effective operating group in spite of the different nationalities of the members. All adapted easily to the common procedures and purpose which were defined in the terms of reference for the Task Force. Russian was the common working language for all members of the group, which also developed its own form of 'Eurosperanto'.

The Task Force had been formed in the last days of January 1992. By April, it was decided to expand the programme to three other critical areas: Chelyabinsk, Nizhny Novgorod and Saratov. Senior German, French and Irish officers were appointed to head the EC Delegations to these areas respectively. The aid programmes to these areas lasted about five weeks from the second half of May.

By the end of June, the Task Force had completed its mission and was disbanded. A small detachment remained to oversee the final administration and as a contingency planning group for the following winter. This team included one Irish officer who remained with the EC in Russia until the end of 1992 when the remaining element was withdrawn. It was evident that the Task Force was an essential and successful element of the aid programme. Among the reasons for its success were the strict application of peacekeeping principles and practices: accurate observation and reporting; absolute and disciplined impartiality; effective international teamwork; and a clear command and control structure.

CSCE MISSION TO GEORGIA

It has been noted that 'with the ending of the Cold War, and the dissolution of the Soviet Union, the nature of the threat to peace has changed. Conflict between states has to a large extent been replaced by conflict within states'.[23] Since the dissolution of the Soviet Union, Georgia, once described as the 'Garden of the Soviet Union', has been threatened with fragmentation on two fronts, Abkhazia and South Ossetia. Georgia has also suffered a bitter civil war.

Unfortunately, it is impossible to outline here the conflicts in Georgia or the roles played by various parties in the unfolding of events which occurred during the fighting. On one front, we can merely note that following fierce fighting the Abkhazians (with external aid) forced the Georgians out of Abkhazia towards the end of 1993. There are up to 300,000 Georgian refugees as a consequence of this fighting.[24] The Abkhazians and Georgians agreed to a ceasefire in May 1994. A predominantly Russian CIS peacekeeping force was interposed. An agreement concerning the return of refugees had been concluded in April 1994, but little progress had been made. In November 1994, Abkhazia declared itself an independent republic, though this status has not received international recognition.

In the case of the Georgian–South Ossetian conflict, the Sochi Agreement of June 1992 achieved a ceasefire between the Georgian and Ossetian belligerents and provided for a peacekeeping force composed jointly of Russian, Georgian and Ossetian troops to occupy the zone of conflict in order to ensure adherence to the ceasefire. This ceasefire has held despite the inadequacies of some local elements of the peacekeeping forces.

In the context of the conflicts that have beset this country the international community is represented by a number of missions which have established offices or operations in Georgia. These include UN agencies, the ICRC and a range of NGOs. The United Nations Observer Mission in Georgia (UNOMIG) is focused on Abkhazia. The CSCE (now OSCE) Mission directs its monitoring efforts towards the situation in South Ossetia.

The current mandate of UNOMIG is specified in UN Security Council Resolution No. 937 of 21 July 1994. It has many of the characteristics of a classic observer mission. The Chief Military Observer is Head of Mission. The strength is 'up to 136 military observers with appropriate support staff'.[25] There are no Irish observers in UNOMIG. The mission's primary task is 'to monitor and verify the implementation by the parties of the Agreement on a Ceasefire and Separation of Forces signed in Moscow on 15 May 1994'.[26] It is also tasked 'to observe the operation of the CIS Peacekeeping Force within the framework of the implementation of the Agreement'.[27]

In contrast, the CSCE Mission is very small. The Head of Mission is a diplomat. Its strength is 17, about half of whom are military. An Irish officer served as mission Chief of Staff from April to December 1994. A second Irish officer has been serving with the mission since then. The mandate of the mission is specified in the *Modalities of the CSCE Mission to Georgia* issued by the Permanent Committee on 29 March 1994.[28]

The tasks of the mission which are specified in the modalities are both wide ranging and precise. The objectives of the mission are:

> to promote negotiations between the conflicting parties in Georgia which are aimed at reaching peaceful political settlement; to promote respect for human rights and assist in democratic institution building throughout the country; to monitor and promote free media principles; to facilitate cooperation with and among the parties concerned and, with their consent, to monitor the joint peacekeeping forces established under the Sochi Agreement of 24 June 1992, in order to assess whether their activities are carried out in conformity with CSCE principles, in particular those mentioned in chapter II.3 of the Decisions of the Rome Council Meeting.[29]

These objectives are then expanded into specific tasks in relation to the Georgian–Ossetian conflict, in relation to the conflict in Georgia/Abkhazia, and in relation to Georgia as a whole.

There is much to compare and contrast between UNOMIG and the CSCE Mission in the context of developments in peacekeeping. No doubt, in due time, such studies will be made. Here I intend to focus solely on the specifics of CSCE peacekeeping as found in the mission to Georgia.

Among the many prescriptive details concerning the CSCE peacekeeping operations, the Helsinki Document states that CSCE PKOs 'may assume a variety of forms including observer and monitor missions'. This is of particular significance to the practitioner on the ground in situations such as those found in Georgia. It will be recalled that UNOMIG is charged to *observe* the CIS peacekeeping forces while the CSCE Mission in Georgia is to *monitor* the joint peacekeeping forces. The difference can be crucially important but is not clearly defined by mandate. Monitoring is more intrusive than observation and therefore requires very close cooperation between monitors and the force being monitored. An initial question might well be, why did the CSCE assign a monitoring task to its mission in Georgia in respect of the Joint Peacekeeping Force (JPKF)? One reason is that the JPKF is keeping the peace in the area of South Ossetia on the footing of a bilateral agreement between Georgia and Russia, the Sochi Agreement. By the terms of this Agreement the force was to be under the control of a Joint Control Commission (JCC). However, the JCC did not meet for over two years from July 1992. As a result there was much concern about the effective political oversight of the force and the exercise of joint command as well as about the unusual composition of the force.

The Joint Peacekeeping Force in the South Ossetia zone of conflict is not a CSCE mission, but since both Georgia and Russia are member-states they can be expected to conform to the principles and norms of the CSCE including those contained in the Helsinki Document. In addition to the Helsinki Document, the fourth council meeting of the CSCE ministers in Rome in December 1993 presented 'principles and considerations essential to CSCE cooperative arrangements as well as to the activities of a third-party military force'. These are:

- respect for sovereignity and territorial integrity;
- consent of the parties;

- impartiality;
- multinational character;
- clear mandate;
- transparency;
- integral link to a political process for conflict resolution;
- plan for orderly withdrawal.[30]

It is these guidelines in particular which defined the monitoring parameters for the CSCE Mission to Georgia and the JPKF. As indicated above, a vital element in the monitoring of forces is the consent of the commanders of the force which is to be monitored. In the case of the JPKF in Georgia this was achieved in a professional and cooperative manner. The commanders understood and accepted the international community's concern that the peacekeeping operation should conform to the desired principles and considerations enumerated in Rome. Equally, the monitors understood that they had no function in the exercise of command of the force. Thus a good working relationship was established between the CSCE Mission and the commanders of the Joint Peacekeeping Forces. On a number of occasions the monitors and diplomats of the CSCE mission were able to assist the JPKF at their request in the defusing of local tensions and in negotiating the release of hostages.

Today the OSCE mission is still actively engaged in its many activities including the monitoring of the Joint Peacekeeping Force. The mission has shown that monitoring can be conducted successfully to the mutual benefit of the peacekeeping force and the international community.

CONCLUSION

These three missions described serve to illustrate to some small degree the diversity of the peacekeeping experiences being undertaken by the Irish Defence Forces. In UNTAG there was the multidimensional experience of a very successful operation. In the EC Task Force in Russia we had the first 'civilian' employment of trained military peacekeepers in a humanitarian and economic support operation. In Georgia we are applying our experiences in monitoring both a third-party peacekeeping force and the conduct of an ongoing CSCE/OSCE Mission.

The strength of our peacekeeping is founded on a combination of many factors. These include detailed lessons which can be learnt from our ever broadening experiences, for in contributing to peace-keeping missions we also learn from them. We endeavour constantly to attain the highest standards of training in the light of our experiences and studies of the evolution in peacekeeping. We fully recognize that peacekeeping requires very specific training and are therefore very pleased to have a school devoted exclusively to the study of and training for peacekeeping operations – the United Nations Training School, Ireland.

NOTES

1. Charter of the United Nations, San Francisco, 26 June 1945, Art. 1, para. 1, United Nations, New York.
2. Ibid., p. 11.
3. For a description and account of UNEF see *The Blue Helmets*, 2nd edn, United Nations, New York, 1990, Chapter 3.
4. D.H. Bowett, *United Nations Forces*, London: Stevens, 1964, pp. 61 ff.
5. Brian Urquhart, *A Life in Peace and War*, New York: Harper & Row, 1987, p. 134.
6. Ibid., p. 135.
7. Mikhail Gorbachev, *Perestroika – New Thinking for Our Country and for Our World*, New York: Harper & Row, 1987.
8. Many of the definitions correspond exactly with definitions used in Boutros Boutros-Ghali, *An Agenda for Peace*, United Nations, New York, 1992.
9. The statistics are compiled by UNTSI on the basis of information supplied by Defence Forces Headquarters, records sections.
10. Maj.-Gen. G.J. McMahon, *The United Nations, World Peace and the Irish Military Experience. An Cosantoir Review*, 1994, p. 120.
11. CSCE Helsinki Document 1992, Chapter III, published by Dept of Foreign Affairs, Ireland, 1993.
12. CSCE Decisions, in *Reference Manual*, Vienna: CSCE, 1993, p. 26.
13. Vienna: CSCE, Doc. 1033/94, p. 1.
14. Boutros Boutros-Ghali, *Supplement to An Agenda for Peace*, General Assembly Doc. A/50/60, 3 January 1995.
15. Ibid., para. 33.
16. Ibid., para. 35.
17. Ibid.
18. For an account of UNTAG see *The Blue Helmets – A Review of United Nations Peacekeeping*, 2nd edn, United Nations, New York, 1990.
19. Col. Michael Moriarty.
20. Comdt John A. Ryan.
21. Lt-Col. David Stapleton was appointed by the Force Commander as Sector Commander for the Southern Sector in Namibia. This was an area about 2.5 times the size of Ireland.

22. The Commissioner of the Civilian Police in UNTAG was Assistant Commissioner Stephen Fanning.
23. University of Limerick, Notification of Conference on Peacekeeping, June 1995: The Aims of the Conference.
24. These are the figures cited by Georgian government sources in mid-1994 to members of the CSCE Mission.
25. UN Security Council Resolution No. 937 of 21 July 1994.
26. Ibid.
27. Ibid.
28. *CSCE Journal of the Permanent Committee*, No. 14, Annex I, Vienna: CSCE, 29 March 1994.
29. Ibid.
30. CSCE Decisions, op. cit., p. 26.

4 India and UN Peacekeeping
Alan Bullion

India has been the most consistent and active supporter of UN peacekeeping operations of all the Third World countries. As is demonstrated in Table 4.1, India has continually participated in UN operations in different parts of the world, and in varying capacities, since 1947. As at 30 June 1994, the Indian contribution to current operations comprised 5,340 troops (7.93 per cent of the total), ranking in third place after Pakistan and France, and ahead of Britain, Canada and the United States.[1]

Table 4.1 Indian participation in UN peacekeeping operations

Place	Operation	Duration	Contribution
Korea	UNTCOK	14.11.1947 to 10.5.1948	Member.
Korea	UNCOK I UNCOK II	10.5.1948 to 21.10.1949	Member.
Korea	Command Military Unit	27.6.1950	One field ambulance unit: 17 officers, 9 JCOs and 300 other ranks, small surgical unit.
Korea	NNRC (Neutral Nations Repatriation Commission)	August 1953 to March 1954	Lt-Gen. Thimmayya as Chairman: 231 officers, 203 JCOs 5,696 other ranks.
Indo-China	Indo-China Supervisory Commission	1954–70	(a) Cambodia: withdrawn after elections – 1958. (b) Laos: medical detachment 1964–68. (c) Vietnam: 970 officers, 140 JCOs and 6,157 other ranks 1954–70.
Middle East	UNSCOP (UN Special Committee on Palestine)	15.5.1947 to 31.8.1947	Member.

Place	Operation	Duration	Contribution
Egypt	UNEF I	15.11.1956 to 19.5.1967	11 infantry battalions – one every year: 393 officers, 409 JCOs and 12,383 others. Maj.-Gen. Rikhye – Force Commander.
Lebanon	UNOGIL	11.6.1958 to 9.12.1958	71 officers
Congo	ONUC	14.7.1960 to 30.6.1964	2 infantry brigades: 467 officers, 404 JCOs, 11,354 other ranks. 36 dead, 124 wounded.
Cyprus	UNFICYP	4.3.1964 onwards	Lt-Gen. Thimmayya died on duty – 18.12.65. Other commanders: Lt-Gen. Gyani, Maj.-Gen. Prem Chand.
West Irian	UNTEA (UN Temporary Executive Authority)	21.9.1962 to 1.5.1963	Maj.-Gen. Rikhye observed ceasefire: 18.8.1962.
Yemen	UNYOM	June 1963 to September 1964	Maj.-Gen. Rikhye was observer, Maj.-Gen. Gyani was a Military Commander.
Namibia	UNTAG	1989–90	20 military observers.
Iran/Iraq	UNIIMOG	1988–90	31 military observers.
Iraq/Kuwait	UNIKOM	April 1991 onwards	15 military observers.
Angola	UNAVEM I	1989–91	30 military observers.
Angola	UNAVEM II	June 1991 onwards	3 military observers.
Central America	ONUCA	1990–92	12 military observers.
El Salvador	ONUSAL	July 1991 onwards	7 military observers.
Yugoslavia	UNPROFOR	March 1992 onwards	Lt-Gen. Nambiar: Force Commander (1992–93).
Cambodia	UNTAC	1992–93	2 battalions: 1,373 all ranks, medical aid.

Table 4.1 (contd.)

Place	Operation	Duration	Contribution
Mozambique	ONUMOZ	December 1992 onwards	940 all ranks, in 1993. As at 31.8.94: 88 troops, 75 civilian police, 18 observers.
Somalia	UNOSOM II	May 1993 onwards	1 infantry brigade/HQ staff: 4,976 all ranks.
Liberia	UNOMIL	September 1993 onwards	20 military observers.
Rwanda	UNAMIR	October 1993 onwards	1 infantry battalion: 800 all ranks.

In this chapter, I will first explore Indian participation since 1947 in these operations. I will then focus on the rationale and explanation for this extensive involvement by India, particularly in areas that do not have a direct bearing on Indian regional security. Finally, I will examine current thinking in Indian security circles on the role of UN peacekeeping in the 1990s and the lessons that can be learnt from contemporary Indian participation in these operations, with special reference to Somalia.

INDIAN PARTICIPATION IN UN OPERATIONS

Korea

India was a founding member of the United Nations and participated as a member of the first UN peace negotiations, on Korea, initially contributing to UNTCOK (UN Temporary Commission on Korea), followed by UNCOK 1 and 2 (UN Commission on Korea). The primary aim of these commissions was to achieve the unification of Korea under an independent government, commencing with the holding of a general election.[2]

However, these negotiations failed and war commenced between North and South Korea on 25 June 1950. India was firmly against participation in a UN military force, being particularly critical of what was perceived as the partisan involvement of the United States, which India regarded as resulting in the internationalization of the conflict.[3]

Despite these strong objections, India did send humanitarian aid to Korea, comprising a field ambulance unit and a small contingent of officers and other troops. It also continued to actively lobby at the United Nations for a peaceful political solution. To this end, India proposed the establishment of the NNRC (Neutral Nations Repatriation Commission), the formation of which was perceived as a crucial turning-point in the conflict. It also served to raise the profile of India at the United Nations.[4]

India became the Chairman and Executive Agent of the NNRC, whose task between August 1953 and March 1954 was to assume custody of prisoners who initially declined to be repatriated. A custodial force (CFI) of Indian troops was also formed to oversee the repatriation of prisoners-of-war. US President Dwight Eisenhower issued a fulsome tribute to Indian Prime Minister Jawaharlal Nehru: 'No military unit in recent years has undertaken a more delicate and demanding peacetime mission than that faced by Indian troops in Korea.'[5] The Indian role in Korea can therefore be regarded as instrumental in establishing the precedents for her participation in subsequent UN operations.

The Middle East

After Korea, India next participated in UNEF (United Nations Emergency Force), which was established on 15 November 1956, to secure the cessation of hostilities between Israel and Egypt and supervise the ceasefire. India had previously served as a member of UNSCOP (UN Special Committee on Palestine) in 1947 and had a particular geopolitical interest in the continued stability of the Middle East.[6]

Under certain specified conditions, India agreed to send a large contingent of troops to participate in UNEF, at one time comprising the second largest force. India regarded the Israeli invasion of Egypt in 1956 as a direct violation of the sovereignty and territorial integrity of Egypt.[7] The Indian presence continued until 1967, when President Nasser of Egypt demanded the withdrawal of UNEF, with which India immediately complied. India argued that without continued Egyptian consent, UNEF would in effect constitute an occupying force without mandate.

Elsewhere in the region, India also participated in UNOGIL (United Nations Observation Group in Lebanon), during the latter half of 1958. It also served in UNYOM (United Nations Yemen Observation Mission) from June 1963 until September 1964. This generally reflected Indian support for fellow members of the NAM

(Non-Aligned Movement) and Arab national self-determination and territorial inviolability in general.

The Congo

India played a particularly pivotal role in ONUC (UN Congo Operation), and provided over one-quarter of the manpower in this operation, which ran from July 1960 until June 1964. India was especially critical of Belgian policy in its former colony and the general lack of preparation of the country for independence.[8]

Although India initially welcomed the formation of ONUC, it was highly critical of the 'limited authority' of the UN force and its general lack of remit to deal with the rising tide of anarchy and lawlessness.[9] It likewise criticized what it perceived as US and British inertia. The UN defended itself against this critique, with the justification that ONUC was a peacekeeping force, not a fighting force, and also that it had no mandate to interfere in internal affairs.[10] India, however, regarded this stance as ambivalent and contradictory.

As a result of continued policy drift, in December 1961, several non-aligned countries withdrew from ONUC, fearful of troop losses and domestic opprobrium. A further turning-point occurred with the assassination of Congolese Prime Minister Patrice Lumumba in February 1961. India urged a strengthening of the ONUC mandate and sent significant numbers of combat troops for this purpose.[11]

However, there was also criticism from Indian opposition parties over the advisability of keeping Indian troops in the Congo. This followed the resignation in June 1961 of an Indian envoy, Mr R. Dayal, who was briefly UN special representative in the Congo. He had been accused of partisanship by Congolese authorities, some of whom were also critical of India's role in ONUC generally.[12] As Indian troop losses increased, opposition in India grew to its continued involvement. Another crucial factor was the growing domestic concern with internal unrest in Nagaland and Goa and mounting border tensions with Pakistan and China.[13] As a result of these tensions, India withdrew the bulk of its troops by March 1964.

India lost a total of 36 troops in the Congo, with a further 124 wounded, its first major losses in a UN operation.[14] It also contributed substantial financial aid and humanitarian assistance to ONUC, despite considerable domestic opposition. India's proactive role in Congo can be contrasted with its subsequent low-key participation in Cyprus and West Irian (Indonesia).

Cyprus

India did not supply troops for UNFICYP (UN Force in Cyprus), which commenced in 1964, primarily because of its preoccupation with domestic security on its borders with China and Pakistan. However, once again it contributed humanitarian aid in the form of medical supplies. It also had a significant number of personnel serving in the UNFICYP HQ in Nicosia, as well as holding the position of Military Commander of the Force on three successive occasions from 1964 onwards, with Lt-Gen. P.S. Gyani, Lt-Gen. K.S. Thimmayya (who died while on duty in Cyprus in 1965 of a heart attack) and Maj.-Gen. D. Prem Chand.[15]

West Irian (Indonesia)

India did not directly participate in UNTEA (UN Temporary Executive Authority) in West Irian (the former Dutch colony of West New Guinea), but it did supply ceasefire observers in 1962, under Maj.-Gen. Rikhye.

India again took an anti-colonial stance on this conflict, as in the Congo, and argued that West Irian should become part of Indonesia, a fellow non-aligned member. However, it has also been posited that her reluctance to provide troops was due to the heavy financial burden resulting from the ONUC and UNEF operations.[16]

Indian peacekeeping after the Cold War

Since the end of the Cold War, India has been engaged in several UN missions, providing military observers in the Iran–Iraq (1988–90) and Iraq–Kuwait (1991) border disputes, Namibia (1989–90), Angola (1989–91), Central America (1990–2), El Salvador (1991) and Liberia (1994).[17] Additionally, sizeable military contingents participated in operations in Cambodia (1992–93), Mozambique (1992–93), Somalia (1993–94) and Rwanda (1994). Lt-Gen. S. Nambiar also served as the first Force Commander and Head of Mission of UNPROFOR in Yugoslavia, from 3 March 1992 to 2 March 1993. It can thus be concluded from this overview that India has usually, whenever requested, provided considerable support and assistance to a wide range of UN peacekeeping operations since 1947.

RATIONALE AND EXPLANATION FOR INDIAN INVOLVEMENT

The reasons for Indian involvement in UN peacekeeping operations have been analysed by various commentators, including several eminent Indian generals who have served on these missions.[18]

First, it has been argued that Indian participation has served its geostrategic interests. This is most notable in the case of the various East and South-East Asian missions in Korea, Indo-China, Indonesia (West Irian) and Cambodia. However, India also perceives the stability of the Middle East and West Asia to be of vital strategic importance and has thus participated in several missions in the region (Egypt, Iran–Iraq, Yemen, etc.). Energy (oil, gas) supplies are an important factor here.

In this context, Somalia, with its pivotal position on the Horn of Africa and close political and economic connections with West Asia, can also be considered of geostrategic importance. It is less clear, however, what direct strategic purpose participation in African missions such as the Congo, Angola, Mozambique, Rwanda and Liberia serves.

Participation in these operations is explained by Parakatil and others as an expression of solidarity with fellow non-aligned countries.[19] Allied to this, India has often taken a stridently anti-colonial stance, as in the Congo and Indonesia, when it regarded the conflict as one of aggression primarily perpetrated by a colonial power such as Belgium or the Netherlands.

India also possesses the fourth largest army in the world and arguably one of the most professionally trained. It is thus well suited to serve in a wide variety of conflict situations. In turn, these operations likewise provide Indian troops with valuable experience which some commentators have more controversially suggested could be utilized for domestic conflict resolution in India.[20]

Other ostensive reasons for participation include humanitarian concern (such as in Rwanda, Yugoslavia, etc.), the desire for international kudos as a major power and also the revenue to be earned by participation in such missions. In this regard, there has been a considerable amount of lobbying by India in recent years to become a permanent member of the Security Council.[21] It is also acknowledged by fellow South Asian nations, Pakistan, Bangladesh and Nepal, who likewise make sizeable contributions to UN missions, that payment by the UN helps them offset the large standing armies they wish to maintain for local strategic reasons.[22] It can also be argued that inter-regional rivalry plays a part in India's wish to retain a major peacekeeping role, with Pakistan as at 30 June 1994 being the largest overall contributor of troops to UN operations (7,290, mostly in Somalia and Bosnia).[23]

PEACEKEEPING IN THE 1990s – THE INDIAN PERSPECTIVE

Indian experience in the Somalia operation (UNOSOM 2) has certainly led to a reappraisal of the future of UN peacekeeping within Indian political and military circles.[24] This can also be seen as a reflection of the wider debate both within and outside the UN on the post-Cold War role of these missions, given the huge increase in their number since 1989 and the changing nature of the conflicts being dealt with, which are increasingly of an 'internal' nature.[25]

Pravin Sawhney, the defence correspondent of the *Asian Age* (New Delhi), has argued that despite its setbacks in Somalia, with the loss of Indian troops and the danger such civil war situations present, India should still continue to contribute large numbers of troops to such missions.[26] Somewhat controversially, he claims that India's experience in Sri Lanka, with its ill-fated IPKF (Indian Peace-Keeping Force) deployment from July 1987 to March 1990, taught her valuable lessons that were subsequently utilized with success in Somalia.[27] Sawhney therefore concludes that while engaged in Somalia, Indian troops were much better equipped and prepared for combat. He envisages that in the future Indian troops will be invited to participate in a wider variety of peacekeeping roles, including in the CIS (Commonwealth of Independent States), where he claims Russia extended an invitation to India during 1994 to provide troops for deployment in the mountainous enclave of Nagorny Karabakh.[28] India also offered troops for the UN Haiti mission in September 1994, when Secretary-General Boutros-Ghali visited the country.[29]

However, in direct contrast to Sawhney's rather sanguine prognosis, the Somalian operation also drew significant criticism from other Indian commentators. On 23 August 1994, several opposition members of the Rajya Sabha (Upper House of the Indian Parliament) tabled a motion demanding the withdrawal of Indian troops, following the loss of seven Indian lives the previous day.[30] Lt-Col. Daljit Singh (Retd), a veteran of the IPKF operation in Sri Lanka, was severely critical of the lack of preparation of Indian troops for possible attack in Somalia.[31] Singh also argues that, as in Sri Lanka, the Indian contingent was handicapped by poor intelligence and being too trusting of the local populace. He concludes: 'Had we learnt from our experiences in the IPKF in Sri Lanka we could have put those lessons to good use in Somalia. But we are bad students of history.'[32]

But there were other positive and tangible benefits from Somalia. Some Somali leaders praised the humanitarian and friendly approach adopted by Indian troops. General Mohammed Liqliquato, a respected neutral Somali leader commented: 'The Indians took pains to understand our culture and tradition. And coming from a developing country, they also empathised with our problems. They are the most effective among the UN troops.'[33]

General Mohammed Morgan, a powerful faction leader and son-in-law of Said Barre, also commented: 'The Indians used to be referred to as tame elephants until they showed how tough they can really be.'[34] Morgan explained that in March 1994, when an Irish convoy being escorted by the Indian troops was ambushed by several heavily armed technicals near Baidao, Indian troops immediately turned on them, destroying three vehicles, killing nine militia and capturing a dozen others. They then called in the clan leaders to explain what had happened and to resolve the issue before it escalated.[35] This was typical of the conciliatory approach criticized above by Lt-Col. Singh. However, it did earn them local respect and confidence, which was not accorded to some other contingents.[36] Indian troops were also engaged in running orphanages, building support systems for schools, digging drinking water wells and other infrastructural projects. 'We have earned the nickname of Friends of Somalia,' Air Force Wing Commander N.K. Upadhaya commented.[37]

India itself had been severely critical of the lack of US resolve in Somalia.[38] The consensus of opinion was that the US had reneged upon its considerable responsibilities and that India and other participants were left to pick up the pieces.[39] Perhaps the greatest surprise for both the Indian and Pakistani armies was that despite their mutual hostility towards each other in normal circumstances on the subcontinent, the two sides formed a surprising degree of camaraderie and goodwill in Somalia. There was a high degree of interaction and rapport between the two sides and troops from each contingent were reportedly dining out together.[39] This novel development demonstrates another positive side-effect of such peacekeeping exercises, when soldiers from normally opposing sides learn to co-operate in unfamiliar terrain. A similar compliment was recently given by Lt-Gen. John Sanderson, the Commander-Designate of the Joint Forces of Australia and Commander of UNTAC, who commented that both Indian and Australian troops had built up a good rapport in Cambodia.[40]

CONCLUSION

India is proud of its long historic links with the UN peacekeeping tradition. It is also generally keen to continue contributing to new situations as they arise.[41] Indian Prime Minister Narasimha Rao is reported to have firmly supported India's continued participation, with the comment that 'the international peacekeeping forces should be selected from regions and areas far removed from where they are to be sent for undertaking credible operations'.[42] This could certainly be regarded as a vindication of Indian participation in Central American peacekeeping operations (ONUCA, ONUSAL), for instance.

However, some of the criticisms raised of recent UN missions have filtered through into Indian policy-making circles.[43] For instance, given the rapid escalation in some conflicts, such as Rwanda and Bosnia, it is generally felt that the UN should be able to respond much more rapidly to these situations.[44] Some Indian commentators have also questioned whether the UN has a sufficiently wide mandate to cope effectively with the increasingly complex ethnic conflicts that are very much on the contemporary agenda.[45] It has been suggested that given India's vast experience of UN operations, it could usefully perform the function of training other potential peacekeeping troops in the future.[46] One such proposal is for a UN staff college for training to be established in India. It is envisaged that this would be modelled on similar lines to other training schemes that now exist in Austria, Canada, Ireland and the Nordic countries.[47] According to a recent report from the Henry L. Stimson Center, Washington, India has a 'low' overall level of specialized training for peacekeeping purposes, despite conducting pre-deployment orientation and unit training.[48] A novel suggestion that might go some way to redress this lacuna is that a comprehensive questionnaire should be carried out among experienced peacekeepers, to create a database that can be drawn upon for further training.[49]

As a further demonstration of India's continuing commitment to UN peacekeeping, in September 1994 it was announced that India had promised to keep at least one stand-by brigade, ready to fly to any part of the world whenever called upon to serve by the UN.[50] This marked a change of policy, as formerly the general consensus of Indian opinion was against having a contingent of stand-by troops ready at short notice, which might siphon off troops urgently required for domestic conflicts.[51]

Overall, India feels that it has performed creditably in such operations. But there is also the perception that its contribution has been undervalued and it would like to participate in a greater share of the decision-making processes of the UN. To this end, it was reported in May 1995 that the US had consulted with India during the formulation of a new draft document for the deployment of UN peacekeeping troops, in acknowledgement of 'India's experience and expertise in peacekeeping, in counter-insurgency, and in mountain and desert warfare'.[52]

First, though, India must also overcome the perceptions and prejudices of others. Some observers have argued that India, along with other Third World countries, has been too willing to participate in recent UN peacekeeping operations. For instance, N. Nanporia contends that 'New Delhi's rather overweening pride in its peacekeeping credentials has clearly played into the West's hands. Flattered by the attention it has received on this count, New Delhi has been uncritically overeager to make its presence felt in places like Somalia, Haiti and Rwanda.'[53] As one observer of UN affairs pointed out after the killing of Indian soldiers in Mogadishu (Somalia) and the humiliating US retreat from Haiti:

> Anyone wanting to provoke trouble knows that attacking American troops is the best way to go about it. If, say, India sees its peacekeepers killed there is not a lot it can do. But because the United States can react, it must, either by retreating or retaliating.[54]

It can be concluded, therefore, that India should undoubtedly continue her laudable policy of support for UN peacekeeping operations. However, she should also adopt a more critical and reflexive stance, judging each new operation on its relative merits and demerits, while demanding an extensive policy input by those Third World powers, such as herself, who continue to contribute the bulk of contemporary peacekeeping troops.

NOTES

1. 'United Nations – the facts', *New Internationalist* (Oxford), December 1994, p. 19.
2. F. Parakatil, *India and the United Nations Peace-Keeping Operations*, New Delhi: S. Chand, 1975, p. 47. Parakatil is the best source on India and its involvement in earlier UN operations. However, his account finishes in 1970 and is also notable for its somewhat adulatory and uncritical tone.
3. Ibid., pp. 58–9.
4. Ibid., p. 63. V.K. Krishna Menon, chairman of UNTCOK, commented that with Korea, 'India emerged as somebody in the United Nations.'
5. Cited in S. Dayal, *India's Role in the Korean Question: A Study in the Settlement of International Disputes under the United Nations*, New Delhi: S. Chand, 1959, p. 196.
6. H.K. Srivastava, 'Indian defence and peacekeeping: are the two competitive or supplementary?', *Indian Defence Review* (New Delhi), Vol. 9, No. 4, October–December 1994, pp. 55–6. Srivastava argues that India has particular strategic interests in West Asia.
7. Parakatil, op. cit., pp. 80–1.
8. Ibid., pp. 107–8.
9. Ibid., p. 110.
10. Ibid., p. 112.
11. A. James, 'The Congo controversies', *International Peacekeeping*, Vol. 1, No. 1, Spring 1994, p. 49.
12. Ibid., p. 50.
13. S. Kodikara, *South Asian Strategic Issues*, New Delhi: Sage, 1990, p. 36. Kodikara suggests that Prime Minister Jawaharlal Nehru received a severe jolt to his *Weltanschauung* (world-view) from the invasion by China, leading to a radical reappraisal of Indian foreign policy and defence strategy.
14. Parakatil, op. cit., p. 124.
15. F. Henn, 'The Nicosia Airport incident of 1974: a peacekeeping gamble', *International Peacekeeping*, Vol. 1, No. 1, Spring 1994, pp. 81–3, gives details of Prem Chand's command in this incident.
16. Parakatil, op. cit., p. 154.
17. Figures are given for these operations in Table 4.1.
18. Lt-Gen. S. Nambiar (Retd), *India's Role in United Nations Peacekeeping*, paper given at Seminar on India's Role in UN Peacekeeping, 16 January 1995, Bombay University; Maj.-Gen. I. Rikhye, *The United Nations of the 1990s and International Peacekeeping Operations*, Southampton: Southampton Papers in International Policy, No. 3, 1992.
19. Parakatil, op. cit., pp. 16–21. See also James, op. cit., p. 49, where he mentions Indian concern for its African diaspora.
20. Srivastava, op. cit., p. 59. See also J. Keegan, 'Better at fighting: How the "martial races" of the Raj still monopolize service in the Indian Army', *Times Literary Supplement*, 24 February 1995, pp. 3–4, where he favourably discusses the suitability of the Indian Army in contemporary ethnic conflict situations, e.g. Somalia.

21. 'Germany wants India on U.N. Council', *The Hindu*, International Edition (Madras), 6 August 1994, p. 3. Editorial, 'Voice for the Third World', *The Hindu*, International Edition (Madras), 15 October 1994, p. 8. Egypt, Brazil, Nigeria and South Africa are other Third World states vying with India for a permanent seat on the UN Security Council.

22. 'United Nations – the facts', op. cit.

23. Ibid.

24. See Nambiar, op. cit., p. 2; Rikhye, op. cit., p. 7; Srivastava, op. cit., p. 56. See also J. Singh, 'To cope with the times: Indian security in a time of global change', *Frontline* (Madras), 28 August 1992, pp. 84–7, on Indian security in the 1990s. Jasjit Singh is a retired Air Commander and is currently Director of the Institute for Defence Studies and Analysis, New Delhi.

25. Among the best of the plethora of papers on this subject are: M. Berdal, 'Fateful encounter: the United States and UN peacekeeping', *Survival*, Vol. 36, No. 1, Spring 1994, pp. 30–50; S. Duke, 'The United Nations and intra-state conflict', *International Peacekeeping*, Vol. 1, No. 4, Winter 1994, pp. 375–93; A. Fetherston, 'Putting the peace back into peacekeeping: theory must inform practice', *International Peacekeeping*, Vol. 1, No. 1, Spring 1994, pp. 3–29; A. Roberts, 'The crisis in UN peacekeeping', *Survival*, Vol. 36, No. 3, Autumn 1994, pp. 93–120; R. Rubenstein, 'Cultural aspects of peacekeeping: notes on the substance of symbols', *Millennium*, Vol. 22, No. 3, Winter 1993, pp. 547–64.

   Useful books include: M. Brown (ed.), *Ethnic Conflict and International Security*, Princeton, NJ: Princeton University Press, 1993; E. Childers (ed.), *Challenges to the United Nations: Building a Safer World*, London: Catholic Institute for International Relations, 1994, esp. Ch. 7; *Wider Peacekeeping*, London: HMSO, 1995, a policy manual, in which the revised procedure of the British Army in contemporary peacekeeping situations is explained.

26. P. Sawhney, 'Despite reverses, Delhi still wants to police Somalia', *Asian Age* (New Delhi), 8 September 1994, p. 9.

27. A. Bullion, 'The Indian Peace-Keeping Force in Sri Lanka', *International Peacekeeping*, Vol. 1, No. 2, Summer 1994, pp. 148–59, gives full details and an analytical overview of the IPKF.

28. Sawhney, see n. 26 above.

29. 'India commits troops for UN duty in Haiti', *Asian Age* (New Delhi), 13 September 1994, p. 1.

30. 'Pull out troops, demands Opposition', *Asian Age* (New Delhi), 24 August 1994, p. 1.

31. Lt. Col. D. Singh (Retd.), 'Complacency responsible for loss of seven lives in Somalia', *Asian Age* (New Delhi), 1 September 1994, p. 9.

32. Ibid. For a fuller exposition of Indo-Sri Lankan relations, see A. Bullion, *India, Sri Lanka and the Tamil Crisis, 1976–94*, London: Pinter, 1995.

33. Cited in R. Chengappa, 'Somalia: An Indian Success Story', *India Today* (New Delhi), 31 August 1994, p. 76.

34. Ibid., p. 78.
35. Ibid., pp. 78–9.
36. 'Somalis want Indian army to stay till peace returns', *Asian Age* (New Delhi), 22 August 1994, p. 5.
37. 'In Somalia, far from the border, India, Pak troops dine together', *Asian Age* (New Delhi), 22 August 1994, p. 5. Similar instances of Indo-Pakistani camaraderie have also been reported with UNTAG in Namibia.
38. Other Voices, 'Failure in Somalia', *Asian Age* (New Delhi), 1 November 1994, p. 6.
39. M. Sommer, 'The price of peace: U.S. undermining U.N. efforts', *Frontline* (Madras), 29 July 1994, pp. 52–3; see also A. de Wall, 'African encounters', *Index on Censorship*, Vol. 23, No. 6, November–December 1994, pp. 14–31, for a scathing indictment of US policy in Somalia: 'Somalia: from humanitarian intervention to military offensive', *The World Today*, Vol. 43, No. 10, October 1993, pp. 184–6, gives a detailed critical overview.
40. Interview with Lt-Gen. J. Sanderson, *Asian Age* (New Delhi), 6 April 1995, p. 15.
41. Personal Interview with Dr L. Singhvi, Indian High Commissioner (UK), 17 May 1995, London.
42. Cited in *Hindustan Times* (New Delhi), 12 August 1994.
43. Nambiar, op. cit.; Rikhye, op. cit.; Singh, op. cit.
44. Nambiar, op. cit., p. 5, where he comments 'waiting for three months for troops to arrive in an area of operations as was the experience with some of the contingents in former Yugoslavia is too ridiculous to be funny.' This lacuna may well be partially addressed by the proposal from UN Secretary-General Boutros-Ghali in June 1995 for the creation of a UN rapid reaction force (RRF) to be deployed in Bosnia and other crisis points; see 'Panel backs UN reaction force', *The Guardian* (London), 20 June 1995, p. 12.
45. Ibid., pp. 5–6; J. Singh, op. cit., p. 86, on Boutros-Ghali's *Agenda for Peace*, and its significance for Indian security.
46. Srivastava, op. cit., p. 58.
47. S. Rangarajan, 'Perils of peacekeeping: training United Nations forces', *Frontline* (Madras), 30 June 1995, pp. 53–5.
48. Ibid., p. 55.
49. Srivastava, op. cit., p. 58, gives details of this suggestion.
50. 'India commits troops for UN duty in Haiti', *Asian Age* (New Delhi), 13 September 1994, p. 4.
51. Nambiar, op. cit., pp. 9–10, discusses training and the proposals and practicalities of operating a 'stand-by' force for rapid response to new conflicts. The long-running debate over the proposal for a UN Permanent Force is also addressed in Parakatil, op. cit., pp. 184–90, where various problems with such a contingency are raised, including (a) what they would do when not engaged on UN operations; (b) whether if they were kept apart from other national military units, they would become incompetent and outmoded; (c) their acceptability in host countries, i.e. whether Indian troops would be more acceptable in

some situations than others, such as other South Asian states. As long ago as 1958, UN Representative Krishna Menon stated: 'It is not possible to put by a number of soldiers and officers and say you are there to go out when there is trouble in the world' (cited in Parakatil, op. cit., p. 187). One possible solution would be to adopt the suggestion by Srivastava, op. cit., p. 59, where such contingents would also have a dual role as in training other peacekeepers and also be utilized for domestic conflict situations.

52. N. Nanporia, 'New Delhi's starry-eyed aspirations at UN', *Asian Age* (New Delhi), 23 May 1995, p. 8. In the same article, it is stated that the US has made consideration of a permanent Indian seat on the UN Security Council dependent upon 'improving relations with Pakistan' and settling the Kashmir dispute.

53. Ibid.

54. J. Leyne, 'From our own correspondent' (Transcript), *BBC World Service* (London), 13 October 1993. This quote neatly chimes with the neo-realist paradigm and its emphasis on the hierarchy of states and their relative military might, as propounded by neo-realists such as Mearsheimer and Waltz. See the discussion by A. Linklater, 'Neo-realism in theory and practice', in K. Booth and S. Smith (eds), *International Relations Theory Today*, Oxford: Polity, 1995, pp. 241–62. The still extant, albeit diminished, hegemony of the United States is exemplified in a speech made by President Bill Clinton at the UN 50th anniversary celebrations in San Fransisco on 26 June 1995: 'The US is still clearly the dominant country in the United Nations, we are still able to do the things we need to do'; see 'Clinton asks UN to clean house', *Asian Age* (New Delhi), 27 June 1995, p. 2.

5 The Perils of Peacekeeping for the US: Relearning Lessons from Beirut for Bosnia*

Grant T. Hammond

INTRODUCTION

The US has used military force abroad on a number of occasions since the end of the Second World War. While many of these interventions have been the direct application of military force into a conflict which it wished to end or keep from spreading (Korea, Vietnam, the Dominican Republic, Grenada, Kuwait), they have also been for peacekeeping operations. These have increased more recently with the end of the Cold War (Lebanon, Somalia, Haiti, Iraq and Bosnia). Without getting into an extended definitional debate about this often confusing term, suffice it to say the purpose of peacekeeping is the *deployment of military forces* to promote or preserve peace or some semblance of it. Peacekeeping is *not the employment of military force* to impose an outcome achieved through force of arms. The first deployment of US ground forces in a peacekeeping operation, and the most costly one in American lives lost, occurred in Lebanon.

US involvement in Lebanon in the form of direct military presence occurred on three occasions in two different time periods. US Marines were deployed for three and a half months in 1958, again from 25 August to 10 September 1982 and then again from 20 September 1982 to 30 March 1984. The purpose in each case was in general a 'peacekeeping' mission. The first was unilateral in nature, the latter two in concert with other forces who intervened as well. In these the US was joined with troops from France and Italy. In addition, the US supported the deployment of the United Nations Interim Force in Lebanon (UNIFIL) – deployed on 22 March 1978 and still there –

*The views expressed in this chapter are those of the author alone and are not policy statements of Air University, the United States Air Force, the Department of Defense or the Government of the United States.

as a part of US policy in the region. Although individual members of the US military were assigned to UNIFIL, neither it nor the Soviets, in keeping with the practices of the Cold War, sent in whole troop units as a part of UN-sponsored peacekeeping forces.

The reasons for US intervention and peacekeeping operations, the environment in which they occurred, US intent, assumptions behind them and the failure to accomplish most of the goals intended are rich in lessons for present and future actions of a similar kind for the US. The decisions and course of events in each case have as much to do with US domestic politics and the actions of allies as they do with adversaries and a concern with regional or global politico-military concerns of national security strategy. They exhibit a rich *melange* of ignorance, ego and diplomatic wishful thinking along with healthy doses of arrogance, a conviction that military power is an effective diplomatic tool for all occasions, and a failure to understand the options – or lack of them – of others involved in the disputes. Alas, from Beirut to Bosnia, despite a great improvement in American tactical ability to accomplish these deployments, the US may not have learned many of the lessons of this first, and in many ways, longest experience with peacekeeping.

This assessment will examine the ways in which the deployment of military forces, both unilateral and multinational, has been used to try and establish or maintain peace in Lebanon, the reasons why these attempts were unsuccessful and the lessons one might learn from this which may have utility elsewhere. If the Americans are to embrace the notion of 'preventive diplomacy' enshrined in the UN's *Agenda for Peace* and the necessity of Military Operations Other Than War (MOOTW) as a necessary part of 'Engagement and Enlargement', the national security strategy of the United States, understanding the fragility of the process and track record of peacekeeping missions is mandatory. Lebanon is the place to begin.

BACKGROUND: THE PLAYERS AND THEIR PROGRAMS

Of all the places in the world, with the possible exception of the Balkans, with which we could become involved, Lebanon is one of the most misunderstood by the US. It was ensnared in a Cold War rivalry with the Soviet Union, overlaid with a more than millennium long dispute between Islam and Christianity, wrapped in regional politics about which Americans knew little and cared less, and embroiled in a colonialist legacy of the West represented by the great powers of Europe who contested for control of the region with the Ottomans. Directly and indirectly, it focused on the existence of Israel as the extension of this colonialist experience, was based on outside support for all the factions in the drama, and was misunderstood by those who most earnestly sought to intervene to end the overlapping conflicts that were contained in the region known as Lebanon.

To the West, Lebanon was 'the Switzerland of the Middle East', a prosperous, Westernized example of a multiconfessional community which was at once Christian (Maronite, Melkite, Greek Orthodox, Catholic) and Islamic (Sunni, Shiite, Druze) in its religion, French and Arab in its culture, and so important to the region as the traders, bankers and middlemen among all these competing tendencies that its position was ensured by its value to all. A nice image, it was more myth than reality. However powerful this constellation of myths and the attraction of 'The Golden Age' of pre-1975, Lebanon neglected the personal ambitions of the *zuama*, the family political and commercial bosses and their various factions, who ran Lebanon as a sort of consortium of Mafia families. It ignored the existence of Israel and the festering sore that it represented to both the Arab and Islamic world. It ignored the territorial designs and political goals of Syria and Hafiz Asad. It ignored the Palestinians and the huge influx of displaced persons caused by the 1948 and 1967 wars. It ignored the impact of a Gamal Abdul Nasser and the defeat of the British and French in the Suez debacle of 1956.

Equally important, this flawed image ignored the fact that the Soviet Union and the United States played out their Cold War rivalry through proxies in the Middle East which they supplied with weapons, money and political support for purposes which had little to do with short-term goals and regional relations. It ignored the realities of regional politics and the overt and covert interventions of Syria, Iraq, Iran, Saudi Arabia, Jordan, Egypt, the PLO and others in Lebanon over the years. It ignored the fact that Lebanon was not a state but a collection of warlord factions and would-be mini-states. It ignored the changing demographic realities of the region, the fiction of the National Pact and the disparate political goals of the various factions forced to share the same piece of territory despite huge differences in political preferences, socio-economic background and desires, religious faiths and means to pursue their ends.

In short, the US presumed a world which shared the biases of the United States instead of the realities of the Middle East. Americans saw processes and institutions working through politics for public welfare. The reality was a feudal social order which placed individuals and patronage over public good, private gain through graft and corruption ahead of public welfare and family, tribal relations and vendettas ahead of even religious faith and conviction. All of this overlay any concept of citizenship in the state. Most Americans did not understand the subtleties of short-term alliances, the length of memories and blood feuds, the strength of *aln* (kin) in Arab cultures nor the nuances of religious differences.

While the US thought it was becoming involved in Lebanese politics, it entered into Lebanese culture and history with little or no understanding of the way things worked – or didn't work. Americans generally had little idea of the complexity and nuances of the individual *zaim* and the rules and routine of Lebanese politics. While the words were the same, the realities were different. While there were elections for the National Assembly, over one-third of the seats had been inherited from a father. The same group of families had virtual locks on certain ministries, an extension of the *Mithaq* (National Pact) agreement regarding the distribution of power within the Lebanese government. The President would always be a Maronite Christian, the Prime Minister a Sunni Muslim and the Speaker of the House a Druze. Nabih Berri, the head of *Amal* (an Arabic word meaning 'hope' and an acronym for *Afwaj al Muqawamah al Lubnanya* – Lebanese Resistance Battalions), once commented that the National Pact 'helped make us build a farm, not a country.'[1] The premiership rotated largely among four Sunni families – the Solhs, the Karamis, the Yafis and the Salams – while the Melkite Taqlas family had as its fiefdom the Ministry of Foreign Affairs and the Druze Majid Arslan held sway over the Ministry of Defence.[2]

Each of the separate confessional communities had rival groups vying for control. The Maronites had the Chamouns, the Gemayels and the Franjiehs and vendettas of long-standing among them. The Chamouns had a longing for fascism and ran a group known as 'the Tigers' which oversaw their business interests and protected their holdings and vassals. The were headquartered in Jouniyeh to the north of Beirut on the coast. In July of 1980, their militia was defeated by that of the Gemayels and Camille Chamoun's son, Dany, prudently went into self-imposed exile in Paris. The Gemayels were head of the Phalange, a rather blue-collar group of thugs that became the largest armed group – some 10,000 strong – among the Maronites. They were headquartered in the south and continued a long running feud with the Franjiehs. The Franjieh's claim to fame was a long-established presence, tough control of their region and protection of their followers, and a personal connection between Sulieman Franjieh (President 1970–76) with Hafiz Asad, President of Syria, which stemmed from a period of exile in Syria. They were headquartered in Zghorta and protected by the Zghorta Liberation Army.

In what became known as the Ehdene Massacre, the feud between the Gemayels and the Franjieh erupted bloodily as Tony Franjieh and Bashir Gemayel maneuvered, and were maneuvered, by their fathers and their supporters to compete for the Presidency. The Gemayels struck first, murdering 34 people, including Tony Franjieh, heir apparent to the clan, along with his wife and children in an attack on his home on 13 June 1978. With symbolism and timing that could not be denied, an assassination attempt on Pierre Gemayel (President 1952–58), the patriarch of the Gemayel clan, occurred exactly one year later, but he survived the car bomb attack. Bashir Gemayel's two-year-old daughter and chauffeur were killed on 23 February 1980 in a car bomb meant for him. His eventual assassination occurred 22 days after becoming President of Lebanon in September 1982. His younger brother, Amin, succeeded him. It had taken five years but the score was finally settled. Unfortunately, Lebanon was further weakened in the process.

Similar rivalries existed in the Muslim communities. Among the Sunnis, the major families which competed with each other were the Karamis of Tripoli and the Salams and Sohls of Beirut. Rashid Karami at age 30 had become Lebanon's youngest Prime Minister in 1953. Karami was the product of conservative religious credentials inherited from his father but was a modernist who survived and became influenced by Nasser. He was Prime Minister during the 1967 war. Riad Sohl was an ardent Arab nationalist and played a major role early in the Republic's history. He had been Lebanon's first Prime Minister and had built up a political consensus with the Maronites. Saeb Salam served as Prime Minister several times during the 1950s. Significantly, both Riad Sohl and Rashid Karami were assassinated, in 1951 and 1970 respectively. Among the Shiites, there were also politically significant families with power – the Asads, Khalils, Zains, Usairans, Haidars and Hamadas – and since there were more of them, their influence was more dispersed. The Druze, with a strategic location in the Shouf Mountains and a 4,000-man militia, were also a force to be reckoned with and politically significant.

They were led by the Jumblatts, Kamal and his son, Walid, who inherited the mantle of leadership after his father was assassinated in 1977.

The PLO, itself a loosely knit coalition of some 29 separate factions, held itself aloof from the others and eventually became the dominant Muslim force in the area, largely as the result of clandestine financial backing from throughout the Arab world and arms supplies from the Syrians, the Soviets and others. It was not too dissimilar from the military supplies being provided by Israel to the Maronites in the 1980s. Yasir Arafat, a former junior high school teacher whose real name is Abdul Rahman Arafat al Qudwa, is the titular head of the federation and has been since its founding in 1964 by the Arab League. Less well known, more prone to terrorist violence and equally as important in many respects was George Habash's Popular Front for the Liberation of Palestine (PFLP), a more radical, Marxist group. He competed with Arafat's Fatah faction in the terrorist years for leadership of the Palestinian movement. Both Habash and Wadi Haddad, an early Arab nationalist, had cut their political teeth at the American University of Beirut in student organizations.

The factions, personalities and policies that were the maelstrom of Lebanese national politics, robber baron capitalism and international intrigue were hard enough for the Lebanese to understand. Outsiders had virtually no chance of understanding the complexities of the egos, vendettas, feuds and alliances which were the substance of the political process. 'Elections were like time bombs.'[3] They tended to be very costly and very corrupt affairs for they confirmed the power of the individual *zaim* who really ran Lebanon. Elections were not determinative, merely punctuation marks that both closed and opened new rounds of struggle, and often violence, as both the winners and the losers tried to exact retribution against the other. Add to this the animosities and vagaries of the politics of Pan-Arabism, regional events, the superpowers and the Cold War, former colonial powers such as Britain and France, the oil boom, regional wars and the existence of Israel and one wonders how to make sense of things even in retrospect.

'THE EVENTS' OF 1958

Though referred to by many as the first Lebanese Civil War, the troubles of 1958 were referred to by many Lebanese simply as 'the events'. These constitute a series of transformations in the region and within Lebanon that threatened the stability of both. They began with events outside of Lebanon with the reaction to Gamal Abdul Nasser's Pan-Arabism and the Suez Canal Crisis in November 1956 and continued through the formation of the United Arab Republic in February 1958. Camille Chamoun, as President of Lebanon at the time, kept aloof from Pan-Arabism, and failed to condemn the Israelis for their role in the Suez war or recall his ambassadors to Britain and France.

The American connection, other than its role in forcing Britain, France and Israel to vacate the Sinai and the Canal in 1956, was through the diplomatic initiative of the Eisenhower Doctrine. This was seen as an extension of the Truman Doctrine to the Middle East and was proclaimed on 5 January 1957 in response to the unsettled nature of the region occasioned by the Suez Crisis. It offered US military and economic assistance to nations believed to be in danger as the result of Communist sponsored invasion or subversion.[4] Lebanon and Iraq were the only states in the region to embrace the Eisenhower Doctrine.

The Eisenhower Doctrine was unquestionably aimed at Egypt and Syria, later joined as the United Arab Republic. Within a month of its passage by Congress, the Eisenhower Doctrine was invoked. On 13 April 1957, King Hussein of Jordan foiled an attempted *coup d'état*. Though Jordan was not a party to the Doctrine nor a member of the Baghdad Pact, the US responded quickly to a Jordanian aid request and sent the Sixth Fleet to the eastern Mediterranean and some $10,000,000 as the first instalment of new military and economic assistance.[5] In that the Soviet Union was seen as Nasser's major backer, any threat to the status quo could presumably be Communist inspired. And the status quo was to be supported in all Western leaning states such as Jordan, members of the Baghdad Pact (Turkey, Iran, Iraq and Pakistan), and those which embraced the Eisenhower Doctrine – Iraq and Lebanon. In this polarized and violence strewn environment, Chamoun's actions alienated the Muslim community in Lebanon – Sunni and Shiite – the Druze, and the small but radical socialist left. As one commentator has remarked, 'The country had been saved from an open religious conflict by Chamoun's genius for antagonizing Christian as well as Moslem members of the establishment.'[6]

'The events' were fuelled internally by the Parliamentary elections of 1957 in which the routine of Lebanese politics was discarded by President Camille Chamoun in an attempt to tie the Maronite leadership closely to the West. In doing so, he was repeating the 1,000-plus year history of looking for foreign saviors for the beleaguered Christian community in Lebanon which dated from the Crusades. Indeed, it was this policy that was so clearly achieved, albeit impermanently, under the French tutelage in the nineteenth century and its protectorate of a mandated territory in the twentieth. But Chamoun's actions destroyed the delicate set of family and confessional balances that called itself a country. He set out to rid himself of the troublesome opposition in Parliament and through a combination of bribery, excessive even by Lebanese standards, and thuggery. Whether caused by ego, stupidity or a go-for-broke attachment to the West, the moves were insensitive, ill-considered and unwise.

The new Parliament was representative of only about 10 per cent of the electorate and was peopled by Chamoun's cronies and those bullied into supporting him. Most of the major families and individual leaders of the last decade or more were ousted. Old-guard politicians such as Karami and Jumblatt were publicly humiliated. Sunni leader Sami Sohl's house was reduced to rubble and Saeb Salam, a former Prime Minister, was beaten by police and thrown into gaol for leading a demonstration. Fifty people were killed in violence surrounding the elections and rumours spread that Chamoun would force a constitutional revision through 'his' Parliament to allow him a second six-year term as President.[7] The violence that surrounded it caused one observer to remark drily that 'though a Lebanese does not have to carry a gun to the polls, it helps.'[8] The carefully contrived, always fragile, but until then functioning, power-sharing arrangements were shattered. It was a new game, and there were no rules.

One result of the turmoil was the uniting of the anti-Chamoun opposition in the National United Front (NUF) formed in April of 1957. After the election the rift only grew and was aggravated by the formation of the United Arab Republic which gave rise to demonstrations for Arab unity and provided a new source of moral and material support for those in Lebanon seeking a voice in Lebanese politics for the majority Arab population. The ratio of 6 (Christian) to 5 (Islamic) in the 1932 census enshrined in the National Pact of 1943 was suspect then. It was an obvious fiction in 1958, if only because of differential birth rates, let alone the tens of thousands of Palestinians who had come to Lebanon after the Arab–Israeli wars, each of which produced a new flood of immigrants. In Lebanon, elections were 'a procedural fiction rather than a constitutional reality' and the hostility aroused served only to make the NUF 'virtually... another government, existing side by side with the legally constituted authorities'.[9]

Tensions increased with propaganda, violence and terrorism from both the government and opposition escalating as charges of foreign assistance, intervention and collusion came from all sides as well. There were efforts at propaganda and suppression of the same from nearly all quarters too and what one observer has called 'the radio war' was a not insignificant part of the slide into civil war.[10] The spark which lit the fuse was the assassination of Najib al-Matni, a left-leaning, anti-Chamoun, Maronite editor of *al Tiligraf*, on 8 May 1958. Tripoli erupted in rioting with 120 casualties in three days. All factions had supporters take to the streets throughout Lebanon and civil authority and basic order dissipated rapidly. When the Druze attacked the Presidential Palace on 13 May, Chamoun was quick to notify the British, French and American ambassadors that he might need to request foreign assistance.

Robert McClintock, the US Ambassador to Lebanon, told Chamoun on the 14th that the US would assist provided certain conditions were met. These were (a) that Lebanon would file a complaint with the Security Council against external interference in its internal affairs (presumably from Egypt and Syria); (b) that Lebanon should seek support from other governments, including some Arab states; and (c) that in the event of American intervention, the US would play no role in Presidential succession.[11] The latter was a very wise requirement. The United Nations also became involved over the next month. On 19 June, the Security Council-created United Nations Observer Group in Lebanon (UNOGIL) was in place to 'insure that there is no illegal infiltration of personnel or supply of arms or other material across the Lebanese border.'[12]

But it was events outside of Lebanon that provoked US intervention. Iraq was solidly pro-Western at the time and trouble from there was unexpected. But early on 14 July, King Faisal and Crown Prince Abdul Illah were assassinated in a *coup d'état* led by Brig.-Gen. Abdul Karim Kassim, a nationalist infected with Nasser's rhetoric and a UAR sympathizer. Simultaneously, rumours spread that King Hussein of Jordan was in danger, and as the opposition in Lebanon celebrated the news, Chamoun felt he too might be deposed. He called Ambassador McClintock to request American intervention –

within 48 hours.[13] Thus commenced Operation BLUEBAT on 15 July 1958. It had as much to do with Iraq and Jordan as it did with Lebanon but Chamoun provided the pretext for a massive display of force in the region. The stakes were bigger than the protection of an unpopular Lebanese President.

US INTERVENTION, 1958

President Eisenhower, despite some opposition from Congressional leaders who thought Lebanon might be on the brink of a civil war in which we had no business, moved quickly to accede to Chamoun's request. In fact, he ordered American units to Beirut with little more than 15 hours' notice. He wanted them in position when he made a television announcement about the matter so that it would be a *fait accompli*. The problem was that several elements of the fleet required for the operation were more than 20 hours away and several units of the Sixth Fleet were steaming away from Lebanon toward shore leave in Athens and Nice. The deployment of troops ashore eventually occurred without incident and roughly on time despite a series of events. There were rumours of a threatened assassination of President Chamoun, requests from General Shihab (Commander of the Lebanese Army) for the Marines to remain on board ship, and uncertainty over where troops were to be deployed. A state of general confusion reigned.

President Eisenhower, in his message to Congress and a radio/television address to the nation, pulled out all the stops and characterized what would come to be a rather formulaic 'one size fits all', series of statements for Cold War crises:

> United States' forces are being sent to Lebanon to protect American lives and by their presence to assist the Government of Lebanon in the preservation of Lebanon's territorial integrity and independence, which have been deemed vital to the United States' national interests and world peace...[14]

> In the second place what we now see in the Middle East is the same pattern of conquest with which we became familiar during the period of 1945 to 1950. This involves taking over a nation by means of indirect aggression; that is under the cover of a fomented civil strife the purpose is to put into domestic control those whose real loyalty is to the aggressor...[15]

I am well aware of the fact that the landing of United States troops in Lebanon could have some serious consequences. That is why this step was taken only after the most serious consideration and broad consultation. I have, however, come to the sober and clear conclusion that the action taken was essential to the welfare of the United States. It was requested to support the principles of justice and international law upon which peace and a stable international order depend... If ever the United States fails to support these principles, the result would be to open the floodgates to direct and indirect aggression throughout the world.[16]

Thus, the US was compelled to act – for Lebanon, for itself, for the United Nations and for the benefit of the world at large. The actual landing resembled more a Gilbert and Sullivan operetta than a Cold War crisis, however. Bikini-clad sunbathers, ice cream vendors, workmen on the beach and villagers who had come to witness the occasion all gathered on the beach, waving and cheering as the Marines waded ashore. As one marine was reported to have said, 'It's better than Korea, but what the hell is it?'[17]

There are numerous accounts of the invasion and its aftermath.[18] It was in the end a quick, short and relatively casualty-free affair for the US. It suffered three dead – one from sniper fire and two drowned while swimming at the beach. But problems were numerous. It was clear that the President thought he knew why we should intervene, but how we were to accomplish those purposes was not at all clear. The problems that befell the US military in carrying out the intervention were enormous and ranged from no doctrine for joint operations, a lack of common radio frequencies, maps based on 1940s information, difficulties in staging the airlift out of Adana in Turkey, poor organization of the men and equipment on the ground, and confused orders and implementation of them.[19] Brigadier-General David Gray in speaking to the men of Task Force Alpha assured them that the prompt and forceful deployment had prevented the collapse of 'the government we wish to support', but as for 'what our future mission may be, I cannot tell you exactly.'[20] Just who the enemy was was not clear and how Communism was a threat to Lebanon even less so. But the US military soldiered on as ordered, however confused and unclear it might have been.

The crisis largely defused itself through the agreement, secured even before US forces intervened, that President Chamoun would not seek re-election. On 31 July, General Fuad Shihab was elected

President of Lebanon. General Shihab, Commander of the LAF, was both a Maronite and a descendant of an important Arab tribe of the amirs who had governed Lebanon for a century and a half earlier in its history, most notably Bashir Shihab II. He was not only the only candidate acceptable to all sides in the context of recent events, he was a man of solid vision and deep understanding of the realities of Lebanese politics.

As he had done before, in the so-called 'Rose Water Revolution' of 1952, he understood that using the Lebanese Army would only increase the bloodshed and political ruination to be suffered. He knew that keeping the Lebanese Army – with a largely Christian officer corps but Muslim majority – out of the struggle was necessary and that calling on it would only make matters worse. A committed secularist, he sought to strike a balance between Christian culture and Arab nationalism, to improve the lot of the impoverished Sunnis and alienated Shiites and to build the power base of the Presidency at the expense of the *zuama*.[21] Regrettably, he was unable to supplant the 'robber baron capitalism' that was Lebanon and to fundamentally change either the politics or the economics which were responsible for the combination of anarchy and order that could not endure forever.

The violence continued, and, though frequent, it occurred on a lesser scale than before. A so-called 'counter-revolution' of September and October restored some balance to the delicate nature of Lebanese politics. The American presence was resented by various sectors of Lebanese society, accepted by others. But by not seeking to stay long, the US gave hopes to all the factions. The Marines began to pull out during the end of August and the Army and Air Force later. By 15 October, the entire 14,000-man force was gone. It was the largest US overseas military deployment between Korea and Vietnam. It was not an experiment in counter-insurgency operations, nor was it peacekeeping. As one observer characterized it, it was 'not war, but like war'.[22] It was an odd deployment of force for demonstration effect under the rubric of the Cold War and the pretext of protecting an American ally – from itself. Had it been opposed, it would have been a disaster. Its greatest success for the US military was in demonstrating how difficult large-scale, no-notice overseas deployments were and the difficulty not only in mounting them, but sustaining them. But that it was 'successful', if the test was the postponement of the Lebanese Civil War, can be argued. So too can the fact that Operation BLUEBAT could not succeed in preventing it – only the Lebanese themselves could do that.

THE LEBANESE CIVIL WAR AND THE SYRIAN
INTERVENTION, 1975–76

Though not directly a part of our concern here, one cannot overlook the massive changes that occurred in the Middle East between the events of 1958 and those of 1975. Without explaining them, a mere listing will bring to mind the sea changes in regional and indeed global, as well as local, politics which occurred in this period. The wars between Israel and her neighbours, both 1967 and 1973, were veritable earthquakes in the region and each sent a renewed stream of Palestinian refugees into Lebanon. The 1967 war expanded Israeli occupied territory into the Golan, the West Bank, the Sinai and Jerusalem, much to the dismay and lamentation of the Palestinians and their Arab backers. The number of terrorist attacks and anti-Israeli organizations increased dramatically and occurred not just in the Middle East, as the events at the 1972 Munich Olympics and elsewhere throughout the world revealed to all.

The 1970–71 Civil War in Jordan essentially transferred the Palestinian commando operations to Lebanon and increased still further the influx of refugees and radicals into Lebanon. There were two impacts of the 1973 war. The first was the spectacular success of the Egyptians in the first three days of the war before suffering an equally catastrophic defeat. But the force of Arab arms had proven successful, even if temporarily, and gave cause for hope against the 'Zionist entity'. The oil price hikes and embargoes to the West during the 1973 war had their real impact in 1974–75 as the price of oil doubled, then redoubled, then doubled again. The economic chaos this caused globally was enormous. Economically, politically, militarily and socially, Lebanon too was becoming more volatile.

The real Lebanese Civil War occurred with all the fury that the pent-up emotions and the changing balance of power both in Lebanon and the region could unleash in 1975. That things had been brewing for some time cannot be denied. Indeed, it was only a matter of time before the pressure cooker that was Lebanon would explode. Events after the 1958 intervention by the US are chronicled elsewhere in detail.[23] Suffice it to say that things became more complicated, not less. The Shihab Administration gave rise to the Phalange Party and the Deuxième Bureau, the military intelligence branch of the Army. The work of both would only complicate things further. It gave way to the Helou Administration (1964–70). Beset by a series of international events – the diversion of the Jordan River by Israel, and the

1967 war – it was bedevilled with an increased radicalization of the Muslim intelligentsia, the rise of Palestinian commando activities and the increasing polarization between the Maronites and Muslims.

A split between Prime Minister Karami and President Helou and the actions of the Lebanese Army and the commandos resulted in an agreement mediated by President Nasser called the Cairo Agreement of 3 November 1969. The essence of the agreement was that Palestinian commandos would be allowed to operate against Israel from Lebanese soil, but only from certain areas and only after coordinating their activities with the Lebanese Army. The Maronites saw this as currying favour with the Muslims and began to increase the efforts to organize, arm and expand their militias. The Muslims in turn saw this as justification for legitimate concern on their part, be they Palestinian, Lebanese or outside radicals.

The fragility of the situation is demonstrated by Sulieman Franjieh's election to President in 1970 – by one vote. The disillusionment of young Shiite students in particular, but the Muslim community in general, continued. It was increased significantly by the April 1973 raid of the Israelis into the heart of Beirut to assassinate the top leaders of *Fath*. Franjieh's two old friends in running the country – Maronite General Iskandar Ghanem, the army commander, and Sunni Prime Minister Saeb Salam – had a showdown with Salam demanding Ghanem's resignation after large anti-government demonstrations over the Israeli action. When Ghanem refused, Salam resigned and things got worse rapidly. If Salam could not control the Muslims, who could? In May of 1973, the Lebanese Air Force took action against Palestinian refugee camps for the first time. Despite efforts at compromise and changes of government, the Maronite–Sunni confrontation only increased. Not to be outdone, the Shiites increased their political clout largely as a result of the leadership and popularity of Musa Sadr.

The spark for the Civil War was a demonstration in support of a strike of local fishermen led by Maaruf Saad, a Sunni leader of the Popular Nasserist Organization of Sidon. 'The strike had been called in protest against the extraordinarily ill-timed formation of an off-shore fishing monopoly sponsored by, of all people, ex-President Camille Chamoun.'[24] Saad was shot and died on 6 March. A violent populist uprising was joined by Palestinian commandos and Lebanese militiamen and prevented the Lebanese Army from establishing control of the city. The Maronites now organized counter demonstrations in support of the army. And the one institution that had saved

Lebanon in the earlier crises of 1952 and 1958 – by not participating – was now engulfed in the struggle that would tear the country apart.[25] Neither the forces of the National Movement within Lebanon nor the efforts of the Syrians were able to put the lid on the tensions that boiled over as a result.

There were essentially four phases to the Lebanese Civil War. The first is a series of clashes between the Phalange militia and radical Palestinians in Beirut between April and June 1975. These were followed by clashes in Tripoli between the supporters of President Franjieh and those of Rashid Karami, Tripoli's Sunni leader and traditional rival of Franjieh. The government fell and an attempt at a military dominated cabinet collapsed as well. In a last ditch attempt to return to politics as usual, a cabinet was formed under Karami who acted as Defence Minister and included Camille Chamoun as Minister of the Interior. It was too late.

By June of 1975 the Civil War had begun in earnest and this phase lasted until January of 1976. The politics of civil war make even stranger bedfellows than usual. Labels are difficult to apply and factions change allegiances throughout. Though having religious labels, the goals and groups were political rather than confessional in nature. There was a predominantly Christian camp which sought to preserve the status quo and the traditional Lebanese political system. A largely but not entirely Muslim camp was a revisionist coalition seeking to overthrow the system. Each made common cause with factions of the other as it suited its purposes to do so in the short run.

Franjieh and Chamoun represented the hard core of the status quo position. This coalition became known as the Lebanese Front and combined the Gemayels' Phalange – the Tigers – the militia of Camille Chamoun's National Liberation Party and Sulieman Franjieh's Zghorta Liberation Army. It was essentially right wing, small, Maronite, well connected and well armed. The younger, more radical and increasingly more numerous Muslims, Sunni and Shiite, represented the hard core of the opposition group. But the opposition was essentially leftist politically, not religious, and sought both a new political order and a new economic one as well. It was known as the National Movement and was a loose association of Kamal Jumblatt's Progressive Socialist Party (the Druze), the Syrian National Party, a curious combination of Greek Orthodox and Muslim, the Independent Nasserites who were Sunni, the Amal which was Shiite, two factions of the Baath Socialist Party, one aligned with Syria and the other with Iraq, and the Lebanese Community Party. This group sought to make Lebanon into an Arab entity and redraw the lines of power both inside and outside Lebanon.

Karami, a leader of the traditional Muslim group but a member of the *zuama* which had brokered ruling Lebanon for a generation was caught in the middle, as was the Lebanese Army. If the Army intervened, it would split the coalition of those attempting to work out some *modus vivendi*. Karami would resign and the Palestinians and Syrians would be left to pick up the pieces. Besieged from all sides, chaos reigned and both the government and the army collapsed in 1976. The wild card in the unfolding drama of the Lebanese Civil War was Syria. It had helped to cause the breakdown by aiding the Palestinian militia groups and training PLO factions which were reinserted into Lebanon so they could attack Israel.

Alternately supporting revisionist elements in the struggle and mediating among the various factions, Asad was determined

> to prevent both Lebanon's partition and a clear cut victory by the radical revisionists and their Palestinian supporters. Such a victory would have sandwiched Syria between two radical neighbors, one of whom, Iraq, was a bitter enemy and would, moreover, probably provoke Israeli intervention on the side of the Christians.[26]

Therefore, Syria intervened – not to create a Greater Syria, but to protect Syrian interests and to broker whatever settlement could be obtained on terms favourable to it. As important, the US acquiesced in this decision and informally brokered an arrangement between Israel and Syria to forestall other, less palatable options.

Under the cover of the Syrian Palestinian Liberation Army, ostensibly affiliated with the PLO but in reality part of the Syrian Army, the Syrians moved in during the second week of January 1976. They tried to separate the factions, impose some semblance of order and call for a truce among the factional participants. They separated the contending forces, established internal checkpoints and monitored the 'Green Line' which separated Maronite and Christian neighbourhoods from Muslim and Palestinian ones. Syria held summits with each side and tried to broker a workable Lebanese system. This proved to be more difficult than imagined and was complicated by the formation of a breakaway Lebanese Arab Army and a coup against Franjieh by the Lebanese Army. A series of truces, ceasefires and agreements were made and broken but Syrian commitment and management, in so far as possible, continued unabated. Unable to achieve a workable circumstance by one means, Asad decided on another.

With Soviet Prime Minister Aleksei Kosygin due to arrive on 1 June, Asad acted to achieve a *fait accompli* and had the Syrian Army invade Lebanon on 31 May. It was a military failure. Both the Palestinian and the Lebanese forces acted against the Syrians and inflicted heavy casualties. The invasion, far from ending an intractable situation, aggravated it even further. But the cooperation between the Maronite militias and the Syrians was overt, for the Maronites joined the Syrian offensive and took the lead. The Sunni majority in Syria resented the Maronite minority in Lebanon and the Alawite minority in Syria, both operating against oppressed Sunni majorities. Asad had created more problems at home without settling those abroad.

A new military attack was launched later in the summer and near collapse of the opposition was achieved in two weeks. But instead of ramming home a military victory achieved by force of arms, Asad went to Riyadh to a conference hosted by the Saudis in mid-October. The meeting joined the Saudis and Kuwaitis with delegations from Syria, Egypt, Lebanon and the PLO to try and end the dispute that had so long paralyzed the Arab world. Another meeting followed soon after in Cairo. The agreements included an immediate ceasefire and a gradual normalization in Lebanon. An Arab Deterrent Force (ADF) of approximately 30,000 men – primarily Syrian – was created to maintain the peace. It was nominally under the President of Lebanon (Elias Sarkis) and financed by the oil producing states. All internal armed forces would return to their pre-1975 positions and all heavy weapons put under control of the ADF. Shootings, random violence and political hostility continued but the all-out war of the previous 18 months subsided.

A semblance of what passed for peace in Lebanon ensued. Over 10,000 people had been killed and massive physical destruction of Lebanon's major urban areas had occurred. Many, mainly Christians, emigrated. Lebanon was forever changed but curiously maintained a relatively stable currency and a certain affluence for those involved in the right kinds of trading. But the government of Lebanon was shattered and existed in name only. It controlled not even half of its capital, Beirut. Warlordism was revived among domestic factions. The Maronites controlled the area north of Beirut with its headquarters at Jounieh; the Palestinians and their Lebanese allies controlled the area south of Beirut; Major Saad Haddad and his pro-Israeli militia vied with the PLO for control of southern Lebanon; the Franjiehs and the Sunnis controlled yet other enclaves. Each port had a different political boss and an administration which collected its own taxes. Even with a massive Syrian military intervention and an Arab imposed regional settlement, Lebanon had ceased to exist in all but name and joined the ranks of the so-called 'failed states'.[27]

THE ISRAELI INCURSION AND THE DEPLOYMENT OF UNIFIL, 1978

An array of political factions bewildering even to the participants was at work after the Civil War of 1975–76 until the Israeli invasion of 1982. Their sheer number, let alone the varieties of their political causes, gives one pause. Among them were:

> Lebanese Rightists – Kata'eb, the National Liberal Party, Guardians of the Cedar, Zghorta Liberation Army (Marada Brigade), Permanent Congress of the Lebanese Order of Monks and Al Tanzim.

> Lebanese Leftists and foreign groups – Progressive Socialist Party, Lebanese Communist Party, Arab Socialist Action Party, Syrian Nationalist Party, Organization of the Ba'th Party, Fath, Popular Democratic Front for the Liberation of Palestine, Sa'iqa, Arab Liberation Front.[28]

The Leftists were a coalition of Lebanese, Palestinians, volunteers and mercenaries from a number of different countries. The Rightists were essentially Christians and were all Lebanese. All the factions longed for and needed outside support to enhance their cause and to make any one 'victorious' against the others, whatever that might mean.

Into this cauldron, the Israelis entered once again. After years of raids and counter-attacks between the PLO and the Israelis for various terrorist acts, shellings of northern Israeli towns and other acts, things turned more serious. In March of 1978, in retaliation for a PLO attack on the Mediterranean coast which killed 34 Israelis and wounded 78, Israel launched a massive retaliatory operation. What was different this time was Prime Minister Begin's drop in popularity (down nearly 20 per cent since December), the continued presence of Syrian troops in Lebanon, and signs of disaffection between the Lebanese and both the Syrians and Palestinians. The irony is that though cross-border incidents had been much higher in the 1975–76 period, there had been a period of relative calm since November of

1977. Indeed, the only Israeli casualty since January 1977 had been a soldier killed on 31 August 1977, while hundreds of Lebanese and Palestinian casualties had occurred in the previous year.[29]

For a variety of reasons, the PLO raid provided the pretext for the 'Litani Operation'. This was an attempt to clear the Palestinians out of their southern Lebanon strongholds and establish a six-mile-wide security zone north of the Israeli border. But Begin's forces went beyond the six-mile zone and moved toward the Litani River in southern Lebanon. The operation was far larger than previous retaliation raids and displaced some 250,000 people and killed 2,000. It gave the Israelis some maneuvering room, diplomatically and militarily. Or so they thought at the time. But the plan backfired in that the US was interested in not offending Arab oil producers and was trying to engineer, along with President Sadat of Egypt and others, a general Middle East Peace accord. More importantly, the US used the UN to pressure Israel as Begin arrived in the US for meetings with President Carter. UN Security Council Resolutions 425 and 426 called upon Israel to withdraw from all of Lebanon, established a United Nations Interim Force in Lebanon – UNIFIL – and spelled out the terms of reference for it. The force was to be at least 4,000 strong and last for six months initially.[30]

But Begin and Israel were outflanked by the US through the UN and were in jeopardy of losing the freedom of action they had enjoyed on the Lebanese border, seeing Security Council interference in the region and a UN model for other occupied areas. All were defeats for Israel. Begin tried to extract as many concessions as possible under difficult circumstances but was frustrated. US President Jimmy Carter threatened to cut off American arms and aid to Israel, and sought to distance the US from Arab charges of collusion with Israel. After discussing this during April, Washington's relations with Israel hit bottom in May when the US Senate approved a sale of planes to Israel – as part of a package deal which also sold planes to Egypt and Saudi Arabia.

When a ceasefire had been established on 21 March, the Israelis occupied an area from Tyre to Mt Hermon across southern Lebanon. It totalled 425 square miles and was one-tenth of Lebanese territory.[31] Eventually, over a period of months, over 6,000 men were deployed as part of UNIFIL to deal with this much larger region. The contingents came from Canada, Fiji, France, Ireland, Iran, Nepal, Nigeria, Norway, Senegal and Sweden. There were now multiple international contingents of armed force in Lebanon in addition to all the armed Lebanese factions. These included 20,000 Israelis, 30,000 members of the Arab Deterrent Force (mainly Syrian), the PLO forces, Iranian SAVAK agents assisting the Shiites, and a Lebanese Army and the southern Lebanese renegade force under Major Saad Haddad attempting to control an area now called 'Free Lebanon'. Slowly, in a series of graduated withdrawals completed by June 13, the Israelis withdrew and the UNIFIL forces were deployed.

Everyone had a hidden agenda, an outside sponsor, an opportunity to cut deals with other factions and agreed that the current circumstances of uneasy truce were not a desirable outcome. There was no sense of finality and little that UNIFIL could do but monitor the situation in a very uneasy environment. There were PLO forces, the Southern Lebanese Army, the Arab Deterrent Force and Israelis all eyeing each other suspiciously with UNIFIL manning border posts, checkpoints and roadways in the midst of all the factions. UNIFIL constrained the PLO's freedom of action and that of the Israelis, was welcomed by some Lebanese and opposed by others, complicated an Arab effort at regional control and settlement, constrained Haddad's forces and his self-proclaimed mini-state, and was in a very precarious position. Without some major, comprehensive settlement of the overlapping issues involved in the Middle East – an Israeli–Palestinian peace, the status of Syria in the region, curtailment of the PLO and terrorist activities, the nature of a Lebanese political entity – UNIFIL could do little but watch and wait. And, indeed, that has been largely its fate.

OPERATION 'PEACE FOR GALILEE' AND THE MNF, SUMMER 1982

Shlomo Argov, the Israeli Ambassador to Great Britain, was shot outside the Dorchester Hotel in London on 3 June 1982. In retaliation – or seizing on a convenient pretext – Israeli jets bombed the Palestinian areas of West Beirut at 3:20 p.m. on 4 June. Somewhere between 50 and 210 were killed and 150 to 250 wounded depending on whose casualty estimates you accept. In a largely ineffective retaliation two hours later, the PLO shelled Haddad held villages in Southern Lebanon and Northern Galilee. The casualty toll was one dead and three wounded. This broke a 13-month-long ceasefire negotiated by US mediator Philip Habib in 1981. Later on 4 June, Israeli Foreign Minister Yitzhak Shamir called for the elimination of the

PLO.[32] The Israeli bombings increased the next day hitting 50 different targets throughout three major areas of Palestinian dominated Lebanon. The UN Security Council voted 15–0 calling for an immediate cease fire. On 6 June, Israel launched a full-scale invasion of Lebanon by land, sea and air. Operation 'Peace for Galilee' had begun.[33]

Its stated objective was to push the PLO back 40 km from the Israeli border. The Israelis announced that the invasion was not aimed at the Syrians and Israeli units would not engage Syrian units unless attacked by them. The Israeli advance was swift and effective. By nightfall on 7 June Israeli forces were somewhat more than 40 km inside Lebanon – they were only 30 km south of Beirut. Prime Minister Begin and Defence Minister Sharon of Israel saw a chance to smash the PLO completely, and they took it. US envoy Philip Habib shuttled back and forth from Israel to Damascus to Beirut trying to arrange a ceasefire. On 9 June, the US vetoed a UN Security Council Resolution which condemned Israel's attack and threatened sanctions if hostilities did not cease. They did not. But, on the 11th Israel declared a ceasefire with Syrian forces and Habib arranged for an Israeli–Palestinian ceasefire on the 12th. Unfortunately, this broke down in less than 24 hours.

Beirut was under siege, attacked by bombs from the air and artillery from the ground. According to Red Cross and a Lebanese official quoted in *The Times*, there were an estimated 600,000 Lebanese and Palestinians – one-fifth of the population – homeless, 14,000 dead and 20,000 wounded. Israel's reported casualties as of 17 June were 214 dead, 1,114 wounded and 23 missing.[34] It was a turning point. Lebanon was being destroyed and Israel had gone from being the oppressed to being the oppressor. The international community began to try and avert even wider bloodshed.

Several realities emerged. First, the Israelis would have to attack Beirut and cause massive destruction to eliminate the PLO from Lebanon. It would be long, bloody and unconscionable in the face of international pressure to avert a bloodbath. But the Israelis were adamant that the PLO must be eliminated from Lebanon. Second, the Arab states of the region were just as adamant that the PLO must be supported and protected. The unlikely combination of pro-American Saudi Arabia and pro-Soviet Syria eventually agreed on 16 July to ask President Reagan and the US to help in a PLO withdrawal from Beirut. The key was an American guarantee of safe extraction of the PLO and Israeli agreement to their withdrawal. Through the work of US envoy Habib, the Israelis reluctantly agreed to this concept on 8 August, after a two-month-long siege of Beirut and a diplomatic stalemate.[35]

The agreement was complicated by the time it took to find another Arab country that would agree to take the PLO and to work out the details of a withdrawal acceptable both to the Israelis and the PLO. Ultimately, the agreement achieved was this. The bulk of the PLO fighters and its administrative apparatus would leave Beirut by ship or plane for Tunis where the Tunisians had agreed to accept them. A smaller group, roughly 6,000, along with some Syrian troops caught in the siege, would be permitted under UNIFIL monitoring to withdraw by land over the Beirut to Damascus highway. The PLO had to turn in their weapons before leaving. Some 8,144 Palestinian guerrillas were evacuated from the port of Beirut by ship accompanied by 664 women and children. The rest of the Palestinian families remained behind.[36]

Into these circumstance the US deployed a detachment of US Marines to the port of Juoniyeh on 23 June 1982 to evacuate American civilians from the area. They had entered a cauldron of both domestic and foreign military forces the size and nature of which they little understood. Among the forces arrayed in Lebanon in the summer of 1982 were the following:

- Domestic military forces (roughly 60,000 men):
  - Palestinian Liberation Organization military forces – approximately 14,000 men well armed with some heavy weapons, concentrated in the Beirut area and the PLO refugee camps;
  - the Phalange (Maronite) – 10,000 men with M-48 tanks and artillery;
  - Druze Popular Socialist Party Militia – 4,000 men with T-54 tanks, artillery, 122 mm rocket launchers, mainly in the Shouf Mountains;
  - Amal Shiite Militia – 2,000 men;
  - numerous other factional militias – all of less than 1,000 men each.
- Foreign military forces (roughly 70,000 men):
  - Syria – 40,000 men in the Bekaa Valley consisting of two armored divisions (the 1st and 3rd), an independent infantry brigade and air defence forces;
  - Syrian proxies – the Palestinian Liberation Army (two brigades of roughly 6,000 men);

- Israel – 20,000 men south of the Awali River consisting of two division groups with the Israeli Air Force on call;
- Israeli proxies – the South Lebanon Army, under Major Saad Haddad, of roughly 3,500 men;
- UNIFIL – a UN sponsored multilateral peacekeeping force which patrolled the Lebanese–Israeli border. It consisted of some 6,000 troops from Fiji, Finland, France, Ghana, Ireland, Italy, the Netherlands, Norway, Senegal and Sweden;
- Iranian Pasdaran Volunteers – 650 men.[37]

Few, if any, of the men deployed in the multinational force were aware of the number of factions and the complexities of the armed forces in Lebanon. Their mission was simply to rescue Americans from the area. They then were given another – to see that the PLO was disarmed and sent out of the country. These forces were to provide what one observer has suggested was 'a multinational shield for a Palestinian sword'.[38]

From 24 August until 10 September, a multinational force (MNF) was deployed to Lebanon. It consisted of US Marines (the 2/8 Battalion Landing Team) deployed to the Beirut area, a French Foreign Legion paratroop battalion deployed to the port of Beirut and an Italian unit which protected the road from Damascus to Beirut. Their purpose was to monitor and assist in the deportation of the 14,000 PLO guerrillas. If the Israelis had not succeeded in exterminating the PLO, they had succeeded in removing them from Lebanon. Close by were ships of the US Sixth Fleet should they be needed. It was essentially a non-combat evacuation and things went very smoothly, despite the numbers and tensions involved. But all was not well, for the US was bitterly resented as Israel's patron and arms supplier. The tensions were obvious, as the remark below indicates. A Palestinian pharmacist turned guerrilla told a Marine as he left:

> I'll tell you what this war taught us. It taught us that the real enemy is the United States. It is against you that we must fight. Not just because your bombs killed our people, but because you have closed your eyes to what is moral and just.[39]

On 10 September, their mission complete, the multinational force withdrew from Lebanon and disbanded. Things were progressing – but not for long.

Four days later, Bashir Gemayel, the newly elected President of Lebanon and head of the Phalange, was speaking to the Ashrafieh branch of the Phalange party. A 200-pound bomb, hidden in the ceiling of the building where he was speaking, was detonated by a Christian member of the Parti Populaire Syrien, Tanious Shartouni, killing the President and collapsing the building.[40] A new round of Lebanon's seemingly endemic violence was begun. Israeli troops moved into West Beirut to try and ensure order and into the neighbourhood of Sabra and the camp of Shatila to flush out any remaining PLO guerrillas who had remained behind. The Phalange, out to revenge the death of their leader, on the evening of 16 September, stole into Sabra and Shatila, now largely inhabited by women, children and old men since their husbands, brothers and sons had just left.

For two nights and a day, as the Israelis stood by, occasionally illuminating the macabre scene with flares, the Phalange exacted their revenge and slaughtered anyone they could catch. Finally the Israeli Defence Forces (IDF) admitted the magnitude of the *dabak* (slaughter) and ordered the Phalange out of the area. As they went, on the morning of the 18th, they attempted to raze the area with bulldozers to cover the carnage they had wrought. The exact death toll will never be known. The Israelis set the number at 700–800, the Palestinians at 2,000.[41] The guarantee of safety for the Palestinians had failed. Within 48 hours, the Marines, and their Italian and French compatriots, were ordered back to Beirut. Both the West and their lackeys, the Israelis, had colluded not only to drive out the PLO but to attempt to exterminate those relatives who remained – or so it seemed to the Palestinians. It was the same place, albeit a very different environment, to which the Marines would return.

US MARINE DEPLOYMENT, SEPTEMBER 1982 TO MARCH 1984

The Marines' mission in their return to Beirut was not as clear or finite as it was the first time. The immediate intention was that they were to prevent any further bloodbaths and serve as an interposition force between the Lebanese government, the warring factional militias and the Syrian and Israeli forces. By implication, it was hoped that they would be able to achieve a withdrawal of foreign forces from the area, restore a stable Lebanese government and remove threats to Israel from Lebanese territory. President Reagan assured them and the American public that they were there 'for a limited period', that they were not to engage in combat but they could exercise

the right of self-defense. Initially, both Muslims and Christians welcomed the Marines as liberators who would stop the bloodletting by
their very presence. And so it seemed. Both the American political
and military leadership did not want the Americans to be labelled as
'peacekeepers' given the ineffectual role of UNIFIL. Instead they
saw the role of the Marines as 'presence'. That mission was not
defined, but presumed.[42]

The decision to go back in was a spur of the moment thing, not
carefully crafted nor well considered. It reflected divisions in the Reagan Administration and the rivalry among personalities, policies
and politics, both foreign and domestic. We sent the force that was
closest – the Marines – with no specific objective, no time limit for the
mission and no carefully crafted rules of engagement (ROE). President Reagan characterized things as follows:

> Their mission is to provide an interposition force at agreed loca-
> tions and thereby provide the multinational presence requested by
> the Lebanese government to assist it and the Lebanese Armed
> Forces. In carrying out this mission, the American force will not
> engage in combat. It may, however, exercise the right of self
> defense and will be equipped accordingly.[43]

Just how one was to avoid combat if fired upon and authorized to
defend oneself was not clear. It was a recipe for disaster. The decision-making process – or lack of it – has been well documented and
serves as insightful background to US policy in Lebanon from 1982
to 1984.[44] The decision to intervene at this time was admittedly a
'Quick Fix'[45] and was occasioned as much by feelings of responsibility and guilt as any well conceived choice from among alternative
courses of action. For better or worse, the Israelis were the responsibility of the US. Another massacre had to be prevented and the
Israelis removed now that the PLO was gone.

The other members of the multinational force were there as well, but
there was no unified chain of command. The 1,200 American Marines
were at the Beirut International Airport, the 2,000 French Foreign
Legion troops were at the port and downtown Muslim West Beirut
and the 2,100 Italians occupied Central Beirut and the gutted Sabra
and Shatila refugee camps.[46] But neither the French nor the Americans
would serve under another's command. Instead, the commanders met
regularly, but ran their own operations. Consultative committees may
be fine for diplomacy, but they are a poor way to run a combined
military operation and exchange timely intelligence information.

The Marines moved into Christian strongholds of East Beirut in their patrols and strengthened their claims of impartiality among the Muslim factions. Over the next 12 months there were 23 changes to Marine deployment and security.[47] One of the most salient was that beginning on 13 December 1982 the Americans began training the Lebanese Army. Eventually, the Lebanese Army even received US Marine Corps uniforms into the bargain. Though understandable on one level, if one wanted to have a stable Lebanese government, by training the Lebanese Armed Forces, a Christian-dominated entity, the Marines 'inadvertently compromised the neutral image they had tried so hard to build'.[48]

The year 1983 brought a series of events which were ominous in their implications. While things became routine in many ways, they were hardly calm. Marines were killed and wounded throughout the year by snipers, artillery fire, car bombs, grenades and rocket attacks. In the spring, there was growing uneasiness in the Muslim communities caused by an increasing camaraderie and joint Lebanese Armed Force (LAF) and US Marine Corps (USMC) patrolling. Then on the afternoon of 18 April 1983 a pickup truck loaded with a ton of high explosives was detonated inside the American Embassy compound destroying an eight-storey building and killing 17 Americans – four Marine guards and 13 civilians – and 44 Lebanese. It was a preview of coming attractions. But not much was done about a significantly increased level of threat.

A month later, on 17 May, an agreement was signed between Gemayel and Begin by which the Israelis finally agreed to withdraw from most of Lebanon. They got to keep a buffer zone in the south held by their client Christian South Lebanon Army. Displaying a clumsy and transparent sense of timing, the US resumed sales of US F-16s to Israel two days later. In an ill-considered fit of wishful thinking, it was supposed that when the Israelis withdrew, the Syrians would too. Why they should have given up on more than seven years of effort invested in Lebanon was not quite clear. And, they did not, electing to stay unless forced out – an unlikely eventuality.

The Marine Amphibious Unit (MAU) Commander as of 30 May 1983 was Col. J. T. Geraghty. He interpreted his mission as 'a diplomatic mission'. In keeping with that interpretation, he thought his men should be seen and not cower in bunkers, that they should not build permanent structures, only temporary ones, and that while they would patrol aggressively, they should avoid combat and if it occurred, they would be ordered to leave.[49] These assumptions were in keeping with the 'presence' aspect of his mission and not illogical in that sense. But given the increasing incidents of violence directed against the Marines and the changing circumstances on the ground, they were unwise.

These assumptions were aggravated by the replacement of Philip Habib with Robert McFarlane as Special Envoy to the Middle East and Deputy National Security Adviser (McFarlane was also a retired USMC colonel). Regrettably, his efforts at mixing force and diplomacy were failures on both counts as he went first too far in one direction and then too far in the other. His actions on the scene in Beirut led to the final break with the Muslim and Druze community and their perception of the Americans not as peacekeepers, but as another warring faction in Lebanon. The LAF had moved into the village of Souk el-Garb in the Shouf, a position they set about occupying as the Israelis withdrew. These were strategic heights overlooking the Marine position at the airport. More importantly, they were the stronghold of the Druze and their militias and had been for centuries.

The LAF got into a firefight (in which eight were killed and 12 wounded). McFarlane ordered the Marine Commander on site to have naval gunfire under his direction fire in support of the LAF. Without assessing an LAF request, McFarlane ordered the naval units offshore to fire 360 rounds from 5-inch guns on ships into the Druze–Syrian–Palestinian positions in the Shouf.[50] Not only was it a tremendously disproportionate response, it was the straw that broke the camel's back. US forces had now earned the hostility of all forces in the region, save those of the Lebanese Armed Forces who were barely able to control half of Beirut, let alone the country. It was only a matter of time before that reality would be brought home.

It happened on the morning of 23 October 1983. Despite supposedly being at Condition II Alert (Attack Probable) at 0622, the time of the attack, two of the 11 guard posts were not manned, six that were had Marines standing watch with magazines out of their weapons and only three were manned (by a total of six men) with their magazines in their weapons. (It was later determined that the Marines were not even at Condition III Alert, and had received no clear instructions on vehicles approaching the compound.) A Mercedes truck carrying five tons of explosives drove through concertina wire and around or through some flimsy barricades and detonated in front of the building which served as the headquarters, sleeping and eating area for the 24th Marine Amphibious Unit (MAU) Battalion

Landing Team (BTL) 1/8. In the resulting explosion, the building was totally destroyed and 218 marines, 18 sailors, three soldiers, a visiting French paratrooper and a Lebanese civilian died and 80 were wounded. It was not an isolated event. A similar attack on the French MNF component the same day took an additional 58 lives. The Israelis would lose 29 to a truck explosion in Tyre on 4 November as well.[51]

> The American response to the tragedy took four forms: unit replacement, major alterations to the rules of engagement, investigations and serious reconsideration of the U.S. goals in Lebanon. But the black mushroom cloud that brewed up from the collapsed BLT headquarters marked the funeral pyre of the American military role in Lebanon. Reagan, McFarlane and Geraghty had gambled and lost. Now it was only a matter of time until the plug was pulled for good.[52]

'Presence' had become very costly. It was also no longer a sustainable option.

There was one more round to the saga of the inept effort to merge force and statecraft. A major increase in firepower in the Sixth Fleet was sent to 'Bagel Station' in the Eastern Mediterranean. The aircraft carriers USS *John F. Kennedy* and the USS *Independence* as well as the battleship *New Jersey* were all sent to the area during the month of November. Some retaliation was deemed appropriate and necessary. On 3 December, two US F-14 reconnaissance aircraft were fired on by Syrian and Druze gunners in the Bekaa Valley with Soviet-made SA-7s. The US decided to respond. An air attack was ordered for the next day. It was a comedy of errors in which nearly everything which could go wrong did, largely because there were 'too many cooks in the kitchen' with orders and changes coming from Washington, London (US Naval Forces Europe), Belgium (NATO headquarters), the Sixth Fleet and Admiral Tuttle's battlegroup.[53] The raid was unimpressive, highly dangerous and the US was lucky to lose only one plane and two pilots (one killed, one captured).

After a series of incidents on a lesser scale and even greater confusion about what the US sought to accomplish in Lebanon and just how it might go about doing it, all US forces were withdrawn by 30 March 1984. President Reagan had said we were not leaving, merely 'redeploying to the sea'. Regardless, we had little to show for the 275 military and civilians who lost their lives in the previous 18 months, either diplomatically or militarily. It is a high cost to pay for an ill-conceived purpose called 'presence'. The largest error made by the US was in not understanding the strategic environment into which it deployed troops and the lack of a clear mission for that force. Stopping a war is difficult for a third party; ending a war that one doesn't understand is wishful thinking.

A perceptive assessment of the breakdown of civil authority that has plagued Lebanon and caused a period of prolonged war is offered by As'ad Abukhalil. He assesses a number of factors which he believes are responsible for the war that has raged intermittently since 1975 and as of 1990 had killed over 150,000 people, wounded over 200,000 and had 20,000 missing.[54] His list of reasons for this prolonged war include:[55]

- the multiplicity of dimensions of the conflict;
- the fact that Lebanon was an arena of foreign conflict and intrigue;
- the absence of any 'neutral' mediator;
- the rise of a war elite whose self-interest lay in continuing strife;
- Syria's belief in the efficacy of 'no victors, no vanquished';
- sectarian agitation and mobilization;
- a fear of the return to the status quo;
- Arab official antipathy to the Lebanese model of democracy;
- the politics of the war generation.

It is a sobering assessment and one which has applicability elsewhere. Its essential insights for policy prescription suggest that if civil strife is not stopped quickly and lasts more than a decade, then it infects the body politic to such a degree that it may become self-sustaining. All factions, foreign and domestic, come to have an interest in, if not prolonging the war, at least not having it end in certain ways. Since no one can control the outcome, the struggle continues, albeit in alternating phases of intense and relatively subdued violence. This may well be a model for other conflicts which share many of the same general attributes of the Lebanese conflict that has existed since the US first attempted a peacekeeping operation nearly 40 years ago.

To these should be added some purely American propensities as well. Americans want to 'do what's right' and that is often defined as 'honoring commitments' in an effort to 'remain credible' as a friend and ally. Because of America's own history and the nature of its revolution, Americans draw hard political lines, but are less know-ledgeable or concerned about social and economic realities. They tend to want to use military force for political ends short of its application in war but often don't really know how to go about doing that. Given the nature of the American political system and decision-making processes, Americans tend to make decisions belatedly and incrementally. What has come to be known as 'mission creep' comes with the territory as Americans learn more about what they have got themselves into this time. Despite the individual differences of culture, geography, society, politics, economics and the military from case to case, Americans have a tendency to involve themselves in other people's civil wars with some frequency – China, Korea, Guatemala, Nicaragua, the Dominican Republic, Vietnam, Lebanon, Somalia, Rwanda, Haiti, Yugoslavia – and not know either what their aims are or how to set about accomplishing them.

Looking back over US actions, Americans have tended to learn much operationally in military terms but little politically or diplomatically over the last 50 years. Ralph Hallenbeck's list of indictments, comparing Vietnam and Lebanon, include the following:[56]

- a marked incongruity between the overarching foreign policy objectives and strategy and the objectives assigned to the military forces;
- a great deal of ambiguity with respect to the outcome that was being sought;
- a lack of unanimity among US policy-makers over both the ends and means of US policy;
- confusion as to whether or not the indigenous political situation could be effectively addressed with the resources at hand;
- a tendency to Americanize the strategy in an effort for American resources to compensate for the failures of the indigenous government;
- a difficulty in applying military ends to accomplish politically limited ends;
- a failure to have meaningful measures of merit to assess the success of the policies being pursued.

While it is true that diplomacy and military force are connected, it is not at all clear just how the US hoped to achieve limited ends through the application of military force in Lebanon – or, indeed, many of the other places in which it has intervened as a peacekeeper or as a peacemaker. Most importantly, the US has failed to make the distinction between the two or understand the significance of changing from one role to the other.

LESSONS WE COULD (SHOULD) HAVE LEARNED

The single overwhelming lesson, with many subcomponents, which the US should have learned in Lebanon, if not well before, is simple: *do not attempt to keep a peace which has no foundation.* That foundation can be achieved in many ways. It can be achieved by military defeat, diplomatic truce, disarmament and arms control, international sanctions and threats of force, military occupation, or victory by one side. All of these can lead to a peace for others to assist in maintaining. That can be done in a variety of ways as well. Economic aid, humanitarian assistance, contributions of 'know-how' for reconstruction of infrastructure, basic constabulary functions of law and order until domestic authorities are able to accomplish these tasks are some among many. But there has to be some definitive basis on which to proceed. If there has not been a catastrophic defeat in war, a ceasefire and serious commitment to peace, a truce or a peace to be kept, then it is hard to accomplish that mission. Merely separating parties shooting at each other is noble, but it is not peacekeeping. It is intervention in the hopes of establishing a peace to keep. To quote a former US Air Force Chief of Staff, 'When hope is your best management toll, you have a big problem.'[57]

If all that is done is to separate warring factions from each other, the effort is likely to be stillborn. If there is no unity, no sense of legitimacy, no recognizable government, no social compact among citizens, no agreement to live at peace in a defined area among those who live there, then peacekeeping is a hope, not a reality, a fiction, not fact. The single overriding requirement is an agreement to pursue a peaceful future in unison for those who live in the territory affected. If migration and partition are the results of the agreement, as they are in the Dayton Accords in Bosnia, then we are merely accomplishing ethnic cleansing in a more acceptable manner. We are monitoring the rearrangement of populations that have publicly admitted that they *cannot* and *will not* live in peace with each other. That realism, while regrettable, is at least a basis on which to act and prepare for the future that is based on things as they are and not wishful thinking. Such was the case in Lebanon, at least in 1978 and 1982, if not 1958.

A corollary to this general principle should be added, that is: *if given a choice, peacekeeping operations should be internationally sanctioned (UN) and multilateral in implementation.* Several reasons exist for this advice. First, the sanction of the international community, or

its representatives in the form of the Security Council or General
Assembly, grants a legitimacy to the operation not often found in
unilateral interventions, however benign the intent. Second, whether
one considers that 'misery loves company' or it is easier to spread the
risk and have someone else to blame for not staying a difficult
course, coalition forces seem to offer a better chance of success.
Despite the difficulties in forming them, coalitions give weight to
one's cause, if only symbolically. Third, they also provide reinforce-
ment in often divided public opinion in the US that others think this
important enough to invest blood as well as treasure.

To this a caveat should be added. There must be a unified military
command and control arrangement. To have large numbers of armed
forces operating in the same area without a single chain of command
invites disaster. Moreover, coordination with civil authorities, such
as they are, is also required, as is cooperation with private voluntary
organizations (PVOs) and the array of international governmental
organizations (IGOs) involved in peacekeeping activities. *All* the
players need to know what the others are doing, where they are and
how to coordinate their activities. Even then, there will be problems,
but they will be neither as numerous nor as serious as they otherwise
might be. The US has learned much about how to handle many of
these problems.[58]

The more specific lessons of the Lebanese interventions by the
United States can be enumerated as follows. All have corollaries in
our actions since Lebanon in Panama, Somalia, Haiti and Bosnia.
American experiences in Lebanon should have warned it about the
folly of attempting to broker peace amid conditions such as it found
there. They lead to the following lessons/injunctions.

1. *One is not likely to settle from without disputes which are essentially family or tribal in nature.* Not knowing and not understanding
the depths of the rivalries among the Maronites and other Christian
groups, the Sunnis, the Shiites, the PLO and the position of the
Druze in the equation of Lebanese politics, the US assumed there
was a legitimate government to restore and bolster (there was not).
Nor was there an army it could train to protect that government –
another fiction. The strongest allegiances are often personal, not political, based on a feudal relationship of fealty and economic protection,
not allegiance to a sovereign entity. Failure to heed this insight led to
our debacle in Somalia and another hasty 'redeployment to the sea'
and eventual withdrawal. There, the mistake was negative, not

positive, in that we characterized Mohamed Farah Aideed as the single villain among many and made elimination of him and his forces the key to success. The US failed to understand the complexities of Somali politics and the pastoralist vs nomad dimension of the society on which it rested.

2. *The overlay of multi-ethnic squabbles in a supposedly multi-confessional society is an invitation to disaster.* Most societies do not function as America does and the role of both democratic processes and institutions, even the concept let alone operationalization of representation, is often, quite literally, foreign. Hence, institutionalization of democratic institutions and practices as a way to settle disputes by negotiation, compromise and incremental agreements is also foreign and smacks of imposition of the will of others, not 'natural' sentiment. There were strong reasons, usually economic and political, for the preservation of separate ethnic and confessional communities under the Ottoman Empire. There are also long histories of favouritism, and recriminations and scores to settle when the opportunity arises. Yugoslavia was no more a state than Lebanon. It was merely a set of boundaries on a map representing distinct territory without regard to how the people and power within those boundaries actually functioned. Whether it is Rwanda or Bosnia, such circumstances are not likely to be susceptible to short-term effective solution by intervention from outsiders. Sooner or later, peacefully or via bloodshed – and probably the latter – the people who live on the territory of these so-called states will have to work things out for themselves. Others may be able to assist from time to time, but should be under no illusions about their ultimate capability to solve the dilemmas that confront those living there.

3. *Do not take sides in the dispute, however tempting it may be.* If one cannot be an honest broker and exude neutrality in the treatment of disputants, one is not involved in peacekeeping. The US had little trouble with the rival factions, even in the cauldron of rivalries that existed in Beirut, until it took sides. When it began training the Lebanese Armed Forces, it traded neutrality and peacekeeper status for favoritism and became a target. The largest loss of life in a single incident since the Vietnam war occurred when the marine barracks were blown up on 23 October 1983. The US did the same thing ten years later in Somalia, with disastrous results. The US chose sides and suffered the consequences. After declaring Mohamed Farad Aideed the source of the trouble in Mogadishu, it set out to arrest him, despite his being the leader of the group which overthrew the

previous Marxist regime and the best organized of the factions in Somalia. The US suffered the largest combat death toll in a firefight – 18 dead and 78 wounded – since Vietnam.

4. *While one may assist in the restoration of law and order as a peacekeeper, do not become responsible for its continuation.* That is the job of a state and the duly constituted agents of political authority, be they local police, a gendarmerie or the National Guard. Patrolling the 'Green Line' and opening the airport in Beirut soon turned into patrolling with the Lebanese Armed Forces whom the US was training and arming. American forces ended up responding to random fire, car bombs and other such incidents. Militaries are not police forces and there is a distinction between constabulary functions and military ones. They should be maintained, not confused. Foreign militaries should not become an agent of the state in which there is little trust and great suspicion and hostility. Doing so means one is no longer impartial or above the fray, capable of investigating impartially the claims of all concerned. The same thing happened with the US intervention in Haiti and the effort to turn a gang of former Tonton Macoutes into a legitimate police force may ultimately only serve to make them more efficient in their terror. If so, it will become morally culpable in the process, regardless of its good intentions.

5. *Do not try and ensure the political succession one desires.* If successful, the regime which follows is forever tainted in the eyes of many of its adversaries, if not its supporters. If the successor regime is unsuccessful, prestige and power are gambled needlessly on circumstances which cannot be controlled. The US certainly decided early on that it wanted a Gemayel regime in Lebanon to succeed and that it was, as far as it was concerned, the Lebanese state. This conviction existed despite the fact that the Parliament which elected him was last elected in 1972, based on an unwritten agreement made in 1943 and that in turn based on a flawed census last taken in 1932, which allowed overseas Maronites to be counted in the six to five ratio of Christians to Muslims, to determine its membership. It bore no reality – religiously, politically, economically or socially – to the reality of the moment. Six years later, after overthrowing Manuel Noriega in Panama, we would install Guillermo Endara as President. Despite having been seen as the winner of an earlier election, his regime was notable in its corruption and inefficiency and he in turn was voted out in 1994. Things rarely seem to be what one hopes they may become in fledgling democracies.

6. *Endemic corruption is a major obstacle for peacekeepers and one which they may not be able to overcome.* As an outsider attempting to control a foreign environment, one has to rely on someone for translation services, information and interpretation of events, and one has a limited amount of expertise about the country and region. To compensate, we must utilize others from the area or expatriates returning to it. All have their biases. And many are products of a system that outsiders essentially do not and, in the short run, cannot understand. Such is the case virtually everywhere to some degree and places those who wish to help from outside at a distinct disadvantage. There are two ways to get things done. Standing in line and waiting one's turn is called 'red tape' and bureaucracy. Giving special favors for some to 'jump the queue' is called graft and corruption. All institutions work with a combination of the two. But in some cases the latter is more widespread, inventive and necessary. If corruption, at least of a sort which one is not used to, is endemic, it is very hard for one to understand how society can function, let alone change it and make it less corrupt, or at least more to one's liking. If outsiders cannot or will not do business this way, stalemate may ensue.

7. *Don't presume there is, or soon will be, a functioning political system similar to those which are familiar with allegiances to political institutions and processes.* In many cases, the functioning relationships of a state are based on allegiances that are personal, communal and feudal in nature. They do not generally reflect Western values, institutions or practices. The notion of swearing allegiance to the constitution or of upholding rules of political processes, and the existence of an independent judiciary and the rights of free speech, press and assembly, are neither universal nor understood by those with little experience of American democratic practices. It is hard enough for Americans to make their multi-ethnic society function with over 220 years of experience. To expect others to learn quickly or to implement reforms and understandings that are born of historic trials and unique cultural solutions is wishful thinking. There is no other system quite like the American anywhere else in the world and Americans tend to forget that all the world is not, and may not want to be, just like the US.

8. *Don't fall victim to the illusion that the demonstration of overwhelming force will have a lasting deterrent impact after we're gone.* The half-life of the demonstration of military capability and power is very short. The array of military assets collected in Lebanon or just offshore proved to be more of a burden than an asset. The shellings

of the Druze strongholds in the Shouf Mountains and the bombing attacks from carrier aircraft were not only singularly unsuccessful in their purpose but had exactly the opposite effect of what we had intended. They made the resistance to US policy aims even more strident and pronounced. Even the crushing military defeat inflicted on Saddam Hussein apparently has had a rather short half-life. And that was in one of history's most lop-sided wars. Peacekeeping efforts in Somalia have also demonstrated this reality and Haiti and Bosnia likely will in time.

9. *Most peacekeeping actions occur in what have come to be called 'failed states' – otherwise, outside peacekeepers wouldn't be there.* There are many areas which we call 'states' in which we discuss unitary 'societies', 'polities' and 'economies' where there are no such things. Because there is a delineated territory on a map and people that are supposed to share a nationality does not make them citizens of a state. They are often little more than extended families, religious minorities, geographic outposts, local robber barons and their supporters who are hardly members of a 'body politic'. If involved in a failed state – a Lebanon, a Somalia, a Yugoslavia (Bosnia) – then reconstructing it will be a long and tortuous process if it can be accomplished at all. It is rather like outsiders – some other king's men – trying to put Humpty Dumpty together again. There can be no guarantee of the result, nor of the time and costs required for such an effort.

10. *Things are not what they seem.* One should undertake peace-keeping operations with the sobering understanding that one does not, and possibly cannot, know what is going on. However much one may think one knows from afar and from outside, things will be different when in-country. Like the photographer and his subject, the behavior of the residents will be different because of the presence of observers. There is little we can do about the latter except to try and understand what the reactions may be. That in turn should be predicated on as keen an understanding as possible before going in. This can be obtained vicariously by a healthy dose of history, cultural anthropology, comparative politics, sociology, psychology and economic analysis in order to know better what we are getting into. But however much one may think one knows, the collective understanding and appreciation of reality will be less than perfect and, in some cases, virtually non-existent. Such has been the case with nearly every American intervention in all parts of the world.

11. *The nation's purpose writ large and its specific policy should (a) fit the circumstances as they are; (b) be obtainable and mutually*

reinforcing; (c) at an acceptable cost; (d) with some reasonably well-defined end state in mind. Americans often come to grips with issues belatedly and in a hurry. They have a tendency to start out slow and gradually escalate their involvement in issues. Doing so often means that their actions are not in harmony with the reality of the moment and therefore dangerously out of step with the forces in being. Peacekeepers need to understand the rapidity with which events change the strategic landscape and limit options. Policies should have obtainable goals, with measures of merit that are relevant. They should also be in harmony with larger purposes in national security strategy and diplomacy so as not to be abandoned half way through the effort. The American intervention in Lebanon in 1958 had as much to do with Iraq and Jordan as with Lebanon, and US Middle East policy in general, the framework of the Cold War and the recent transformations in the Middle East beginning with the Suez Crisis. The US was fortunate to extricate itself quickly and easily. It was not so fortunate in its second visit in 1982.

Peacekeeping operations are likely to be open-ended affairs. Neither UN intervention in Cyprus (32 years) nor Operation PROVIDE COMFORT II (five years) were to last as long as they have. The US did not expect to stay in Lebanon for 18 months when it went back a second time in 1982. Duration alone can change costs enormously. So can casualties. There were only three US Marines killed in the US intervention in 1958 – one to sniper fire and two to drowning while swimming off a Beirut beach. There were 241 in one incident on 23 October 1983 in the third time American forces went to Beirut. How much in blood and treasure will the nation commit and expend if necessary should be considered beforehand, not after the fact. In virtually any deployment of military forces, let alone their employment in a hostile environment, there will be casualties. Even the Gulf War had more non-combat deaths than ones caused by hostile fire. Lastly, there needs to be a vision of the preferred end state and an exit strategy for both success and failure. Not to do so risks being overtaken by events and at the mercy of others' choices rather than one's own. This end state may well be defined, as the US deployment to Bosnia was, by a time limit alone. While a strategic detriment in the formulation of policy, such a requirement may be the price to be paid in a democratic society for the deployment of large peacekeeping forces.

12. *Just as in medicine – a helping profession – there should be the equivalent of a Hippocratic Oath for peacekeepers – 'First, do no*

Harm'. Whatever the mission or operation, there will be casualties and unintended as well as unexpected consequences. But one should operate in such a manner that the presence of peacekeepers does not further destabilize an already dangerous situation or make for a wider war than the one they seek to end. Such was not the case with the US military intervention in Lebanon in 1982, despite its good intentions. And although it was occasioned by the horrors of the Sabra and Shatila Camp massacres, ultimately the intervention only ensured a continuing and wider war. The US and the UN may well do so again in Bosnia. They have already done so in Somalia.

WHY WE DO NOT LEARN

However interesting and summative, if unspectacular, the lessons mentioned above, the more relevant and important question is: 'Why do we not learn from our past mistakes?' The answers to that are far more difficult. They are also speculative on my part. I cannot prove them, only assert them at this juncture. These hypotheses will be tested later as part of another study. If true, they represent a much greater problem than the rules of engagement, the deployment capability and even the diplomatic climate in which military forces are used in operations other than war, specifically peacekeeping operations. Some have given sharply critical assessments for what they deem 'military incompetence' and the perils of 'groupthink'. Some of it may be true, however strident and tendentious the tone.[60] Much of it is wide of the mark, though some points are worth pondering. I don't wish to review such claims and counter-claims here, Rather, I seek to provide some tentative hypotheses to answer the question highlighted in this section. Why do we not learn from our past mistakes?

First, there is little or no continuity. I suspect the military and the political leadership of the country do not learn very well from the past because rarely are the same group of decision-makers confronted with similar crises. The political leadership tends to turn over every four years. President Clinton is the first Democrat to be elected to two terms since Franklin Roosevelt. Though Eisenhower, Nixon and Reagan were two-term Presidents, as with most, many of their cabinet officers and principal advisers changed. Eisenhower and Nixon each had two Secretaries of State and three Secretaries of Defense. Reagan had a record seven National Security Advisers. The situation in the military is even worse. Rarely does a Chairman or Service Chief serve more than a two-year term and it is not at all uncommon for many general officers to be rotated every 18 months or less from one job to the next as they are promoted. There is not much continuity at the top – the institutional memory is wanting.

Second, Military Operations Other Than War (MOOTW) have not been seen as important by the military services, with the possible exception of the Marine Corps. MOOTW is not deemed an important or a routine part of the military's role. The existence of MOOTW is neither necessary nor sufficient for the US military's existence, *esprit de corps* and capabilities. While this attitude existed throughout the Cold War and can certainly explain why we didn't learn from Operation BLUEBAT in 1958 and the 30 or so years thereafter, it has only been since the end of the Gulf War with Operations PROVIDE COMFORT and SOUTHERN WATCH in Iraq, DENY FLIGHT in Bosnia, RESTORE HOPE in Somalia and RESTORE DEMOCRACY in Haiti that MOOTW has become a rather steady diet for the US military.

Third, there is no constituency for MOOTW in the military. There is the old attitude of the Cold War which some have characterized as 'I don't do windows.' Despite the fact that MOOTW is what militaries do in peacetime and they are generally good at it, they don't like it. Gradually, there has been a grudging acceptance of MOOTW as a legitimate military mission. But even so, it is seen as a sidebar to the main focus on fighting and winning the nation's wars – or at least deterring them – as the legacies of the Cold War. However great the need for and frequency of Military Operations Other Than War are *outside* the military, there is no constituency for them *inside* the military. Those in uniform define themselves as warriors. They may be required to impose a peace by force of arms, but they do not see themselves routinely responsible for keeping a peace by *not* using arms. Their scorecard says if it isn't war, it doesn't really count.

Fourth, and an even more pernicious reason, is that the US military is very ethnocentric and in many ways anti-intellectual. It routinely studies war, not MOOTW. The nation's command and staff colleges and its war colleges spend far more time studying war than MOOTW. On one level, this is understandable because of the need for institutional *esprit de corps*, the need for glorification of military heroes and accomplishments. Moreover, the US military studies its wars, not those of others. Few if any hours are devoted to studying the Falklands/Malvinas War, the Iran–Iraq War or the Soviets' misadventures in Afghanistan. More importantly, the military tends to study its successes, not its failures.[61] The Second World War and the Gulf War dwarf the time spent on Korea and Vietnam. But far more can be learned from studying one's failures and shortcomings than glorifying one's successes. Rarely does senior leadership play a wargame in which Blue (the US) loses – it always wins against the enemy (Red) forces. If that's the arrogance of the way the US military feels about war, imagine how it feels about MOOTW? And it is a question of emotion, not belief. The military doesn't like MOOTW and didn't volunteer to be the world's nanny. Intellectually, MOOTW takes a distant second place to war in the mind of the military. Increasingly, though, it is now recognized as important. But many still don't like it.

Happily, this is likely a generational phenomenon which is changing even now. Younger troops and officers have less of a problem with MOOTW missions than do their older leadership. The one generation was socialized during the Cold War. The newer one represents a post-Cold War reality. One grew up with nuclear deterrence, interventions against the spread of communism and a peer competitor in the Soviet Union. The other has come of age in an era in which 'preventive diplomacy', 'engagement and enlargement' and humanitarian intervention are the watchwords of the day. It will take some time, but things will improve and get better.

CONCLUSIONS: FROM BEIRUT TO BOSNIA

The deployment of a nation's military forces abroad carries with it the status and prestige of the nation. It also risks the employment of these forces. What one calls somewhat euphemistically 'Military Operations Other Than War' are often just the opposite. They are military missions which *risk* war. Pretending that they don't or hoping that they won't may be wishful thinking. Peacekeeping missions are fraught with dangers, the full extent and significance of which one can never understand, strategically or tactically, before becoming involved. One therefore enters into these sorts of missions at great risk and should do so with great care. While they appeal to both sides of the somewhat schizophrenic national will of Americans – a desire to serve as a passive example for others to emulate and a desire to go off on Wilsonian crusades to remake the world in its image – one should not enter into them lightly or expect more from intervention than is possible.

The American track record from Beirut to Bosnia is hardly one of unmitigated success. The US experience in Lebanon was a failure as was its effort in Somalia in the long run. In both cases it stopped a course of death and destruction – at least temporarily – but made no lasting impact on the disputants or the conflict. As of this writing, the jury is still out on American deployments to Haiti and Bosnia. But the accomplishments, however significant in the short run, may be short lived. If the problems had been easy to solve, they would have been solved. A regional hegemon, a regional coalition, a neighboring state would have already imposed a solution if that were possible. What we are dealing with are those cases which may prove to be intractable, at least for the foreseeable future, or those in which the antagonists are so closely balanced that even force of arms cannot declare a victor and impose an end to violence by the application of overwhelming force. If inducements of other kinds – military, economic, technological, political – have failed, what makes one think that one can solve the disputes at issue?

Most importantly and fundamentally, if what is at issue is the inability of disparate communities to live together and function as members of a state, then the solution may well be partition of some kind and the admission of a failed state. That can be negotiated, achieved by ethnic cleansing via death, destruction or relocation, imposed from without or achieved from within. But the effort to preserve something which no longer exists – a 'state' which is a failed political entity, in the absence of civil authority, with the dissolution of bonds of social affection or acceptance, amid pervasive economic catastrophe – is a fool's errand. Anarchy is anarchy. Where it exists, there may be lives to be saved by stopping the killing, humanitarian aid to prevent greater loss of life, respite for the removal of those caught in the crossfire, but there is no peace to keep, no state to preserve, or basic social order on which to build. Failure to understand this will guarantee failure of future peacekeeping interventions and lead to the defeat – moral and physical – of those nations foolish enough to try and preserve what no longer exists.

There have been many periods in history and many regions of the world in which, despite moral protestations, neither the US nor other Western nations became involved in foreign disputes of political or human significance – Tibet, East Timor and much of Africa come to mind. And there are strong cases made for a reconsideration of isolationism.[62] And yet, there are equally strong calls for exercising the responsibility of great power and the mantle of leadership, sought or not, thrust upon the US. 'If not now, when and if not here, where?' echo the cries for intervention. There is no easy way, no litmus test for deciding when and where to attempt to wield power, influence, access or control. There is only the effort that emerges from the intersection of political and other forces at any given time which are dependent as much on personality and politics as on policy and purpose.

Might may or may not make right, but it has proven to be the most effective way to create a modicum of order, be it democratic, authoritarian or totalitarian. In the words of Charles Tilly, 'States made wars and wars made states.'[63] They may also make peace, but generally only after war. Preserving that state is no easier now than it has been for much of human history. Thinking it can be done from without, by the deployment of armed forces, however well intentioned, and that it is somehow a neutral act, without local, regional or global significance, is a delusion one can ill afford. One makes enemies by actions and inactions, whatever the choices made. But a calculation on the likely success of the enterprise, the cost and consequence from a variety of perspectives *other than one's own*, and an effort to practice the conservation of enemies would serve all well. So too would a healthy dose of humility rather than hubris. A sense of its limitations should balance the plaintive repetitions of the phrase that the US is the world's 'sole remaining superpower'. The lessons of Lebanon suggest that one's efforts at preventive diplomacy and engagement and enlargement should be carefully selected, limited and tempered by the admission that there are many wrongs in the world which one cannot right. Caution rather than confidence should be the order of the day.

NOTES

1.   Augustus Richard Norton, *Amal and the Shi'a: Struggle for the Soul of Lebanon*, Austin, Tex.: University of Texas Press, 1987, p. 80.
2.   Among some fairly general sources on Lebanese history and politics see Helena Cobban, *The Making of Modern Lebanon*, Boulder, Colo.: Westview Press, 1985; P.K. Hitti, *A Short History of Lebanon*, New York: St. Martin's Press, 1965; Samir Khalaf, 'The case of nineteenth century Lebanon', in Milton J. Esman and Shibley Telhami, (eds), *International Organizations and Ethnic Conflict*, Ithaca, NY: Cornell

University Press, 1995; Don Peretz, *The Middle East Today*, 2nd edn, Hinsdale, Ill.: Dryden Press, 1971.

3. Sandra Mackey, *Lebanon: Death of a Nation*, New York: Anchor Books, 1989, p. 117. This is a highly readable and very detailed commentary on the fate of modern Lebanon.

4. See excerpts from President Eisenhower's Message to Congress on 5 January 1957 proclaiming the Eisenhower Doctrine in M.S. Agwani, *The Lebanese Crisis, 1958: A Documentary Study*, New Delhi, for the Indian School of International Studies by Asia Publishing House, New York, 1965, pp. 4–13.

5. Roger J. Spiller, *'Not War But Like War': The American Intervention in Lebanon*, Leavenworth Papers No. 3, Ft Leavenworth, Kan.: Combat Studies Institute, US Army Command and General Staff College, January 1981, p. 9. This is the most detailed account of the military aspects of the intervention.

6. Walid Khalidi, *Conflict and Violence in Lebanon: Confrontation in the Middle East*, Cambridge, Mass.: Center for International Affairs, Harvard University, 1979, p. 38. The most serious breach by Chamoun was offending Msgr Paul Meouchy, the Maronite Patriarch.

7. Mackey, op. cit., p. 122.

8. Peretz, op. cit., p. 329.

9. Fahim Qubain, *Crisis in Lebanon*, Washington, DC: Middle East Institute, 1961, pp. 55, 58.

10. Ibid., pp. 80–1.

11. Robert McClintock, 'The American landing in Lebanon', *United States Naval Institute Proceedings*, Vol. 88, No. 10, October, 1962, pp. 66–7.

12. Agwani, op. cit., pp. 98–9.

13. Spiller, op. cit., p. 17.

14. President Eisenhower's Message to Congress, 15 July 1958, cited in Agwani, op. cit., p. 229.

15. Extract from President Eisenhower's radio-TV address, 15 July 1958, cited in Agwani, op. cit., p. 231.

16. Ibid., p. 233.

17. Reported in the *New York Times*, 27 July 1958, Part 4, p. 1, cited in Jack Shulimson, *Marines in Lebanon, 1958*, Washington, DC: Historical Branch, G-3 Division, HQ, US Marine Corps, n.d., pp. 12–13. This is a highly detailed typescript report of the Marine portions of Operation BLUEBAT.

18. Among the numerous accounts of 1958 and its aftermath, other than those already cited, see Erika G. Alin, *The United States and the 1958 Lebanon Crisis: American Intervention in the Middle East*, Lanham, Md.: University Press of America, 1994; Marius Deeb, *The Lebanese Civil War*, New York: Praeger, 1980; and Agnes Korbani, *U.S. Intervention in Lebanon, 1958 and 1982, Presidential Decisionmaking*, New York: Praeger, 1991.

19. Spiller, op. cit., pp. 28–39.

20. Cited in Spiller, op. cit., p. 38.

21. Mackey, op. cit., p. 133.

22. A comment made by a Pentagon spokesman, quoted in the *New York Times*, 16 July 1958, p. 1, cited in Spiller, op. cit., p. 24.
23. For a synopsis of the events after the 1958 intervention see Cobban, Khalidi and Mackey for their different, but informative assessments.
24. Khalidi, op. cit., p. 44.
25. Ibid., p. 45.
26. Itamar Rabinovich, *The War For Lebanon, 1970–1983* Ithaca, NY: Cornell University Press, 1984, p. 48.
27. Gerald B. Helman and Steven R. Ratner, 'Saving failed states', *Foreign Policy*, No. 89, Winter 1992/93, pp. 3–20.
28. Korbani, op. cit., p. 60.
29. Khalidi, op. cit., p. 127.
30. Ibid., pp. 131–2.
31. Ibid., p. 133.
32. Selim Nassib with Caroline Tisdall, *Beirut: Frontline Story*, Trenton, NJ: Africa World Press, 1983, p. 27.
33. For a succinct overview of these events, see Ch. 8, 'The battles of Beirut (1982–4)', in Cobban, op. cit., pp. 181–208.
34. Nassib, op. cit., p. 52.
35. See Raymond Tanter, *Who's At the Helm? Lessons of Lebanon*, Boulder, Colo.: Westview Press, 1990.
36. See Mackey, op. cit., pp. 178–82, and Daniel P. Bolger, 'Fire in the Levant: operations in Lebanon', *Americans At War, 1975–1986: An Era of Violent Peace*, Novato, Calif.: Presidio Press, 1988, Ch. 4, pp. 191–260, especially pp. 194–5.
37. This information, in different formats, is cited in ibid., pp. 192, 194 and 201, and is drawn from the Institute for Strategic Studies, *Military Balance, 1983–1984, Air Force Magazine*, December 1983, pp. 97–100, and Chaim Herzog, *The Arab–Israeli Wars*, New York: Random House, 1982, pp. 387–93.
38. Tanter, op. cit., p. 193.
39. Quoted in Mackey, op. cit., p. 181.
40. Ibid., p. 183.
41. There are many commentaries on the massacres, most of which are highly partisan and biased. Among those that are less so are Cobban, op. cit., Mackey, op. cit., and Rabinovich, op. cit. Useful, if strident, is Nasib and Tisdall, op. cit.
42. For a detailed description and chronology of these operations and an assessment of them see Ralph A. Hallenbeck, *Military Force as an Instrument of U.S. Foreign Policy: Intervention in Lebanon, August 1982–February, 1984*, New York: Praeger, 1991.
43. President Ronald W. Reagan, message to Congress, 29 September 1982, cited in Bolger, op. cit., p. 240.
44. See Tanter, op. cit., Hallenbeck, op. cit., and Korbani, op. cit., for assessments of the failures in US decision-making related to various aspects of our third (second in 1982) involvement in Lebanon.
45. Korbani, op. cit., p. 79 and Chapter 6 entitled 'The 1982 interventions: policy of a "Quick Fix"', pp. 79–100.
46. Mackey, op. cit., p. 189.

47. Bolger, op. cit., p. 229.
48. Ibid., p. 200.
49. Ibid., p. 208.
50. See Tanter, op. cit., pp. 217–25.
51. Little is made of these other events by most US commentators who focus on this particular American tragedy and the larger loss to the exclusion of the pattern of such incidents which both preceded and followed it.
52. Bolger, op. cit., p. 230.
53. See ibid., especially pp. 233–7, Tanter, op. cit., and Hallenbeck, op. cit.
54. Information from the *New York Times*, 10 March 1992, cited in As'ad AbuKhalil, 'The longevity of the Lebanese Civil War', in Karl P. Magyar and Constantine P. Danopoulos (eds), *Prolonged Wars: A Post Nuclear Challenge*, Maxwell AFB, Ala.: Air University Press, 1994, p. 63, note 1.
55. Abukhalil, op. cit., pp. 48–62.
56. Hallenbeck, op. cit., pp. xii–xiii.
57. Remarks made by Gen. Michael J. Dugan, USAF (Retd) to members of the faculty at the Air War College during a visit in November 1995.
58. An excellent reference in this regard is John Mackinlay (ed.), *A Guide to Peace Support Operations*, Providence, RI: The Thomas J. Watson Institute for International Studies, Brown University, 1996.
59. See Joint Pub. No. 3–07.3, *Joint Tactics, Techniques and Procedures for Peacekeeping Operations*, Washington, DC: US Government Printing Office, 29 April 1994.
60. See, for example, the work of Norman Dixon, *The Psychology of Military Incompetence*, New York: Basic Books, 1976; Irving Janis, *Victims of Groupthink*, Boston: Houghton Mifflin, 1972; and Richard Gabriel, *Military Incompetence*, New York: Hill & Wang, 1985.
61. The excellent work done by Eliot Cohen and John Gooch, *Military Misfortunes*, New York: Vintage, 1991, is an exception to the rule and a great contribution to military history.
62. See Eric A. Nordlinger, *Isolationism Reconfigured: American Foreign Policy for a New Century*, Princeton, NJ: Princeton University Press, 1995.
63. Charles Tilly, 'Reflections on the history of European state-making', in Tilly (ed.), *The Formation of National States in Western Europe*, Princeton, NJ: Princeton University Press, 1975, p. 42. See also the excellent discussion of this point in Bruce D. Porter, *War and the Rise of the State: The Military Foundations of Modern Politics*, New York: Free Press, 1994.

6 Learning from the Failure of Disarmament and Conflict Resolution in Somalia*

Clement E. Adibe

INTRODUCTION

On 2 March 1995, the United Nations completed the withdrawal of its troops and civilian personnel from Somalia. This action formally ended a long ordeal for the premier international organization which began three years earlier with an international demand for organized intervention to stop the massive starvation that was claiming the lives of Somalis. On the day of the UN's forced exit from Somalia under unfavourable circumstances dictated by warlord General Mohamed Farah Aideed, UN Secretary-General Boutros Boutros-Ghali announced, with regrets, that the hopes for a new international order that blossomed at the end of the Cold War had evaporated. In the future, he said, the United Nations would have to 'contract out' more operations to regional organizations or multinational forces led by major powers with special interests in disputes. As we now know, this is already happening in the former Yugoslavia where NATO has assumed peacekeeping functions following the success of negotiations in Dayton, Ohio. But should that be the lesson of Somalia? If not, then, what *should* the failure of the Somali operation teach international institutions and national governments about multilateral conflict resolution? This is the central problem I propose to discuss in this essay. I shall argue that far from functional devolution of peace tasks to regional organizations, the lesson of Somalia is that there is an urgent need for the consolidation and harmonization of the principles and guidelines for UN peace missions through a programme of combined training for all national contingents prior to deployment in

---

* This chapter is based on research conducted at the United Nations Institute for Disarmament Research (Disarmament and Conflict Resolution Project) in Geneva between January and June 1995. The chapter draws heavily upon two previous publications: *Managing Arms in Peace Processes: Somalia*, Geneva: United Nations, 1995; and 'Somalia: lessons of a failed intervention', *Gravitas*, Vol. 2, No. 3, Winter 1995, pp. 23–6.

118

an operational theatre. This essay is divided into three sections. The first section briefly discusses the conflict that invited international intervention. The second section examines the major phases and activities of multinational peacekeeping forces in Somalia, while the third and concluding section discusses the lessons of the failed mission in Somalia.

THE ANARCHY IN SOMALIA

Some scholars have argued that the conflict and violence that prompted international intervention in Somalia between 1992 and 1995 was due to the warlike and ethnocentric *nature* of Somalis. In one such explanation, Andrew Natsios argued that 'the Somalis are *by instinct* a remarkably ethnocentric culture,' with deep-seated traditions and folklore that promote and perpetuate antagonism: 'Me and Somalia against the world, Me and my clan against Somalia, Me and my family against the clan, and Me against the family.'[1] Such 'First Image' characterization of the ordinary Somali as inherently violent neglects crucial 'Second Image' considerations of political dynamics and regime-type that brought Somalia to its knees.[2] Not unlike similar cases of state collapse in Africa, Somalia progressively slid into anarchy two decades earlier with the military overthrow of constitutional government by General Siad Barre. The logic of military dictatorship compelled Barre to rely on the use of force to settle political disputes. The strength of Barre's regime, bolstered heavily by Cold War superpower rivalry in the strategic Horn of Africa, made political opposition and legitimate dissent a deadly game indeed. As long as superpower support lasted, Barre's regime enjoyed sufficient moral (albeit by default), financial and military resources to crush and deter any opposition, thus maintaining a facade of stability. However, the end of the Cold War at the beginning of the decade assured the irrelevance and consequent weakening of client-authoritarian regimes, such as Barre's in Somalia. It therefore took a minor push by Somali opposition forces to crack the once formidable dictator.

Opposition to Barre's regime came from two major sources. The first was the Somali National Movement (SNM), at the core of which were exiled Isaaq patriots who had borne the brunt of Barre's violence since Somalia's defeat by Ethiopia in the Ogaden conflict of 1977. In 1989, the SNM was joined in opposition to Barre's regime by a second group, the United Somali Congress (USC), which was based mainly in the south around Mogadishu. In 1990, the two groups took advantage of Barre's weakness to launch increased guerrilla attacks on government facilities in both the north and the south. Although Barre retaliated in kind, his demoralized and ailing army could not match the strength and determination of opposition militia forces operating from all sides of the vast country. In desperation, Barre resorted to arming the masses while also exploiting the interclan divisions within the opposition.[3] The consequence was catastrophic for Somalia. Barre lost power and fled to Nigeria in December 1991 as his army was routed by opposition forces. However, in arming the masses and dividing the opposition along clan lines, he succeeded in making Somalia ungovernable by the victorious opposition militia groups.

The splintering of the USC, which controlled Mogadishu, into two competing factions was largely responsible for the scale of the mayhem that attracted international attention. In the struggle for supreme political power between the two key figures in the USC, General Mohamed Farah Aideed and Mr Ali Mahdi, Mogadishu was laid waste by the armed activities of the two warlords and their subclans, the Habre Gedir-Hawiye and Abgal-Hawiye.[4] Therefore, contrary to Natsios's argument that the conflict was the product of the intrinsically anarchic qualities of the Somali person, Mohammed Sahnoun offered a more plausible explanation when he argued that the disintegration of Somalia resulted from uprisings which were

> fueled both by clan-based rivalries and by wider political and economic considerations. The northern part of Somalia, home of a large clan, the Isaak, as well as other smaller tribes, came to resent the leadership of the southern tribal groups, whom they consider to have monopolized political power since Siad Barre took over in a coup in 1969. The inhabitants of the northern regions perceived themselves to be wronged and *without the possibility of democratic redress*. Their revolt was led by the Somali National Movement (SNM). Government forces, unable to prevent the uprising, unleashed a bloody repression against the civilian population, using aircraft and heavy weapons.[5]

The death and famine which spread throughout Somalia *because* of this conflict prompted widespread demands for concerted international efforts to restore order and contain the human tragedy in the Horn.

THREE PHASES OF INTERNATIONAL INTERVENTION IN SOMALIA

The United Nations reluctantly stepped into the Somali crisis after it became obvious in the spring of 1992 that uncoordinated efforts by all international humanitarian agencies of all shapes and sizes would do little to provide the assistance required by Somalia's desperate population. Once initiated, the UN involvement in Somalia took on a dynamic of its own. The UN intervention in Somalia between 1992 and 1995 may be categorized into three distinct phases, each with its own mission objective. These are:

(a) the first United Nations Operation in Somalia (UNOSOM I), an observer mission which was characterized by the relentless search for a credible role for the UN in Somalia;

(b) the Unified Task Force (UNITAF) in which the United States, empowered by the Security Council in accordance with Chapter VII of the UN Charter, organized and led a 'non-blue-helmeted' multinational force to enforce peace in Somalia;

(c) the second United Nations Operation in Somalia (UNOSOM II) which saw the return of blue helmets for an essentially peacebuilding operation in Somalia.

Each of these phases will be discussed in some detail below.

PHASE I: THE FIRST UNITED NATIONS OBSERVER MISSION IN SOMALIA (UNOSOM I)

The immediate outcome of the technical team's visit to Somalia was the Secretary-General's proposal for a 90-day Plan of Action for Emergency Humanitarian Assistance to Somalia, which was presented to the Security Council for consideration and approval.[6] This was in response to the unanimous request by Somalia's warring factions for 'an urgent and largely humanitarian assistance operation, as well as an important recovery programme'.[7] On 24 April, the Security Council adopted Resolution 751 approving the Secretary-General's plan to establish the United Nations Operation in Somalia (UNOSOM), charged with the responsibility of directing all UN activities in Somalia. The Resolution also requested the Secretary-General 'immediately to deploy a unit of 50 United Nations Observers to monitor the ceasefire in Mogadishu'.[8] Four days after the passage of the Resolution, the Secretary-General appointed Mr Mohammed Sahnoun, an Algerian diplomat, as his Special Representative in Somalia.

Upon arriving in Mogadishu in May to commence the implementation of Resolution 751, Mohammed Sahnoun was confronted with a rapidly changing security situation in Somalia. Rather than the groups of warring militia fighting against each other for control of Mogadishu, Sahnoun observed that humanitarian relief workers and their storage depots had become the principal targets of organized violence in Somalia. Following extensive discussions with the different warlords, Sahnoun shared their concern that 'they would lose control of some of the young militia, who might join other unruly youths already engaged in looting' if nothing was done to stem the famine.[9] In light of this concern, therefore, Sahnoun sought to control the availability and use of weapons through a programme of food-for-arms. Thus began the first but unsuccessful disarmament initiative to be undertaken in Somalia without any military support.

In explaining the rationale for the food-for-arms initiative, Sahnoun argued that:

> Since arms and ammunition were easily available,...[m]any Somali leaders had requested UN assistance in disarming the population. However, the Somalis would *voluntarily* bring in their weapons only if the food basket was sufficiently attractive. It was also necessary to use some other forms of inducement, such as temporary employment or other activities.[10]

For Sahnoun, therefore, the appropriate strategy would be to 'flood' Somalia with food for 'food scarcities further contributed to the atmosphere of general insecurity that now prevailed within the country'.[11] Accordingly, he proposed to deliver a minimum of 50,000 metric tons of food per month for the duration of the Secretary-General's 90-day Emergency Plan of Action. The problem, however, was that UN humanitarian agencies could not meet the food target, and even the meagre supplies that were arranged could not be delivered effectively because of logistical inadequacies. As a consequence, the shortage of food amidst worsening mass starvation served only to increase the level of violence in Somalia. According to the Secretary-General's report on the issue:

> ...in the absence of a government or governing authority capable of maintaining law and order, Somali 'authorities' at all levels of

society compete for anything of value in the country. Armed threats and killings often decide the outcome. Looting and banditry are rife. Amidst this chaos, the international aid provided by the United Nations and voluntary agencies has become a major (and in some areas the only) source of income and as such is the target of all the 'authorities,' who may sometimes be no more than two or three bandits with guns. *In essence, humanitarian supplies have become the basis of an otherwise non-existent Somali economy.*[12]

On the security front, the implementation of resolution 751 also ran into serious obstacles. The agreement on the deployment of 50 *unarmed* UN observers in Somalia was contingent upon successful 'consultations with the parties in Mogadishu' by the SRSG.[13] Pursuant to this requirement, Sahnoun initiated a lengthy process of consultations with the leaders of the major warring factions as well as the traditional rulers of Somalia's major clans. The purpose of this approach, which has been referred to as the 'bottom-up' strategy, was to weaken the increasingly over-demanding authority of the warlords by building grassroots support for UN activities through the medium of traditional elders. In Sahnoun's own words:

> Our delegation pursued a strategy of putting the clan system to work for Somalia. Agreements among local elders gradually helped to reduce the fighting and allowed food deliveries into the interior of the country. After arduous discussions, and with the help of the elders, we arranged a deal with Ali Mahdi, M.F. Aideed and other faction leaders for the deployment of 500 Pakistani peacekeepers in Mogadishu.[14]

Notwithstanding the obvious advantages of the bottom-up approach, such as the confidence and trust it generated among the warring parties in the UN mechanism, even Sahnoun would concede that the strategy proved to be extremely time-consuming, especially when compared with its results, for 'the warlords, particularly Aideed, were in no mood to passively accept the plucking of their feathers'.[15] Their success in resisting the gradual erosion of their authority resulted in a significant loss of time. For instance, '[i]t took two months just to persuade Mahdi and Aideed to accept the deployment of the 50 UN observers.'[16] The team of observers, drawn from Austria, Bangladesh, Czechoslovakia, Egypt, Fiji, Finland, Indonesia, Jordan, Morocco and Zimbabwe, arrived in

Mogadishu in July 1992 under the command of Brig.-Gen. Imtiaz Shaheen of Pakistan as the Chief Military Observer (CMO) of UNOSOM.[17]

Somalia's warlords took advantage of the two-month gap between the adoption of Resolution 751 and the deployment of the UN observers to rearm and strengthen their military position in anticipation of a major showdown. In the process, they would further tarnish the reputation and impartiality of the UN. According to Sahnoun, in one case of rearmament which occurred in mid-June, 'a Russian [Antonov] plane with UN markings, chartered by a UN agency [the World Food Programme] had delivered currency and military equipment to the north of Mogadishu, apparently to troops supporting interim president Ali Mahdi.'[18] According to the Secretary-General's assessment, this incident had a backwash effect on the processes of negotiations between Mr Sahnoun and General Aideed (spelled Aidid) for the deployment of UN observers:

> General Aidid's faction thereupon accused United Nations personnel of bias and suspended the deployment of United Nations observers. United Nations Headquarters instructed the CMO to remain at his post, whereupon the USC delivered an 'expulsion notice' to him and his party.[19]

The consequence of the clash of wits between the UN and General Aideed was the rapid deterioration of the political and security environment in Mogadishu. This was evidenced by the increased hostility towards foreigners, especially UN and relief workers. Generally speaking, as the frequency and intensity of violence against humanitarian personnel increased amid increasingly critical media scrutiny, UN officials in New York became increasingly impatient with Sahnoun's inability to achieve any significant improvement in the humanitarian and security conditions in Somalia. On his part, Sahnoun increased pressure on UN headquarters to show 'good faith' to all the warring parties in Somalia, especially General Aideed, in view of past and continuing acts which were eroding the faith and confidence of ordinary Somalis in the neutrality of the UN.[20] But he also accelerated discussions for the deployment of UN security personnel to escort humanitarian convoys, in accordance with Resolution 751. The success of these negotiations was relayed to the Secretary-General who, on 12 August, informed the Security Council that he was ready to deploy 500 'blue berets' to Mogadishu as part of UNOSOM.

Obviously, the coordination of logistics and information between field operations in Somalia and UN headquarters must have been inadequate. According to a recent report, 'Sahnoun was answerable to three UN Under-Secretaries, and unifying the various UN activities in the field was nearly impossible. His requests for greater autonomy and flexibility were [also] not met.'[21] In Sahnoun's own words: 'I still cannot understand why people in New York (who knew nothing of the realities in the field) made hasty and uncalled-for decisions, and still persist in having them implemented despite evidence of misjudgment and the strong objection of the people in the field.'[22] Indeed, these gaps in communication and coordination would result in a series of miscalculations by the UN Secretariat, all of which combined to worsen the humanitarian and security conditions in Somalia. According to Sahnoun:

> ... the UN headquarters in New York tended to ignore our advice and warnings in sensitive matters related to security. It took a great deal of time and difficult negotiation for our team to reach an agreement for the deployment of 500 UN troops. We were hoping that they would be deployed right away. After all, this was just a small battalion. There is no doubt that had these 500 troops been fully deployed as late as a month after the agreement, i.e. the beginning of September, it would have made an appreciable difference. However, bureaucratic delays (and skirmishes at the headquarters between different departments) led to total confusion. *Hence the 500 troops had not even arrived when an announcement was made in New York that over 3800 troops would be sent to Somalia.* This statement was made *without* informing the UNOSOM delegation in Mogadishu and the leaders of the neighbouring countries, and, worse still, without consulting the Somali leaders and community elders as we had done before.[23]

The first group of UNOSOM troops, comprising a lone unit of Pakistani soldiers, arrived in Mogadishu on 14 September 1992, to confront a hopelessly anarchic environment. Their task was made even more difficult by the fact that the marauding groups of militia under General Aideed had already considered them to be anti-Aideed. The reason for this perception is rooted in the UN's actions since August which blatantly negated prior understandings reached between Aideed and Sahnoun. Robert Patman underscored the nuances underlying this perception:

Aideed appeared to drag his feet [on the] negotiations [preceding]
the deployment of the UN security force...Mahdi [by contrast]
accepted with alacrity...The protracted discussions reflected
Aideed's concern that the introduction of peacekeeping troops
would not only erode his competitive position with Ali Mahdi in
Mogadishu – his faction exercised control over the lucrative
Mogadishu harbour and airport facilities – but also affect his
political base elsewhere in Somalia. Eventually, on 12 August,
four months after Resolution 751, Aideed and his SNA allies
signed an agreement with Sahnoun for the deployment of the 500
peacekeepers. *As part of the agreement, Sahnoun stated that any
increase in the number of UN troops would require the consent of
Aideed's SNA leadership.*[24]

New York's announcement of a major increase in the strength of
UNOSOM, without adequate consultation with the SRSG, would
further undermine the credibility of the latter in future negotiations
with Somalia's warring factions. It certainly amounted to a breach of
the agreement between Aideed and Sahnoun. But, even more fundamentally, that UN headquarters announced such an increase in
UNOSOM's force structure without the prior *consent* of all the
parties to the conflict in Somalia was too significant a move which
was bound to foul the delicate relationship between UN field personnel and local Somali militia and consequently alter the direction
and status of the mission as a Chapter VI operation. This raises
the following question: why did the UN take such a precipitate
action?

As I have mentioned earlier, Sahnoun's 'bottom-up' negotiating
strategy had resulted in considerable loss of time without producing
the desired impact on the dire security and humanitarian situation in
Somalia. Meanwhile, at the UN Secretariat some senior officials were
not only dissatisfied with Sahnoun's progress, but were also suspicious of his actions and intentions in Somalia. According to Patman,
'a suspicion existed within the UN Secretariat that Sahnoun was *mis-
reading* the Somali situation. With thousands of Somalis dying from
hunger each week and warlords like Aideed effectively exercising a
veto on UN action, the organization perceived it faced a crisis of
credibility.'[25]

The Secretariat's response to the crisis of credibility took two
forms. First, on 22 July the Secretary-General submitted a report to
the Security Council explaining 'the complex political and security

situation in Somalia' and a 'comprehensive approach' which the situation required.[26]

> I have therefore come to the conclusion that the United Nations must *adapt* its involvement in Somalia. Its efforts need to be *enlarged* so that it can help bring about an effective cease-fire throughout the country, while at the same time pressing forward with parallel efforts to promote national reconciliation. This will require the Organization to establish a presence in all regions and to adopt an innovative and comprehensive approach dealing with all aspects of the Somalia situation, namely the humanitarian relief and recovery programme, the cessation of hostilities and security, the peace process and national reconciliation, in a *consolidated framework*.[27]

This proposal set forth four principal functional objectives for UNOSOM: (a) humanitarian relief assistance; (b) ceasefire monitoring; (c) security, demobilization and disarmament; (d) national reconciliation through conciliation, mediation and good offices.[28] These objectives were predicated on the understanding that 'a framework for the security of humanitarian relief operations is the *sine qua non* for effective action.'[29]

This message was further reinforced in another report submitted a few weeks later to the Security Council. In view of the worsening famine situation and widespread looting of relief materials by armed gangs, the Secretary-General in this report recommended an immediate enlargement of ongoing airlift operations into Somalia and the establishment of 'preventive zones' on the Kenya–Somalia border. Because of the massive refugee flows generated by the Somali conflict, the programme of establishing and maintaining preventive zones was intended to 'reduce significantly cross-border movements of people in search of food' a well as 'contribute to a decrease in frictions that are growing in the border area.'[30] By the Secretariat's own estimate, this proposal would require the deployment of 'four additional United Nations security units, each with a strength of up to 750, to protect the humanitarian convoys and distribution centres throughout Somalia.'[31] These requests were approved by the Security Council in Resolution 775 of 28 August 1992.[32] One week later, the Security Council approved yet another proposal from the Secretary-General to increase the strength of UNOSOM by the deployment of three logistic units comprising 719 personnel.[33] These increases brought the total strength of UNOSOM to 4,219 persons by 8 September 1992.

In addition to substantially increasing its profile in Somalia through unilateral measures, the UN Secretariat also effected major changes in its field operations staff in Somalia. In this regard, Mohammed Sahnoun, who had strongly protested against the Secretariat's deployment of additional UNOSOM troops 'without proper consultation', was forced to resign his appointment as the Special Representative of the Secretary-General (SRSG) on 27 October.[34] His replacement was Ismat Kittani of Iraq whose task was to cope with increasing demand for coordination among expanding UN agencies as well as national contributions to UNOSOM. Above all, he also had to contend with the worsening famine condition and the deteriorating security environment in Mogadishu and elsewhere in Somalia.

Upon his arrival in Mogadishu in October 1992, Ambassador Kittani met a far more volatile situation than did his predecessor. As might have been expected, General Aideed had reacted negatively to the announcement, without prior consultation, of additional UN troop deployment by New York. Therefore, '[c]onvinced that the UN announcement contravened his August agreement with Sahnoun, Aideed threatened to send UN troops home in bodybags.'[35] Like many Somalis, he saw the announcement as a prelude to UN 'invasion' of their country. In a distress letter dispatched to the President of the Security Council on 24 November 1992, the Secretary-General underscored the danger to UN operation of such 'widespread perception among Somalis that the United Nations has decided to abandon its policy of cooperation and is planning to "invade" the country.'[36] This perception, along with Aideed's strong opposition to the increased UN military presence, was strengthened further by the sudden replacement of Mohammed Sahnoun – ostensibly because of his consensual diplomatic approach in Somalia – with Ismat Kittani as the SRSG in Somalia.[37]

The consequence of this development was that the general security environment in Somalia rapidly deteriorated at a pace that required a complete re-evaluation of the principles and methods of UNOSOM. In reporting to the Security Council the new security challenges brought about by the pervasive 'invasion syndrome' in Mogadishu, the Secretary-General submitted that the situation cannot be halted by the military resources currently available to UNOSOM, and recommended 'the deployment... of the four additional UNOSOM battalions... as quickly as possible.'[38]

PHASE II: 'OPTION 4', THE UNITED STATES, THE UNIFIED TASK FORCE (UNITAF) AND 'OPERATION RESTORE HOPE' IN SOMALIA

Despite concerted efforts by officials in Washington to treat the Somali crisis as a humanitarian issue best handled by international relief agencies, the intensity of American media focus on the failure of ongoing UN humanitarian efforts in Somalia finally brought the subject to the attention of the White House towards the end of summer 1992. By the beginning of autumn, a consensus began to emerge in Washington (and the UN Security Council as well) that '[o]nly a dramatic change in the security situation could hold back the deadly slide toward national self- destruction' in Somalia.[39] Andrew Natsios, who served as President Bush's coordinator of the relief programme in Somalia, has argued that the turning point in US policy towards the Somali crisis was an Oval Office meeting of the President's National Security team in mid-November 1992.[40] At that meeting, President Bush instructed his top national security advisers 'to do *whatever was necessary* to stop the starvation in Somalia'.[41]

The outcome of this process was the Bush Administration's decision to dispatch a sizeable contingent of US forces led by the First Marine Expeditionary Force (1 MEF) to Mogadishu to ensure the safe delivery of humanitarian aid.[42] This decision was communicated to the UN Secretary-General by the US Acting Secretary of State, Lawrence Eagleburger, on 25 November 1992. According to UN sources, Eagleburger informed the Secretary-General that 'should the Security Council decide to authorize Member States to ensure the delivery of relief supplies, *the United States would be ready to take the lead in organizing and commanding such an operation*, in which a number of other Member States would also participate.'[43] On the strength of this information, the Secretary-General proposed a set of policy options for consideration by the Security Council.

The Secretary-General's five options for renewed UN response to the complex humanitarian and security situation in Somalia

Four days after Eagleburger's visit, the Secretary-General submitted to the Security Council a new situation report on Somalia, in which he reviewed 'the basic premises and principles of the United Nations effort in Somalia' and laid out the following five options for a country-wide enforcement action to 'create conditions for the uninterrupted delivery of relief supplies to the starving people of Somalia.'[44]

Option 1: Strict adherence to the principles and practices of traditional UN peacekeeping
This option would force the United Nations to stay the course of traditional peacekeeping under Chapter VI of the Charter, requiring the consent of the parties to the conflict. That being the case, the objectives and practices of the UNOSOM mission would proceed as planned with the authorized deployment of an additional 4,200 blue helmets *if* an agreement to that effect was reached with General Aideed. The problem with this option, however, was that:

> Several of the de facto authorities, including especially General Aidid, have refused to agree to the deployment of United Nations troops in areas where the need for humanitarian relief is most acute. Even when they have agreed, their subsequent cooperation with UNOSOM has been at best spasmodic and, by their own admission, they do not exercise effective authority over all the armed elements in the areas which they claim to control.[45]

Put simply: '[t]he reality is that there are at present very few authorities in Somalia with whom a peace-keeping force can safely negotiate an agreed basis for its operations.'[46] Essentially, therefore, traditional peacekeeping does not and cannot work in a stateless society.[47] That being the case, the Secretary-General concluded that Option 1 'would not in present circumstances be an adequate response to the humanitarian crisis in Somalia.'[48]

Option 2: Immediate cessation of the experiment in humanitarian intervention
This option calls for the immediate pull-out of UN military personnel in Somalia as the first step towards abandoning the idea of using international military personnel to protect humanitarian activities as envisaged by proponents of humanitarian intervention.[49] In the light of initial objections to the introduction of military personnel in Somalia by some humanitarian NGOs, the Secretary-General reckoned that this option would allow the humanitarian agencies in Somalia 'to negotiate the best arrangements they can with the various faction and clan leaders.'[50] Like Option 1, the Secretary-General highlighted the weaknesses of this arrangement. While acknowledging the merits associated with Option 2, especially in the eyes of

some important non-governmental relief organizations, the Secretary-General rejected it less on grounds of practicality than on principle as well as the model's negative long-term impact. In his own words:

> The experience of recent months has been that, without international military protection, the [humanitarian] agencies have felt obliged to pay what is in effect protection money to the various factions, clans and sub-clans. *If the international community were to allow this to continue, it would be committing itself to an endless process in which less and less of the aid it provided would reach vulnerable groups and in which lawless trading in that aid would become, even more than at present, the foundation of Somalia's economy.* Such an outcome would encourage further fragmentation and destroy hopes of national reconciliation.[51]

Accordingly, the Secretary-General argued for measures that would involve stronger military presence because, in his view, '[t]he current difficulties are due not to their [i.e. UN military personnel] presence but to the fact that not *enough* of them are there and that they do not have the *right mandate*.'[52]

Option 3: Deterrence through the deployment of a massive military force under UN command and control
This option would allow the UN to deploy and maintain in Somalia a significant military presence beyond the level envisaged in any of the existing resolutions. Such a force would have the means and authority to create the conditions for the safe delivery of humanitarian relief as well as deter local factions 'from withholding cooperation from UNOSOM'. Such massive deployment would be based on the belief that 'a determined show, and if necessary use, of force by UNOSOM would be enough to convince those who are currently abusing and exploiting the international relief effort that they should cease their lawless activities.'[53]

Essentially, therefore, the purpose of Option 3 is to extract consent from Somalia's warring factions through intimidation or, failing that, to secure their cooperation with the United Nations through the instrument of coercion. If this option smacks of Machiavellian diplomacy, it is because, as the following report describes it, the military scenario in Somalia had become one of survival of the *fittest*:

> The troops in the city number several thousand when counting all the clans, sub-clans and free-roaming bandits. In Mogadishu

South alone, there are approximately 150 'technical' vehicles. Each
vehicle carries a heavy machine gun or 106 mm RR anti-tank gun.
In each of these vehicles there are 8 to 12 soldiers armed mainly
with AK 47s, G3 rifles and anti-armour RPG-7s. The local forces
have no uniforms and no communication...The state of training
of these troops is unknown but almost all would have some kind
of combat experience and they know how to operate all their
weapons. The condition of their weapons is surprisingly good;
ammunition is old but plentiful and still operational. In addition,
they have several operational armoured wheeled vehicles with can-
nons of 20 mm and dump trucks with twin 30 mm AA guns. It
must be assumed that the equivalent military force exists in Mogadishu North. Both sides have indirect fire capabilities (mortars,
field guns and free flight rockets).[54]

In the view of the Secretary-General, Option 3 suffered from one
major defect, and that was that the United Nations lacked the
resource and organizational capacity to embark on a military operation on a scale wide enough to create 'conditions throughout Somalia
for the secure delivery of relief supplies'.[55]

*Option 4: Recourse to a country-wide enforcement operation under-
taken by a group of member-states authorized to do so by the Security
Council*
This option had all the benefits of Option 3 without its attendant risk
of failure arising from the resource as well as the command and control limitations. Barring any difficulties in assembling a group of
member-states with the capacity and willingness to undertake such a
mission, Option 4 had the advantage of accomplishing the mission of
providing security for humanitarian supplies in Somalia with limited
financial burden on the United Nations. But it also presented its own
logistical and legal problems, and risked the possibility of degenerat-
ing into some form of unilateralism.

In light of these limitations, the Secretary-General cautioned that
'[i]f the members of the Security Council were to favour this option,
my advice would be that the Council should seek to agree with the
Member States who would undertake the operation on ways of
*recognizing the fact that it had been authorized by the Security Council
and that the Security Council therefore had a legitimate interest in the
manner in which it was carried out.*'[56] He then recommended various
ways of responding to these weaknesses:

The enabling resolution could underline that the military operation was being authorized in support of the wider mandate entrusted to the Secretary-General to provide humanitarian relief and promote national reconciliation and reconstruction in Somalia. The initial authorization could be for a specific period of time and the Member States concerned could be asked to furnish the Security Council with regular reports, on the basis of which the Council would, at specified intervals, review the authority it had given for the operation to take place. It could also be stated in the enabling resolution that the purpose of the operation was to resolve the immediate security problem and that it would be replaced by a United Nations peace-keeping operation, organized on conventional lines, *as soon as the irregular groups had been disarmed and the heavy weapons of the organized factions brought under international control.*[57]

These proposals, aimed at limiting the action and duration of the military operation undertaken by a group of member-states, were based on the assumption that those states would be willing to commit their forces for an extended period of time. The events of the weeks that followed would contradict this assumption.

Option 5: Country-wide enforcement action under UN command and control

This option would underline the collectivity of international peace and security under the aegis of the United Nations. However, like Option 3, the reality is that the United Nations lacks the resources, mechanisms and capability for any meaningful independent enforcement action on any significant scale. According to the Secretary-General: 'The Secretariat, already overstretched in managing greatly enlarged peace-keeping commitments, does not at present have the capability to command and control an enforcement operation of the size and urgency required by the present crisis in Somalia.'[58] Based on this assessment, he argued and recommended that

the Security Council take a very early decision to adjust its approach to the crisis in Somalia... The focus of the Council's immediate action should be to create conditions in which relief supplies can be delivered to those in need. Experience has shown that this cannot be achieved by a United Nations operation based on the accepted principles of peace-keeping. *There is now no alternative but to resort to Chapter VII of the Chapter*... If forceful 'action is taken, it should preferably be under United Nations command and control. If this is not feasible, an alternative would be an operation undertaken by Member States acting with the authorization of the Security Council. In either case the objectives of the operation should be precisely defined and limited in time, in order to prepare the way for a return to peace-keeping and post-conflict peace building.[59]

As might have been expected, the Security Council chose Option 4. The Council's adoption of Resolution 794, by unanimous vote, on 3 December 1992 marked a watershed in the history of United Nations efforts in the area of conflict resolution. Based on the argument that the 'complex and extraordinary' character of the Somali conflict called for an 'immediate and exceptional response', the Security Council determined that 'the magnitude of the human tragedy caused by the conflict in Somalia, further exacerbated by the obstacles being created to the distribution of humanitarian assistance, *constitutes a threat to international peace and security.*'[60] Accordingly, the Council, '*[a]cting* under Chapter VII of the Charter of the United Nations, *mandated* the Secretary-General and Member States cooperating to ... use all *necessary means to establish as soon as possible a secure environment for humanitarian relief operations in Somalia.*'[61] In accordance with the recommendation of the Secretary-General, the Security Council ceded command and control of the forces to 'the Member States concerned', but requested the first of regular reports on the progress of the operation within 15 days of the passage of Resolution 794.[62]

The day following the adoption of Resolution 794 by the Security Council, US President George Bush formally announced the commencement of 'Operation Restore Hope' (ORH) which would be directed by a Unified Task Force (UNITAF), under the command of Lt-Gen. Robert Johnston of the US Armed Forces. The first elements of US military contingent to ORH landed on the beaches of Mogadishu on 9 December 1992, and in no time UNITAF was able to establish a military presence sufficient enough to deter and punish, when necessary, the warring factions in Somalia (see Table 6.1).

By definition, UNITAF was a 'non-blue helmeted' operation, that is 'an operation in which the Security Council authorizes or requests Member States voluntarily to take certain actions' in maintenance of international peace and security.[63] Usually, the states initiating such operations bear the financial burden, in exchange for a non-UN

Table 6.1 The composition of UNITAF* (at 7 January 1993)

Country	Troop contribution
United States	21,000
Belgium	572
Botswana	303
Canada	1,262
Egypt	270
France	2,783
Germany	60
Italy	2,150
Kuwait	43
Morocco	1,356
New Zealand	42
Saudi Arabia	643
Turkey	309
United Kingdom	90
Maximum force strength	*37,000 (including 8,000 US troops stationed at sea)*

*Troops forming an advance party for UNITAF were also drawn from the following countries: Australia, India, Nigeria, Pakistan, Sweden, Tunisia and Zimbabwe.

command and control structure.[64] In the case of UNITAF, the United States wrote the mandate, and it did so with the advantage of accumulated lessons of experience from previous international military interventions, particularly Operation Desert Storm. According to students of US military strategy, the Pentagon plan for UNITAF was based on the 'Powell Doctrine' which calls for the deployment of massive military force in a US operation adjudged to be 'military doable', with a clear political authority (mandate), and a defined plan for entry and exit.[65] According to Lt-Gen. Barry McCaffrey, Director for Strategic Plans and Policy for the US Joint Staff, this doctrine is especially important in cases of 'aggravated peacekeeping' operations, such as Somalia, which are complicated by the 'intransigence of one or more of the belligerents, poor command and control of belligerent forces, or conditions of outlawry, banditry, or anarchy.'[66] Based on these considerations, the mandate for UNITAF was cautiously drawn up to be limited in scope, time and objective. Consistent with its mandate, UNITAF's operational mission statement defined the objectives of Operation Restore Hope as:

(a) securing seaports, airstrips and food distribution points;

(b) providing security for relief convoys and the operations of relief agencies;

(c) assisting UN agencies and non-governmental organizations (NGOs) in providing relief to the famine-stricken population.[67]

To accomplish these mission objectives, American military planners developed a 'three-track' approach to the problem of anarchy in Somalia. According to Lt-Gen. McCaffrey, military actions were planned, in phases, to focus on the following tasks:[68]

(a) Establishing security in Mogadishu and other famine-stricken parts of Somalia. This would involve a programme of voluntary disarmament and cantonment of militia in exchange for material rewards and retraining for civilian life.

(b) Assisting NGOs and private volunteer organizations in the delivery of humanitarian relief. This would involve providing military escort for humanitarian relief supplies, thus putting an end to the use of Somali 'technicals' by humanitarian agencies for providing security.

(c) Commencing early efforts to restore some semblance of law and order by encouraging the creation of an indigenous political authority and police force. This would involve establishing contact with, and encouraging dialogue between, the remnants of Somalia's political, religious and traditional elites as well as the leaders of the military factions. For this task, the UNITAF military command sought and obtained a visible civilian equivalent in the form of the US Liaison Office (USLO), headed by Robert Oakley.[69]

The US Central Command (USCENTCOM), which was in charge of the Somali operation, planned ORH in four phases. In the first phase US marine amphibious forces, assisted by elements of UNITAF, would secure the airfield and seaport in Mogadishu. Thereafter the forces would move inland to secure Baledogle and prepare for similar operations in Baidoa. The second phase would involve the deployment of a brigade of US Army and UNITAF forces to secure the famine-stricken town of Baidoa and three other relief centres: Oddur, Belet Weyne and Gialassi. Under phase three, USCENTCOM planned to advance further south to secure the port and airfield at Kismayo, Bardera and the land route from Bardera to Baidoa. In the fourth and final phase of the operation, US planners hoped to 'transfer...the responsibility for maintaining a secure environment for the delivery of humanitarian relief to United Nations peace-keeping forces.'[70]

For reasons of domestic politics, President Bush was unwilling to commit American troops for an extended period of military action in Somalia. Indeed, barely one week after the commencement of Operation Restore Hope, Washington declared its Somali mission a success and began to urge the United Nations to commence planning for early deployment of blue helmets to take over from UNITAF as early as March 1993. This request was formalized in a report circulated to members of the Security Council by Edward Perkins, US Ambassador to the United Nations, on 17 December 1992 – just one week after the first elements of US forces landed in Somalia. In this report, the US government indicated that the Somali operation was 'proceeding generally as planned' and pointed to 'positive indications that operations will continue successfully'.[71] It then suggested that the transfer of responsibility could proceed ahead of schedule: 'This transfer may occur concurrently with other phases as peace-keeping forces are available to assume responsibility for secured areas.'[72]

The problem of transition from UNITAF: differing perspectives from the UN Secretariat and the United States government

US Ambassador Perkins's letter to the United Nations was the first official and public indication of the disagreement between the UN Secretariat and the Bush Administration over the objectives and duration of the US-led multinational operation in Somalia. The disagreement centred on three critical issues: (a) the timing and scope of disarmament; (b) the geographical limits of the UNITAF mission; and (c) the duration of Operation Restore Hope. As I stated earlier, disarmament was not an integral component of US military planning for the Somali mission. The reason is simply that the political consultations that had taken place in Washington between the White House and the Congressional leadership underscored caution, doability and the necessity for avoiding mission creep as the defining variables in mobilizing the support of the American public for US military involvement abroad, even in a desperate humanitarian situation as in Somalia.[73] As far as the White House was concerned, the basis of US political consensus on Somalia would be eroded if disarmament was inserted into the mission mandate. Such a mandate would increase the length of the US mission as well as the risk factor, that is the greater likelihood of American casualties. On account of the latter, the Bush Administration did not want to tarnish its impressive military record with an ambitious intervention in Somalia with little promise of generating political capital for his outgoing regime. But the administration also saw the need for some form of disarmament to be undertaken once the mission was under way. In that case, the decision of when and to what extent Somalis would be disarmed would be made in conformity with the military situation on the ground. Put simply, Washington's view was that disarmament was not a priority but could be undertaken if deemed necessary by the US military in Somalia and, even so, it would be limited, voluntary and conducted on an *ad hoc* basis.[74] By contrast, the UN Secretariat viewed disarmament as a priority programme which must be accomplished by UNITAF *before* a transition to UN command could be effected. This position was underscored by the UN Secretary-General in a letter he dispatched to President Bush on 8 December 1992:

> ... any forceful action by the international community in Somalia must have the objective of ensuring that at least the *heavy weapons* of the *organized factions* are neutralized and brought under international control and that the *irregular forces and gangs* are disarmed. Without this action I do not believe that it will be possible to establish the secure environment called for by the Security Council resolution...[75]

The consequences of these differing positions for the disarmament process in Somalia will become obvious later in the discussion. Meanwhile, it suffices to mention that preparations for a transition to a post-UNITAF operation proceeded in spite of the inability of the UN and the US government to resolve their conceptual and practical differences on this important subject. Similar disagreements over whether the UNITAF operation should cover the whole of Somalia, and whether the mission should last longer than Washington's original plans, were not resolved until the transition to the second phase of UNOSOM in the spring of 1993.

PHASE III: THE SECOND UNITED NATIONS OPERATION IN SOMALIA (UNOSOM II)

At the insistence of the United States, the UN Secretariat reluctantly began planning for a transition from UNITAF to a second United Nations military operation in Somalia in late January 1993. At that time, the general perception was that the non-blue-helmeted forces had brought some order to Mogadishu and surrounding areas, thus paving the way for a more effective distribution of relief aid to the local population. In the words of the UNITAF command, 'all areas are stable or relatively stable.'[76] The reality, however, was that the security situation in Mogadishu and much of Somalia remained quite dicey. According to the Secretary-General:

> Whilst the general security situation has improved considerably, the security threat to the personnel of the United Nations, UNITAF and non-governmental organizations (NGOs) is still high in some areas of the city of Mogadishu and other places, including Bardera, Bale Doble [*sic*] and Baidoa. Inter-clan fighting still tends to break out from time to time, along with sniper attacks.[77]

> [In short], the unique features of the situation [in Somalia] continue to prevail. There is still no effective functioning Government in the country. There is still no organized civilian police force. There is still no disciplined national armed force... [T]he atmosphere of lawlessness and tension is far from being eliminated.[78]

Given such an environment, a post-UNITAF operation had to assume the limited security tasks of the multinational force under Operation Restore Hope *in addition* to the responsibilities for rebuilding Somali state and society in accordance with the principles enshrined in Boutros-Ghali's *An Agenda for Peace*.[79] This was precisely what the Secretary-General recommended for UNOSOM II.

UNOSOM II mission mandate

The mandate for UNOSOM II is as extensive as the Secretary-General's analysis of the problem of Somalia. In recommending the mandate for the approval of the Security Council, the Secretary-General explained that:

> The mandate for UNOSOM II... would confer authority for appropriate action, including enforcement action as necessary, to establish *throughout* Somalia a *secure environment for humanitarian assistance*. To that end, UNOSOM II would seek to complete, through *disarmament and reconciliation*, the task begun by UNITAF for the restoration of peace, stability, law and order. The mandate would also empower UNOSOM II to provide assistance to Somali people in rebuilding their shattered economy and social and political life, re-establishing the country's institutional structure, achieving national political reconciliation, recreating a Somali

state based on democratic governance and rehabilitating the country's economy and infrastructure.[80]

This broad mandate required UNOSOM II to undertake the following military tasks:[81]

(a) to monitor existing ceasefire agreement between the warring parties;

(b) to prevent any resumption of violence and, if necessary, to take 'appropriate action against any faction that violates or threatens to violate the cessation of hostility';

(c) to maintain control of the organized factions after their disarmament and encampment in transition sites;

(d) to secure and maintain a register of small arms seized from all unauthorized armed elements in Somalia;

(e) to maintain security at all ports, airports and lines of communication required for the delivery of humanitarian assistance;

(f) to ensure the protection of personnel, installations and equipment belonging to the UN and humanitarian agencies;

(g) to continue with the programme of de-mining in the most affected areas;

(h) to assist the repatriation of refugees and displaced persons.

This mandate was given legal backing by the Security Council with the adoption of Resolution 814 of 26 March 1993. UNOSOM II thus became 'the first operation of its kind to be authorized by the international community' under UN command. It also became an eloquent expression of the determination of the international community 'not to remain a silent spectator to the sufferings of an entire people for no fault of their own'.[82] Put succinctly, UNOSOM II became the first empirical test of Boutros-Ghali's UN-centred theory of international community as entailed in *An Agenda for Peace*. Pursuant to the new mandate, the Secretary-General appointed Admiral Jonathan Howe (Retd) of the United States as his new SRSG in Somalia, and Lt-Gen. Çevik Bir of Turkey as the Force Commander of UNOSOM II.

By April 1993, UNOSOM II had attained a significant military presence following the deployment of about 18,000 multinational forces out of a projected maximum force strength of 28,000 troops (see Table 6.2). With forces contributed by about 33 states, UNOSOM II became the largest multinational force ever assembled under the direct control of the United Nations Secretary-General. This fact,

Table 6.2   The composition of UNOSOM II (at 30 April 1993)

Country	Troops
Australia	67
Bangladesh	940
Botswana	423
Canada	2
Egypt	1,666
India	4,925
Ireland	82
Malaysia	955
Nepal	311
New Zealand	50
Nigeria	702
Pakistan	7,057
Romania	231
Zimbabwe	993
Total	*18,404*

Source: DPI, *United Nations Peacekeeping*, New York: United Nations Department of Public Information, 1994, p. 123.

in addition to the extraordinarily wide mandate entrusted to it, would create enormous problems for the mission, especially in the area of command and control. Soon after it assumed operational command from UNITAF in May 1993, UNOSOM II was embroiled in a series of combat actions with Somali militia due mainly to a combination of political misjudgements and military miscalculations.

Between June and October 1993, UNOSOM II suffered heavy and humiliating casualties on a wide scale, thereby prompting international pressure initially to increase its firepower (see Table 6.3), and later to review its approach towards the Somali crisis. The consequence of such review was the rapid, but largely *de facto* and unilateral downsizing of the mission strength and mandate throughout 1994. The pull-out of many national contingents from the mission, especially those of the Western countries, severely weakened the military and psychological capability of UNOSOM II to accomplish its mission in Somalia. It therefore became only a matter of time before the mission would be formally terminated. On 4 February 1994, the Security Council passed Resolution 897, 'reaffirming the objective that UNOSOM II complete its mission by March 1995.'[83] The UN pull-out from Somalia was begun and completed ahead of schedule.

Table 6.3 The composition of UNOSOM II (at November 1993)

Country	Force nomenclature and task description	Total contribution
Australia	Movement control	48
Bangladesh	Infantry battalion	945
Belgium	Brigade (BDE) HQ infantry battalion	948
Botswana	Infantry company	326
Canada	Staff personnel	4
Egypt	Infantry battalion	1,100
France	BDE HQ, infantry battalion, aviation unit and logistical battalion	1,107
Germany	Logistical units	1,726
Greece	Medical unit	102
India	BDE HQ and 3 infantry battalions	4,937
Ireland	Transport company	79
Italy	BDE HQ, 3 infantry battalions, aviation unit, logistical/engineering unit and one medical unit	2,576
Kuwait	Infantry company	156
Malaysia	Infantry battalion	871
Morocco	Infantry battalion and one support unit	1,424
Nepal	Security company	311
New Zealand	Supply unit	43
Nigeria	Recce battalion	614
Norway	Headquarters company	130
Pakistan	BDE HQ, infantry battalions, 4 tank squadron, signal unit and support	5,005
Republic of Korea	Engineer battalion	252
Romania	Field hospital	236
Saudi Arabia	Infantry battalion	757
Sweden	Field hospital	148
Tunisia	Infantry company	142
Turkey	Infantry battalion	320
United Arab Emirates	Infantry battalion	662
United States	Logistical units	3,017*
Zimbabwe	Infantry battalion and signal company	958
Composite	Military police company	100
Composite	Headquarters staff	240
Grand total		*29,284*

*This figure is only for US forces under the United Nations Command. There were also about 17,700 troops (including the Quick Reaction Force) belonging to the United States Joint Task Force in Somalia, but under the sole command of the United States.

By 2 March 1995, all UN personnel had been evacuated from Somalia, albeit without accomplishing their mission of disarming the factions and bringing an end to the conflict. In declaring the UN Somali mission closed, the Secretary-General lamented the failure of the Organization to achieve its objective in Somalia: 'If there is not the political will among the protagonists, we cannot achieve peace.'[84] What, then, can we learn from the failure of the Somali operation?

CONCLUSIONS: LEARNING THE LESSONS OF SOMALIA

By many accounts, the failure of the Somali operation is really about the failure of UNOSOM, as distinguished from UNITAF. UNOSOM II faced two fundamental problems. The first, which is a matter of practical consideration, was the contradiction between the expansion of its tasks and the drastic reduction of its resource pool. The second but more serious difficulty faced by UNOSOM II was conceptual or philosophical. It relates to the idea of 'neutrality' which has been embedded in UN peace operations since 1956. It means that, unlike traditional armies or such state-led coalition forces as UNITAF which are guided by national military doctrines, UN forces face no 'enemies' in the theatre of operation. By their actions, UN forces should endear themselves to opposing combatants – a possibility that is best enhanced by a conscious effort on the part of UN forces to refrain from inflicting collateral damage of any kind. Based on this principle, according to one military scholar, 'the challenge for UNOSOM II [was] to accomplish the expanded mission without becoming embroiled in the factional fighting to the point of backing one faction against the others.'[85] It is this particular limitation on UNOSOM II that would account for many of the problems encountered during the UN phase of enforcement actions in Somalia, especially from June 1993 to the embarrassing termination of the mission in 1995.

Perhaps nowhere did the conceptual and resource limitations of UNOSOM II reveal themselves with more tragic consequences than in the area of disarmament. Originally conceived by the Secretary-General as the pillar of any international intervention in Somalia, the disarmament of warring factions did not interest the Bush Administration and was therefore excluded from UNITAF's mandate. However, it came to occupy a central position in UN peace efforts in Somalia from the spring of 1993. Despite strong concerns within the Force Command that the United Nations lacked the financial wherewithal to embark on voluntary disarmament based on a weapons buy-back scheme, and the military capability to push through a coercive disarmament scheme, UNOSOM II Commander General Çervik Bir authorized various 'disarmament wars' designed to weaken the fighting machine of the warring factions. Indeed, between May and October 1993 the United Nations engaged different Somali militia – especially the strongest among them, General Aideed's forces – in a series of combat actions. Each of these engagements resulted in significant UN casualties and much heavier casualty figures on the Somali side. Each battle steeped the UN higher on the escalatory ladder as Aideed exploited every opportunity to wreak considerable havoc on the morale and capability of UN forces. Surprisingly, rather than de-escalate or, failing that, formally abandon the pretensions of UN neutrality in order to ensure for its forces an uninhibited pursuit of military victory, UNOSOM II continued to play catch-up with General Aideed's self-orchestrated guerrilla warfare. As we now know, the result was catastrophic as the UN fell victim to Aideed's bait by embarking upon an eleventh-hour manhunt which ended tragically in October 1993 when elite US Army Rangers were shot down over the skies of Mogadishu while attempting to apprehend Aideed's principal aides.[86]

The failure of UN peace efforts in Somalia, therefore, demonstrates the fundamental problem posed by the continuing tension between the idealism of Pearsonian peacekeeping in conditions of *inter*-state conflict and the Hobbesian realism of contemporary peace operations in conditions of *intra*-state conflict.[87] The world has changed considerably since 1956 when Lester Pearson developed the idea of United Nations peacekeeping as a method of international conflict resolution. The classic embodiment of Pearsonian peacekeeping, the first United Nations Emergency Force (UNEF I), differs markedly from what the UN has sought to do since it began intervening in civil conflicts, beginning with the Congo crisis of 1960. According to Paul Diehl, Pearson's peacekeepers were 'an interposition force between the protagonists' who were easily distinguishable by geography and a distinct command and control apparatus.[88] Such a force was 'strictly neutral... in action and purpose, in addition to troop composition. The force was not designed to affect military balance in the area or to favor one side or the other in its activities.'[89] Above all, it was deployed *after* the conclusion of a ceasefire agreement by the protagonists. Consequently, the function of the force was limited to supervising or monitoring the implementation of such an agreement.

Clearly, none of these conditions existed in Somalia. There was no authority in Mogadishu with which to negotiate; violence was widespread and uncoordinated. The absence of a clear line of demarcation between protagonists rendered redundant the notion of interposing a neutral force in Somalia. Consequently, once the UN decided to intervene in Somalia mainly out of humanitarian concerns, it did so aware that it would have to create, defend and enforce the peace in ways that would compromise its 'neutrality'. Yet, the UN promoted the facade of neutrality even as it sought to wrest power from Somalia's ruthless warlords. Perhaps the sad history of the Somali intervention would have been different had the United Nations identified the 'bad guys' as the enemies of peace and treated them accordingly. The type of humanitarian emergency that prompted multinational military intervention in Somalia should not be attempted without a prior readiness on the part of the interveners to punish those whose fatalistic arrogance led to the human tragedy in the first place. To pretend that there are no bad guys in such conflicts is to provide a recipe for the kind of disaster that befell the United Nations in Somalia.

In terms of operational considerations, the Somali operation also suggests an urgent need to improve coordination and communication among national contingents. Unless future peacekeeping operations are to be undertaken by one national army or a unit within it (as is inherent in the idea of 'mission subcontracting'), there is need for improved coordination and harmonization between disparate national contingents. In Somalia, for instance, there were 33 national contingents of varying sizes and capability, and differing languages, operational doctrines and *esprit de corps*. The widely publicized dispute between Gen. Bruno Loi, the commander of the Italian contingent to UNOSOM II, and the overall Force Commander demonstrated the weakness of operating multinational peacekeeping operations like some kind of feudal fiefdom.[90] A subset of this requirement is the necessity of maintaining effective coordination among units of a national contingent. In Somalia, the lack of adequate coordination between the commanders of different US units in Somalia was partly responsible for the ill-fated manhunt operation of October 1993. According to one reliable account, the use of Special Operations forces in Somalia under the exclusive command of USCINCENT in mainland United States meant that Maj.-Gen. Montgomery, the commander of US forces in Somalia, could not exercise operational control over their activities in Somalia.[91] Worse still, because Gen. Montgomery was not privy to the combat plans of Special Operations forces, intelligence and operational objectives could not be harmonized, thereby setting the stage for the tragedy that occurred in October 1993.

Obviously, greater force cohesion is required for future operations. This could be achieved through a programme of training for participating contingents before deployment into a theatre of operation. Such training will afford the troops the opportunity to be commonly educated about the culture of the people they hope to save from self-destruction, the mission objective, mandate, rules of engagement, as well as the purpose and types of equipment to be used during the mission. Existing training facilities in many countries, such as Finland, Canada and the United States, could be designated by the UN Department of Peacekeeping Operations as centres for the compulsory training of future peace personnel.

Somalia also teaches us that not every soldier is a peacekeeper. Peacekeeping is fast becoming a cottage industry for many of the world's armies. Many cash-starved regimes have been known to ship off their favoured troops to peacekeeping operations where they would earn hard currency. Yet many other regimes, particularly the authoritarian type, have employed peacekeeping missions as a way of 'exiling' soldiers who are more likely to oppose the status quo in their countries. It is the moral duty of the United Nations to set the highest ethical standards for soldiers selected for peacekeeping duties. Accordingly, there should be no room in the United Nations peace force for hate-mongering soldiers, and there is no reason to request or accept troop contributions from dictatorial regimes. It is sinister to rely on soldiers who engage in human rights abuses in their own country to build a peaceful, law-based society in another.

In conclusion, Somalia teaches us that there is greater need for preventive diplomacy today than ever before. Somalia-type conflicts have preoccupied the United Nations since the Congo crisis. Such conflicts do not just break out. Rather, they are the inexorable consequences of a prolonged pattern of large-scale human rights abuses that usually begin with the dismantling of democratic institutions. Current thinking on how the international community might best respond to this problem remains rudimentary. What is clear, however, is that devising an international mechanism to stop such regimes early on before they consolidate their power base would require greater creativity and foresight than has so far been displayed.

APPENDIX: UN INTERVENTION IN SOMALIA
A CHRONOLOGY OF MAJOR EVENTS, 1991–95

Date	Description of events
27 December 1991	After due consultations with incoming UN Secretary-General, Boutros Boutros-Ghali, outgoing Secretary-General Javier Pérez de Cuéllar formally informs the Security Council of his intention to launch a UN peace process in Somalia.
3 January 1992	The first high-level UN team, led by Under Secretary-General James Jonah, arrives Mogadishu to discuss UN humanitarian and peacebuilding proposals with the leaders of Somalia's principal warring factions.
23 January 1992	UN Security Council adopts the proposal of the Secretary-General in the form of Resolution 733 which imposes a complete embargo on the delivery of weapons and military equipment to Somalia.
12–14 February 1992	General Mohamed Farah Aideed and Ali Mahdi, the leaders of the two principal warring factions in Somalia, meet with officials of the UN, OAU, LAS and OIC at the UN Secretariat in New York to discuss the principles of an immediate ceasefire agreement.
3 March 1992	In Mogadishu, Aideed and Mahdi sign a ceasefire agreement which provides for a UN security presence to ensure the safe delivery of humanitarian supplies to Somalia's famine-stricken population.
24 April 1992	The Security Council adopts Resolution 751 establishing UNOSOM. Subsequently, the Secretary-General unveils a 90-day Plan of Action for Emergency Humanitarian Assistance to Somalia and appoints Mohammed Sahnoun, an Algerian diplomat, as his Special Representative in Somalia.
27 July 1992	The Security Council adopts Resolution 767, requesting the Secretary-General to 'make full use of all available means and arrangements' to facilitate UN humanitarian efforts in Somalia. A few days later, the Secretary-General authorizes airlift relief operations to Somalia. This is followed immediately by the deployment of an advance party of 50 *unarmed* UN observers in Mogadishu.

Date	Description of events
28 August 1992	Security Council adopts Resolution 775 which authorizes the enlargement of UNOSOM by 3,800 troops to stem the deteriorating security situation in Somalia. Surprised by the move, Aideed reacts angrily to the news of UN troop reinforcement and so does Sahnoun who threatens to resign as the SRSG.
October 1992	Under pressure from his bosses in New York, Sahnoun resigns as the SRSG and is replaced by Ismat Kittani, an Iraqi diplomat, amid rising violence against UN personnel in Mogadishu and elsewhere in Somalia.
25 November 1992	Amid increasing media reports of the Somali famine and UN bungling of token relief efforts, Acting US Secretary of State Lawrence Eagleburger visits the UN to communicate to the Secretary-General his government's decision to organize and lead a multinational force to secure Somalia for effective delivery of humanitarian aid.
3 December 1992	Acting under Chapter VII of the UN Charter, the Security Council adopts Resolution 794, authorizing the US-led coalition to use force to secure a conducive environment for the distribution of humanitarian aid in Somalia.
9 December 1992	The first elements of US Marines that form the bulk of the 37,000-strong Unified Task Force (UNITAF) secure a beachhead in Mogadishu at the start of a complex military/humanitarian mission code-named 'Operation Restore Hope'.
4–15 January 1993	UN Secretary-General convenes another session of Somali peace talks in Addis Ababa. Attended by 15 Somali political groups, representatives of the Countries of the Horn and the Secretaries-General of OAU, LAS and OIC, the Addis Ababa conference produces an agreement on the general disarmament of the warring factions.
27 February 1993	In accordance with its timetable, the US withdraws part of its forces in Somalia and promises to follow through with its original plans to pull out the bulk of its forces by May.
3 March 1993	The Secretary-General reports to the Security Council the success of the UNITAF mission and proposes the transition from non-blue-helmets to blue-helmets under UNOSOM II. He proposes the expansion of

Date	Description of events
	the mandate of UNOSOM II to cover the whole territory of Somalia in the following areas: (a) ceasefire monitoring; (b) preventing any resumption of conflict; (c) maintaining control of weapons brought to it in accordance with agreements reached on disarmament; (d) seizing the small arms of all unauthorized militia in Somalia; (e) securing or maintaining security at all sea and airports as well as other lines of communication for the delivery of humanitarian assistance; (f) protecting UN and NGO personnel and installations; (g) clearing of mines; (h) assisting in the repatriation of refugees.
8 March 1993	Violent inter-clan conflict erupts in Kismayu, killing more than two dozen Somali civilians and wounding several more, including humanitarian aid workers.
9 March 1993	Rtd Admiral Jonathan Howe assumes responsibility of UN operation in Somalia as the new SRSG. His task is to oversee the transition of operations from UNITAF to UNOSOM II. The Secretary-General also appoints Lt-Gen. Çevik Bir of Turkey as Force Commander of UNOSOM II.
17 March 1993	Following strong accusations by Aideed of UN complicity in the capture of Kismayu by anti-Aideed forces led by Gen. Hersi 'Morgan', the UN suspends national reconciliation talks which had begun in Addis on 15 March.
26 March 1993	Security Council adopts Resolution 814, approving the Secretary-General's proposal for the transition from UNITAF to UNOSOM II with an enlarged mandate.
4 May 1993	The US formally hands over command of the multilateral enforcement action to UNOSOM II. It leaves behind, however, a sizeable number of its troops and equipment in Somalia and offshore to assist UN operations if and when needed.
5 June 1993	24 Pakistani troops on a scheduled disarmament verification mission are killed in an ambush. Aideed's faction is implicated in the incident in which 40 other Pakistanis were wounded, 5 taken hostage, 35 Somalis killed and 130 wounded. This marks the return of wide-scale violence against foreign presence in Somalia. It also becomes a turning-point for the entire UN operation.

Date	Description of events
6 June 1993	Security Council reacts to the ambush of Pakistani troops with Resolution 837, which condemns the 'treacherous act' and demands 'firm and prompt action' against 'the perpetrators of this crime'. This sets the stage for the progressive escalation of violence in the months that follow.
12 June 1993	In response to the killing of the Pakistani soldiers, UNOSOM II begins a series of punitive actions against Aideed's forces and installations. US Cobra helicopter gunships are called in to participate in a series of bombing raids against known and suspected positions and installations of Aideed's forces, including Radio Mogadishu.
17 June 1993	SRSG Admiral Jonathan Howe orders the arrest of General Aideed for his involvement in the death of Pakistani peacekeepers. Thereafter extreme violence erupts as Aideed militia successfully seek every opportunity to frustrate UNOSOM II and inflict heavy casualties on UN peacekeepers.
24 June 1993	Frustrated by the inability of his forces to apprehend Aideed, SRSG Admiral Howe commits a cultural blunder by announcing a US $25,000 reward for information leading to the capture of General Aideed. Meanwhile, US helicopters engage in low-level flights searching for Aideed and also distributing offensive leaflets announcing a ransom for Aideed's capture. All these lead to the further degeneration of the security environment in Somalia to an all-time low.
24 August 1993	The US dispatches 400 of its elite Army Rangers to Mogadishu to facilitate the manhunt for General Aideed. This action not only increases the US profile in the exercise but adds urgency to the task of capturing General Aideed – a task to which Force Command devotes much of its military and political capital.
5–30 September 1993	UN and Somali militia engage each other in a series of high-profile gun battles resulting in more casualties suffered by Nigerian, Pakistani, Italian, American and Malaysian contingents, among others, including Somali civilians.
3 October 1993	Somali militia shoot down two US helicopters carrying elite US Army Rangers on a mission to capture an unspecified number of top aides to

Date	Description of events
	General Aideed. Five of the Rangers are killed instantly while 18 others die in an ensuing battle with Somali militiamen. When the battle is over, 75 US soldiers have been wounded, and Michael Durant, the pilot of one of the downed helicopters, and Shakanli of the Nigerian contingent are taken prisoner by Aideed's militia which suffers much heavier casualties.
4 October 1993	In a move that would have further escalated the tension in Somalia, the US government responds to the high-profile downing of its helicopters by ordering the immediate deployment of additional reinforcements of 5,300 US troops and equipment, including advanced AC-130 'Spectre' helicopter gunships to Somalia. Soon after, Washington reverses its policy and begins a downward review of its objectives and commitment in Somalia – a process which will result in unilateral termination of its involvement and a recourse to diplomatic solution to the conflict.
10 October 1993	President Clinton announces the appointment of Robert Oakley as his special envoy to Somalia. Oakley's mandate is to secure the release of Durant, and initiate a diplomatic process for the resolution of the Somali conflict. Four days after Oakley's arrival in Mogadishu, and following extensive discussions with local leaders, Aideed's militia releases Durant and Shankali. Aideed will later be flown by US pilots to attend a new round of peace meetings in Ethiopia.
29 October 1993	Security Council adopts Resolution 878, extending the UNOSOM II mandate to November to allow for more time for the preparation of an 'in-depth' review of the Somali operation.
16 November 1993	Security Council adopts Resolution 885, authorizing the establishment of a Commission of Inquiry to investigate armed attacks against UNOSOM II personnel, and the suspension of arrest actions against General Aideed. Accordingly, the Secretary-General inaugurates the Commission which comprises Hon. Matthew S. Ngulube, the Chief Justice of Zambia, as Chairman; Rtd General Emmanuel Erskine of Ghana, member; General Gustav Hagglund of Finland, member; and Winston Tubman of the UN Legal Office as Secretary. Two days later, on 18 November, the Council adopts Resolution 886, extending the mandate of UNOSOM II by six months.

Date	Description of events
4 February 1994	Security Council adopts Resolution 897, extending the life of UNOSOM II to March 1995 but with a significantly downsized mandate and military strength. The new mandate limits UNOSOM II to 'traditional' peacekeeping: assisting Somali parties in implementing cooperative disarmament and in reaching a political settlement; protecting major air and seaports and essential infrastructure; providing humanitarian relief; assisting in re-establishing a Somali civil police force and judicial system; helping in the repatriation and resettlement of refugees and displaced persons, etc.
March 1994	The United States completes the withdrawal of its troops from Somalia, marking the beginning of the end of the entire UN operation in Somalia. Soon afterwards, a number of Western states, including Italy, Germany, Turkey and Norway, also pull out their forces from Somalia. This leaves UNOSOM II psychologically and materially weak even for the execution of its drastically reduced mandate.
2 March 1995	With logistics support provided by the United States military, the UN completes the pull-out of its military and civilian personnel from Somalia, three weeks ahead of schedule. This event marks the formal termination of UNOSOM II operation. Speaking two weeks earlier in New York about the pull-out operation, Mr Kofi Annan, Under Secretary-General for Peacekeeping Operations, said the decision was 'deliberate and painful'. The world community, he said, can only 'facilitate, encourage and assist, not impose or coerce peace'. In his reflection on the UN pull-out from Somalia, the Secretary-General, speaking in Vienna, says he believed that the hopes for a new international order that blossomed at the end of the Cold War had evaporated. He adds that he foresees the need to 'contract out' more operations to regional organizations or multinational forces led by major powers with special interests in disputes.

NOTES

1. Andrew S. Natsios, 'Food through force: humanitarian intervention and U.S. policy', *The Washington Quarterly*, Vol. 17, No. 1, 1993, p. 136 (emphasis added).
2. For a discussion of 'First' and 'Second Images' of the international system, see the original formulation by Kenneth N. Waltz, *Man, the State and War: A Theoretical Analysis*, New York: Columbia University Press, 1959. For further discussions, cf. Michael Doyle, 'Kant, liberal legacies and foreign affairs, Part I', *Philosophy and Public Affairs*, Vol. 12, No. 3, 1983, pp. 205–35; 'Liberalism and world politics', *American Political Science Review*, Vol. 80, No. 4, 1986, pp. 1151–69; E. Weede, 'Democracy and war involvement', *Journal of Conflict Resolution*, Vol. 28, No. 4, 1984, 649–64; Francis Fukuyama, *Democratization and International Security*, London: International Institute for Strategic Studies, Adelphi Papers No. 266, 1991/92; Robert Lathum, 'Democracy and war-making: locating the international liberal context', *Millennium: Journal of International Studies*, Vol. 22, No. 2, 1993, pp. 139–64; Z. Maoz and N. Abdolali, 'Regime type and international conflict, 1816–1976', *Journal of Conflict Resolution*, Vol. 33, No. 1, 1989, pp. 3–35; and Jack S. Levy, 'The causes of war: a review of theories and evidence', in Philip Tetlock et al. (eds) *Behavior, Society and Nuclear War*, Vol. 1, New York: Oxford University Press, 1988, pp. 209–333.
3. Jeffrey Clark, 'Débâcle in Somalia: failure of the collective response', in Lori Fisler Damrosch (ed.), *Enforcing Restraint: Collective Intervention in Internal Conflicts*, New York: Council on Foreign Relations, 1993, p. 210.
4. Mohammed M. Sahnoun, 'Prevention in conflict resolution: the case of Somalia', *Irish Studies in International Affairs*, Vol. 5, 1994, pp. 8–9.
5. Ibid., p. 7 (emphasis added).
6. Report of the Secretary-General on the Situation in Somalia, Document S/23829/Add. 1, New York: United Nations, 21 April 1992.
7. Sahnoun, op. cit., p. 9.
8. UN Security Council Resolution No. 751, Document S/RES/751, New York: United Nations, 24 April 1992, para. 3.
9. Sahnoun, op.cit., p. 9.
10. Ibid. (emphasis added).
11. Ibid.
12. Letter from the Secretary-General to the President of the Security Council, Document S/24859, New York, 24 November 1992, p. 3 (emphasis added).
13. See Ioan Lewis (1993), 'Misunderstanding the Somali Crisis', *Anthropology Today* 9, August, p. 2; and Robert Patman (1995), 'The UN Operation in Somalia', in R. Thakur and C. Thayer, eds, *UN Peacekeeping in the 1990s*. Boulder, Colo.: Westview Press, p. 100.
14. Ibid., p. 10.
15. Robert Patman, 'The UN operation in Somalia', in Ramesh Thakur and Carlyle Thayer (eds), *UN Peacekeeping in the 1990s*, Boulder, Colo.: Westview Press, 1995, p. 100.

16. Ibid.
17. For details, see the Report of the Secretary-General on the Situation in Somalia, Document S/24343, New York: United Nations, 22 July 1992, esp. pp. 3–4.
18. Sahnoun, op. cit., p. 11. See also the Report of the Secretary-General, Document S/24343, op. cit., p. 3.
19. Ibid.
20. Sahnoun pointed to several incidents of UN chartered flights with 'mysterious cargo' which undermined the impartiality of the organization and his subsequent pleas for a thorough investigation of these incidents which went unheeded by New York. In his own words: 'What is incredible is that although the UN name and reputation were at stake, no serious investigation was undertaken and no legal action for redress was pursued.' See ibid., p. 11.
21. The United States Institute of Peace, *Restoring Hope: The Real Lessons of Somalia for the Future of Intervention*, Washington, DC: USIP Special Report, 1995, p. 7. For a detailed account, see Mohammed Sahnoun, *Somalia: The Missed Opportunities*, Washington, DC: USIP Press, 1994.
22. Sahnoun, 'Prevention in conflict resolution', op. cit., p. 13.
23. Ibid., p. 11 (emphasis added).
24. Patman, op. cit., pp. 100–1 (emphasis added).
25. Ibid., p. 102 (emphasis added).
26. DPI, *The United Nations and the Situation in Somalia*, 1994, p. 3. See also the Report of the Secretary-General, Document S/24343, New York, 22 July 1992 United Nations.
27. Ibid., p. 11, para. 56 (emphasis added).
28. Ibid., pp. 11–12, para. 57.
29. Ibid., p. 12, para. 59 (emphasis in the original).
30. Report of the Secretary-General on the Situation in Somalia, Document S/24480, New York: United Nations, 24 August 1992, p. 5, para. 22.
31. DPI, op. cit., p. 4.
32. United Nations Security Council Resolution 775, Document S/RES/775, New York: United Nations, 28 August 1992, para. 3.
33. For detailed analysis of the deployment of these troops, see Samuel Makinda, *Seeking Peace in Somalia*, Boulder, Colo.: Lynne Rienner, 1993.
34. See Sahnoun, 'Prevention in conflict resolution', op. cit., p. 12.
35. Patman, op. cit., p. 101.
36. Letter from the Secretary-General to the President of the Security Council, Document S/24859, New York: United Nations, 24 November 1992, p. 1.
37. On this, Robert Patman, citing a senior UN official, writes that upon arrival in Mogadishu, Kittani, Sahnoun's successor, 'soon reached the conclusion that Aideed would never agree to a substantial UN peacekeeping presence' (op. cit., p. 102). The deterioration of the security situation afterwards would therefore support the general assessment that Sahnoun's consultative or consensual bottom-up approach to the

conflict had endeared him to the locals, including the warlords, and that this had contributed to the lack of major war between the warring factions and UN forces as had occurred after his departure. For further details, see Clark, op. cit., pp. 224–5; Makinda, op. cit.; Patman, op. cit., p. 102.

38. Letter from the Secretary-General to the President of the Security Council, Document S/24859, New York: United Nations, 24 November 1992, p. 4.

39. Natsios, op. cit., p. 135.

40. Ibid., p. 144, fn. 11. Present at this meeting were President Bush (presiding); General Colin L. Powell, Chairman Joint Chiefs of Staff; General Brent Scowcroft, National Security Adviser; Dick Cheney, Secretary of Defense; and Lawrence Eagleburger, Acting Secretary of State.

41. Ibid., p. 135 (emphasis added).

42. Initial orders to prepare for possible deployment in Somalia were sent by the Joint Chiefs of Staff to 1 MEF on 20 November 1992. That gave Lt-Gen. Robert Johnston, Commander of 1 MEF, 19 days to plan to for the deployment of his forces by 9 December. For details, see F.M. Lorenz, 'Law and anarchy in Somalia', *Parameters: US Army War College Quarterly*, Vol. 23, No. 4, Winter 1995, pp. 27–41.

43. DPI, op. cit., p. 6 (emphasis added).

44. Letter from the Secretary-General addressed to the President of the Security Council, Document S/24868, New York: United Nations, 29 November 1992, p. 1.

45. Ibid., p. 2.

46. Ibid.

47. Cf. Marrack Goulding, 'The evolution of United Nations peacekeeping', *International Affairs*, Vol 69, No. 3, 1993, pp. 451–64; Brian Urquhart, 'Beyond the "Sheriff's Posse"', *Survival*, Vol. 32, No. 3, 1990, pp. 196–205; John Mackinlay, 'Powerful peace-keepers', *Survival*, Vol. 32, No. 3, 1990, pp. 241–50; Thomas G. Weiss, 'New Challenges for UN military operations: implementing *An Agenda for Peace*', *The Washington Quarterly*, Vol. 16, No. 1, 1993, pp. 51–66.

48. Letter from the Secretary-General, Document S/24868, op. cit., p. 2.

49. For detail, see especially Thomas G. Weiss and Jarat Chopra, 'Sovereignty is no longer sacrosanct: codifying humanitarian intervention', *Ethics and International Affairs*, Vol. 6, 1992, pp. 95–117; David J. Scheffer, 'Toward a modern doctrine of humanitarian intervention', *University of Toledo Law Review*, Vol. 23, Winter 1992, pp. 253–93; and Gunter Lewy, 'The case for humanitarian intervention', *Orbis*, Vol. 37, No. 4, 1993, pp. 621–32.

50. Letter from the Secretary-General, Document S/24868, op. cit. p. 2.

51. Ibid., p. 3 (emphasis added).

52. Ibid. (emphasis added).

53. Ibid., p. 4.

54. Report of the Military Adviser to the Secretary-General, quoted in Letter from the Secretary-General, Document S/24868, op. cit., p. 4.

55. Ibid.
56. Ibid., p. 5 (emphasis added).
57. Ibid. (emphasis added).
58. Ibid.
59. Ibid., p. 6 (emphasis added).
60. United Nations Security Council Resolution 794, Document S/RES/794, New York: United Nations, 3 December 1992, Preamble.
61. Ibid., para. 10 (emphasis added).
62. Ibid. Cf. paras 8, 12 and 18.
63. Madeleine K. Albright, US Ambassador to the United Nations, Speech to the US Congress, USIA Wireless Service, 9 March 1995.
64. Ibid.
65. See contributions on the subject by US officers in Dennis J. Quinn (ed.), *Peace Support Operations and the US Military*, Washington, DC: National Defense University Press, 1994; and Dick Cheney and Colin Powell, 'US mission to Somalia is necessary and clear', *USIA East Asia/Pacific Wireless File*, 4 December 1992, p. 12; Natsios, op. cit., pp. 139–40. The Powell Doctrine forms the centrepiece of Presidential Decision Directive 25 (PDD 25) – the official policy of the United States government in matters relating to US involvement in UN peace-keeping operations. For details see the US State Department, *The Clinton Administration's Policy on Reforming Multilateral Peace Operations*, Washington, DC: Department of State, Bureau of International Organization Affairs, Publication 10161, May 1994; and Donald C.F. Daniel, *U.S. Perspectives on Peacekeeping: Putting PDD 25 in Context*, Newport, RI: US Naval War College, Strategic Research Department Research Memorandum 3–94, 1994.
66. Barry R. McCaffrey, 'US military support for peacekeeping operations', in Dennis J. Quinn op. cit., p. 5.
67. Natsios, op. cit., pp. 132.
68. McCaffrey, op. cit., p. 6.
69. Details of the activities of the civilian component of 'Operation Restore Hope' are the subject of a volume by Robert Oakley and John Hirsch, *Somalia and Operation Restore Hope: Reflections on Peacemaking and Peacekeeping*, Washington, DC: USIP Press, 1995.
70. Letter from the Permanent Representative of the United States of America to the United Nations addressed to the President of the Security Council, Document S/24976, 17 December 1992, Annex, p. 2.
71. Ibid.
72. Ibid. (emphasis added).
73. See especially Oakley and Hirsch, op. cit.
74. Author's interviews with military personnel who served in Somalia, Geneva, February–May 1995.
75. Quoted in the Report of the Secretary-General to the Security Council, Document S/24992, New York, 19 December 1992, p. 8 (emphasis added).
76. Quoted in the Report of the Secretary-General to the Security Council, Document S/25354, New York: United Nations, 3 March 1993, p. 2, para. 6. UNITAF activities were limited to the southern and central

parts of Somalia, which collectively amount to 40 per cent of the country's territory.

77. Report of the Secretary-General to the Security Council, Document S/25168, New York: United Nations, 26 January 1993, p. 4, para. 21.
78. Report of the Secretary-General, Document S/25354, op. cit., p. 21, para. 100.
79. For a wider perspective on the extended mandate of UNOSOM II, cf. Boutros Boutros-Ghali, *An Agenda for Peace: Preventive Diplomacy, Peacemaking and Peacekeeping*, New York: United Nations Press, 1992.
80. Report of the Secretary-General, Document S/25354, op. cit., p. 19, para. 91 (emphasis added).
81. Ibid., p. 13, para. 57.
82. Ibid., p. 22, para. 101.
83. Security Council Resolution 897, Document S/RES/897, New York, United Nations, 4 February 1994, p. 2.
84. Boutros Boutros-Ghali, quoted in *The New York Times International*, 5 March 1995.
85. Lorenz, op. cit., p. 40.
86. UN Security Council Document S/26738, New York: United Nations, 12 November 1993.
87. Cf. Paul F. Diehl, *International Peacekeeping*, Baltimore, Md.: Johns Hopkins University Press, 1993, Chapter 1; Goulding op. cit.; and John Mackinlay and Jarat Chopra, 'Second generation multinational operations', *Washington Quarterly*, Vol. 15, No. 3, 1992, pp. 113–31.
88. Diehl, op. cit., p. 31.
89. Ibid.
90. See *The Guardian* (London), 17 July 1993.
91. F.M. Lorenz, 'Rules of engagement in Somalia: were they effective?', draft manuscript for *Naval Law Review*, May 1995, p. 4.

7 Voices from Warzones: Implications for Training UN Peacekeepers*
A. Betts Fetherston

With so close a relationship between fear and corruption it is little wonder that in any society where fear is rife corruption in all forms becomes deeply entrenched.[1]

INTRODUCTION

As recently as six years ago the UN deployed a largely anonymous force of 10,000 blue helmets. Today peacekeepers in the field number over 60,000. A great deal has been written about these 'peace' armies, where and when they should be deployed, how they should be organized and overseen, what they should and should not be doing, how they should be trained and so on. Even with all of this increased attention, however, little thought has been given to understanding the complexities of the warzone environment (psychological, social, cultural, political) within which peacekeepers work. As a result little is known about the impact peacekeepers have on the people they are sent to 'help'. This is especially apparent when one reviews the content of training programmes which have been set up recently for prospective peacekeepers. On these courses far more time (up to 90–95 per cent) is spent learning how to fill in UN forms, handle four-wheel drive vehicles, recognize mines and deal with all the administrative matters involved in sending troops overseas than on inter-cultural relations, human rights, consequences of violence, issues of power, sensitivity to gender issues or mediation and negotiation skills. Given the long-term abuse of people living in warzones at the hands of military and paramilitary groups it is important to consider carefully the impact of sending yet more military personnel to an already highly militarized environment.

Especially disturbing, in light of the experiences of people in warzones, are reports of a range of abuses by UN peacekeeping personnel.

Issues such as the use of military personnel to act as agents of peace, the ethics of intervention and the appropriateness of the threat or use of force all have important implications for the long-term recovery of war-torn societies. Moreover, the very apparent militarization of peacekeeping over the last several years and propensity of the international community and peacekeepers to fall back on the use of force as a means of settling conflicts needs to be questioned. Left out of the endless analyses on peacekeeping and enforcement are issues of transformation, which go far beyond short-sighted and short-term arrangements for re-establishing political authority and look to base activity in warzones over the long term on the needs of the people who live there.

In this chapter I want to make three basic points. The first is that conflict management as it is currently practised is not an effective means of reducing the prevalence of violent conflict or going further and building long-term stable peace. The second point is that part of the reason conflict management is ineffective is that it is based on assumptions about protracted violent conflict which do not reflect the everyday experiences of people living in warzones. This is most obvious when one looks at the lives of people living in warzones on the one hand, and the activity of peacekeepers (as representative of a broader peace process) in warzones on the other. The third point is that in order to become more effective we need to base the theory and practice of conflict management far more firmly within the context of the complex realities of warzones. The overarching implication of doing this is to call into question conflict management in general – a problem I have taken up elsewhere.[2] In this chapter, I want to focus on how such a re-analysis brings into question the role of peacekeeping and more specifically the training and preparation of peacekeepers.

I will argue that the psycho-social impact of persistent and widespread violence on people living in warzones has far-reaching consequences for both indigenous and outside attempts to facilitate peace. And that peacekeeping does not adequately account for these consequences to the extent that they may be doing more harm than good in the long run. This chapter begins by addressing three interrelated issues: conflict management as understood and practised by the international community, peacekeeping as part of that conflict management system and a critique of this 'traditional' approach using the work of French sociologist, Pierre Bourdieu. I will then turn to a discussion of cultures of violence in warzones and the impact of peacekeeping on this complex environment. The chapter concludes with some discussion of the implications of this analysis for training peacekeepers.

CONFLICT MANAGEMENT: CONCEPTS AND CRITIQUE

Assumptions underlying traditional conflict management

In both the theory and practice of conflict management, the state is assumed to be the primary actor. From this it follows that diplomatic activity (peacemaking) is a *conflict settlement* process, and its focus is on the elite of groups in conflict to the exclusion (whether intentional or not) of other levels of interaction. Assumptions of conflict settlement include: violent conflict is inherent (either biologically or because of resource scarcity); violent conflict takes place on a battlefield between opposing military groups and the costs of war are counted in the numbers of 'battle-related' deaths; since violent conflict is inherent, that is, we cannot get rid of it, our management options are to 'control' or 'moderate' it; violence is a legitimate means of conflict control; outcomes of conflict settlement are a priori limited to win–lose possibilities which most often closely resemble the pre-existing status quo. These assumptions lead to particular practices so that the general characteristics of settlement activities include: elite or 'top'-focused initiatives and top-down directed 'solutions'; short-term involvement generally focused on what can be called the 'containment-to-vote' time period; overall goal of re-establishing a 'recognizable' political authority through democratic elections. As a result of the narrow focus of conflict settlement strategies, even after a 'successful' process (normally culminating in a 'vote'), the potential for the re-emergence of violent conflict continues since in re-establishing a status quo, the problems that caused the conflict initially remain largely in place.

These assumptions and characteristics directly affect peacekeeping in that it is most often in relation to peacemaking efforts (which almost always attempt some kind of conflict settlement) that peacekeeping missions are deployed. As such peacekeeping is seen as an *adjunct* to the peacemaking process rather than as an activity in its own right. For example, peacekeeping can be the direct outcome of a peacemaking process (such as with the operations in Cambodia or Namibia), or it can be an attempt to 'buy time' for diplomacy (as in the case of Cyprus). Alternatively, peacekeeping can be a stopgap measure in the wake of significant humanitarian emergencies either before, during or after attempts at diplomatic solutions (as in the cases of Somalia, Bosnia and Rwanda). In any event, peacekeeping is embedded in the theory and practice of conflict settlement and its activities are, therefore, limited.

Habitus as a basis for criticism

Most state-based conflict management which includes peacekeeping only becomes seriously involved in conflicts once they reached an overtly violent stage, and often only after they have become pro-tracted. Peacekeepers are, therefore, asked to function in highly milit-arized and complex environments. In such contexts recognizing and understanding the social and cultural influences on action – answer-ing the question, 'why do people behave the way they do?' – becomes increasingly salient. The work of French sociologist Pierre Bourdieu provides an analysis of human behaviour from the point of view of an individual's lifeworld. In his work, Bourdieu tries to explain whyparticular social practices become understood as 'normal' or as 'common sense' to the exclusion of other alternatives.

Bourdieu's work is significant here for three reasons. First his ana-lysis helps us better understand warzones and, more specifically, the impact of protracted violence on social practices. Second, his work provides some insights into the impact peacekeepers have on those social practices. Finally, Bourdieu's perspective provides a basis for criticizing our own conflict management efforts by seeing them not as universally applicable and apparent, but as particular, socially embedded and constructed, and, therefore, not necessarily useful practices.

Individuals, according to Bourdieu, are socialized throughout their lives to function within a particular social system with its own cul-ture, history and understanding of the world. This socialization, or inculcation, produces within individuals certain sets of dispositions towards ways of acting or interacting in different types of social situations. Inclinations derived from socialization are often taken for granted as 'natural' or 'normal' and are not the subject of conscious reflection. Further, these inclinations reinforce particular practices which, in turn, reinforce the sets of inclinations. This is an important point because it leads to the argument that in dealing with present situations we are guided by past practices even though in many cases the circumstances which produced the practice no longer exist. If practices 'seem determined by anticipation of their own consequences,' Bourdieu argues, 'the fact is that, always tending to reproduce the objective structures of which they are the product, they are determined by the past conditions which have produced the principle of their production...'[3]

These social practices are not, by virtue of repetition, necessarily constructive or rational. Put another way, the existence of particular social norms does not confer any particular rightness (or effectiveness) on those practices. An especially cruel example of this is female circumcision. Bourdieu contends that *habitus* '... in imposing different definitions of the impossible, the possible, and the probable, cause[s] one group to experience as natural or reasonable practices or aspirations which another group finds unthinkable or scandalous, and vice versa.'[4]

Applying Bourdieu's analysis to the present topic, I argue that many of the ideas that guide our present conflict management efforts are more a product of *habitus* than of rational decision and, moreover, are based on ideas of conflict that are no longer appropriate for present circumstances. Three points from Bourdieu's analysis are especially salient for this discussion. First, individuals function within particular social environments which tend to inculcate certain sets of dispositions or certain ways of understanding and acting within that social space. So, for example, a member of a military organisation has a set of dispositions which increases the tendency that a soldier will act and react to particular situations in particular ways. This is also as much the case for diplomats, conflict researchers or for those living in violent conflict environments. Second, this *habitus* is not often consciously considered, but rather appears as the common sense or natural way of being within the social environment. These modes of behaviour are not necessarily more rational or effective, but are more embedded and, therefore, more acceptable or comfortable to the individual. Third, *habitus* produces and is produced by practices which are relevant to past situations, but which may not be relevant to present ones.

What application does the foregoing analysis have in relation to the practice of peacekeeping and for conflict management more generally? I argue that the implications are fundamental to our understanding of how to cope with the violent and hugely destructive conflicts afflicting various areas of the world. Further, what is most urgently needed beyond present practice is a kind of thinking about conflict management that is directly relevant to the needs of people in warzones and that is capable of moving toward the transformation of highly contested and complex environments rather than content with re-establishing the *habitus* of a particular political status quo.

VOICES FROM WARZONES: ACCOUNTING FOR EVERY-DAY EXPERIENCE

The character and practice of war has changed significantly since the United Nations was founded in 1945 when wars were generally conducted between states. By 1993, 34 major armed conflicts were in progress around the globe and not a single one could be described as a war between two states.[5] In this post-Cold War world, characterized by complex, non-interstate conflicts, fault lines are difficult to establish and many issues beyond relations between political elites are salient. Yet the international community has been unable to move beyond its traditional formula for conflict management developed in a previous era and adapt to the immense challenges posed by this so-called 'new world disorder'. A closer examination of the range and severity of problems facing societies which have experienced protracted violent conflict suggests that this continuing emphasis on 'containment-to-vote' strategies is inadequate.

The proportion of civilian war-related deaths, which had averaged around 50 per cent since the eighteenth century, increased to 73 per cent in the 1970s and was close to 90 per cent in 1990.[6] The devastation in Rwanda will, no doubt, raise the percentage of that depressing statistic. Anthropologist Carolyn Nordstrom argues that the increase in civilian deaths is directly related to 'increasing reliance on dirty war tactics'. She argues that '[d]irty wars seek victory, not through military and battlefield strategies, but through horror. Civilians, rather than soldiers, are the tactical targets, and fear, brutality, and murder are the foundation on which control is constructed.'[7] Human rights abuses worldwide support this argument.[8] Statistics on the widespread use of rape as a tactic of terror and control in war provide further evidence.[9]

Further complicating any third-party intervention at the site of conflict, as Nordstrom's research shows, is that battlefields are set in the centre of civilian society, and combatants and noncombatants are difficult to distinguish.[10] People move in and out of actual battlefields, and as violence generates internally displaced people and refugees that warzone expands.[11] This is not the actual place of bullets and explosions, but is in the instability of people's lives that only begins where the traditional notion of 'battlefield' ends. Describing the consequences of such lived experience from the Guatemalan context, Green suggests how fear becomes part of everyday life and how cultures of violence become part of social practices.

> Fear divides communities through suspicion and apprehension not only of strangers but of each other...Denunciations, gossip, innuendos, and rumors of death lists create a climate of suspicion. No one can be sure who is who. The spectacle of torture and death and of massacres and disappearances in the recent past have become more deeply inscribed in individual bodies and the collective imagination through a constant sense of threat.[12]

The enormity of such social issues is further exemplified by this excerpt taken from a 1992 UNICEF report on the situation in Cambodia.

> Every family has experienced loss of loved ones. The majority of adults have experienced or witnessed torture and have lived with extreme deprivation of food and water. Many adults have witnessed brutal murder, including instances where their own children were the victims and others at the hands of children. The country suffers the loss of the majority of their professional and educated classes who were targeted for elimination...The effects of such tremendous loss and violation on social networks and on human behaviour must be understood and addressed.[13]

Violence, in these situations, becomes part of the 'normal' and the 'sense of reality' becomes guided by a new 'set of limits' of what is socially acceptable behaviour. These 'sets of limits' are a new *habitus* formed within a violent and fearful world and are the basis of the development of cultures of violence. These experiences of violence and the cultures of violence that become embedded in social structures have to become a central part of both the theory and practice of conflict management, not marginal issues.

Limited understandings of both cultures of violence and conflict management can be seen clearly running through the thinking of much of the international community. The focus on confined and delimited battlefields leads to emphasis on ceasefire agreements, peace accords and the reinstitution of *political* stability when the fighting ends. Further, understanding the cost of war goes far beyond counting 'battle-related deaths'. The cost in life expands to include those who disappeared, were murdered or massacred, but beyond that our understanding must also account for the impact of violent conflict on the living, the survivors. The Bosnian, Mozambican and Cambodian women who experienced and witnessed repeated rape, beatings and torture carry the warzone with them beyond the cease-fire, beyond the implementation of peace agreements and beyond the 'vote'. It is to these experiences that I will now turn. Since it is estimated that of the 90 per cent civilian war-related deaths, 70 per cent are women and children, I focus most of my attention on their experiences.

(Re)populating concepts and practices of conflict management

Rape was used systematically in Bosnia as a means of demoralizing government forces, but also as a means of ethnic cleansing through impregnation of mainly Muslim women by Serb men. Melia Kreit-mayer, a Muslim doctor and member of an ethnically mixed medical team that worked with rape survivors in Bosnia, argued that, 'these women were raped not because it was the male instinct. These women were raped because it was the goal of war.'[14] Recent UN findings support Kreitmayer's claim and as a result rape has been classified a war crime.[15] Much of the data that were and are being collected in Bosnia which have added to the pressure to make rape a war crime only came to light because of the strength and determination of women who had suffered through these experiences to try to do something to prevent it happening to others. One 17-year-old Muslim women said, when asked to tell of her experience of being raped repeatedly by Serb soldiers, ' "I wouldn't want anyone else to have the same experience. It is worse than any other punishment in the world".'[16]

The suffering of Cambodia in the 'killing fields' is well known. Under the Khmer Rouge, murder, torture and massacres were part of everyday life. What is less well-known is that rape and sexual violence were 'commonly practiced under the Khmer Rouge'.[17] Attempts to escape did not often improve living conditions and refugee camps themselves became places of abuse presenting, according to one report written by two psychologists for the United Nations Border Relief Operation (UNBRO), 'every kind of human vice that can be imagined.'[18] There was, in many cases, literally no safe place to go. The same report found signs of severe psychological and social dysfunction among refugees living in these camps. One coping mechanism identified by the researchers was a state of psychological withdrawal, which, they noted, had often been mistaken by Western aid providers as 'Khmer "toughness", "stoicism", "callousness", "dishonesty", or "corruptness".[19]

Psycho-social scars last long beyond the physical fact of brutality. This is true not just for each individual but for society when rape, murder and torture have been a part of everyday experience. It is the insecurity and fear generated by such acts that makes dirty war so effective. And, it is this that accounts for cultures of violence which make recovery a long-term and difficult process. Nordstrom recounts one Mozambican woman's response when asked to speak of her experiences of repeated rape and brutality: 'I do not have anything of importance to say, you do not want to hear my words. I have no value, no worth. I am nobody, less than nothing.'[20] Some research indicates that for individuals who have experienced violence and depravation it can take 15–20 years for problems even to *surface*.[21] Little research is available indicating how long it takes for communities and societies to begin to heal. Further complicating any recovery process is the fact that perpetrators as well as survivors will be expected to coexist in a post-peace agreement society.

It is this part of conflict, more complex than the problems of physical and political reconstruction, that is not accounted for in most understandings of conflict and conflict management. Traditional conflict management with its short-term emphasis on 'containment-to-vote' does not begin to cope with the range of complex issues generated from analyses of cultures of violence. More specifically, the significance of the existence of cultures of violence for peacekeepers, who often carry weapons and wear uniforms into these conflict areas, needs to be carefully considered.

Peacekeeping in warzones

The practice of peacekeeping is something of a paradox. On the one hand, there are numerous examples of its lack of effectiveness and of practices guided by *habitus*. On the other hand, the practice of peacekeeping also provides glimmers of hope, where individuals (and in a few cases whole missions) have found innovative and facilitative ways to further transformative processes. On the whole, however, peacekeeping is still embedded in its traditional conflict management roots with, in all too many cases, negative consequences.

In keeping with a conflict settlement approach, few, if any, commentators suggest that peacekeeping itself could not only have an important and positive impact on the conflict, but also on the peacemaking process. This is directly related to the conceptual understanding of the practice of peacekeeping within a conflict settlement regime. At a more specific level, peacekeeping, it is argued, functions with consent, impartiality and the non-use of force except in self-defence. And although such ideas are hardly congruent with the normal functions of military organizations, peacekeeping is seen mainly as a military activity, understood and implemented using military personnel. There is an obvious contradiction here, but it goes unexamined to the extent that basic military training is still widely considered the best means of producing effective peacekeepers.

What impact does the influx of UN military personnel have on local populations who have experienced years of violence and terror most often at the hands of uniformed military or paramilitary groups? Six out of every seven peacekeepers are soldiers and peacekeeping missions are made up overwhelmingly of military personnel. Over 70 countries have contributed troops to UN peacekeeping operations. Some of those troops have been trained specifically in counter-insurgency tactics. An elite Indonesian battalion, for example, who had been involved in the suppression of East Timor was sent to Cambodia as UN peacekeepers. There is no switch inside a blue helmet that automatically turns a soldier trained for war-fighting into an individual prepared to work non-violently and with cultural sensitivity in a highly militarized environment. Peacekeepers enter the complex and already militarized conflict environment with their own *habitus* or sets of dispositions learned from within a military milieu for handling conflict. Moreover, they come physically equipped with uniforms and, usually, guns. From a military perspective solving problems comes down to greater (or perhaps better strategically applied) force. The message that force is effective in achieving ends is reinforced in a context where peacekeepers, paradoxically, are supposed to represent 'peaceful means'.[22]

One direct outcome of the influx of military personnel under the UN flag in Cambodia was a rapid increase in prostitution and an alarming growth in the sex industry. One estimate suggests that in Phnom Penh alone the number of prostitutes increased from 6,000 in 1991 to 20,000 by 1992 with similar increases observed in provincial towns.[23] Child prostitution was particularly popular because of the better chance that younger prostitutes would not yet have contracted the HIV virus. Child 'virgins' were sold to UN peacekeepers for as much as £500 after which these children were 'worth' considerably less, getting paid on average £10 per soldier.

According to a recent article in *Ms* magazine, Yasushi Akashi, head of the UN mission in Cambodia, when confronted with questions about this problem, responded by saying 'he was not a "puritan", [and] that "18-year-old, hot-blooded soldiers" had a right to drink a few beers and chase after "young beautiful beings of the opposite sex".'[24] In response to Akashi's comments, an open letter of protest accusing UN personnel of intimidation and sexual harassment was sent to Akashi and UN Secretary-General Boutros Boutros-Ghali. The letter was signed by 170 individuals including Cambodians, NGO and UN staff. Among other things, the strongly worded letter maintained that 'sexual harassment occur[ed] regularly in public restaurants, hotels and bars, banks, markets and shops to the point where many women [felt] highly intimidated.' The letter went on to point out that, 'inappropriate behavior by male UNTAC personnel often leaves women with a feeling of powerlessness. These men hold positions of authority on behalf of the international community and should be setting an example for others.' The letter also noted the there were 'very few women represented in high level positions in UNTAC' and few included overall in the mission. This was in contrast to the fact that women make up 60–65 per cent of the Cambodian population. What kind of example, the letter asked, does this set for a future Cambodia? In response to this letter a liaison officer was appointed to a deal with complaints, but this was a full year after UNTAC had been in Cambodia. Such issues led one NGO observer in Cambodia during the UNTAC operation to ask: 'Is it possible to use the institutions that have coordinated our wars to build a world that has less violence? In particular, are personnel of those institutions, trained in the systematic use of violence, the most appropriate agents of peace?'[25]

Akashi now heads the peacekeeping mission in former Yugoslavia where there have been a range of similar problems. Reports detailing black marketeering, gun-running, drug-dealing, theft and prostitution by UN troops surfaced in mid-1993 and centred around abuses by Kenyan, Ukrainian and French troops and have since been levelled at Russian troops, leading to the recent removal of a Russian contingent commander. The 1993 allegations forced the UN to investigate, yet instead of opting for an independent, unbiased assessment they sent an Austrian major-general and former UN peacekeeper to head the inquiry. One of the most serious allegations made contended that UN troops regularly visited a Serb-run brothel which forced captive Croatian and Muslim women into prostitution. The full UN report on these allegations was never made public, although three months following its completion, the UN appointed another ex-UN peacekeeper as its first force inspector in former Yugoslavia.

In Mozambique UN troops have been accused of involvement in child prostitution and their presence led to an overall increase in prostitution in the country. Residents of Nampula, Mozambique, sent a letter of protest to newspapers and the UN head of mission, Aldo Ajello, accusing Portuguese UN soldiers stationed in their town of racism, violence and sexual abuse. Residents who signed the letter said that while 'they did not want to go as far as Somalis have gone against UN forces,' they added that, ' "we will not allow Portuguese blue helmets to beat us up and humiliate our girlfriends as if they were tramps. If they continue, we will take action ourselves at our own risk".'[26] While an investigation of these allegations led to the expulsion of some UN troops from Mozambique, the soldiers sent home were not prosecuted.

In Somalia a UN Canadian battalion was sent home after a series of incidents. One company, in particular, had been involved in the torture and murder of a 16-year-old Somali, Shidane Arone. A Canadian tribunal handling the inquiry was told that Arone was beaten with a wooden baton, a metal pipe, fists and boots and the soles of his feet were burned with cigarettes. One of the soldiers involved was court martialled and sentenced to a five-year gaol term for his part in the torture and death of Arone. A second Canadian soldier was sentenced to 90 days in a military gaol and demoted to corporal for his part in the fatal beating. This public disciplinary action (lenient given the seriousness of the offence) is rare among troop-contributing countries.

To the author's knowledge no UN soldier has yet to be prosecuted or sentenced to a gaol term for child prostitution or rape. Neither the UN nor the country within which the peacekeeping operation takes place have jurisdiction over UN peacekeeping personnel. This power remains solely in the hands of the national governments of troop-contributing countries. They have distinguished themselves by their unwillingness to punish those responsible or to take steps to ensure such behaviour is not repeated. The lack of action suggests collective head-nodding of the upper echelons of diplomatic and military corps when statements like Akashi's are reported. An attitude seems to prevail that peacekeeping operations, like war, involve a unique set of circumstances that excuse a certain amount of 'wild' behaviour.

Beyond the physical fact of uniforms and guns, soldiers bring with them particular ways of interacting in the social world. Military organizations inculcate ways of behaving that may be appropriate for situations of war (this too could be questioned) but which are inappropriate for situations undergoing the delicate and complex process of transformation from violence to peace. Learning how to fight, kill and win establishes particular ways of seeing the world in terms of us/them, friend/enemy, human/non-human. Underlying all military training is the connection between the use of force and gaining power and control over the 'enemy', i.e. winning. This is illustrated most clearly in the 'anything goes' frontier behaviour of some soldiers who act like the conquering armies their training has taught them to be.

That soldiers behave in accordance with their training should come as no surprise. What is surprising is how little importance is attributed to re-training soldiers from war-fighting to peacekeeping. This is obvious when one considers that the basic principles of peacekeeping – consent, impartiality and the non-use of force – are inimical to the assumptions which underlie military activity. It is not that military personnel are incapable of behaving appropriately within a peacekeeping milieu – in fact, many behave admirably in often extremely testing circumstances. But socialization does tend to limit the range of alternative actions in and reactions to circumstances and the number of abuses by peacekeepers clearly demonstrate that many soldiers are not able to adjust. If, however, soldiers have been created through rigorous training and adherence to particular assumptions and codes, so too can peacekeepers.

TRAINING FOR PEACEKEEPING: OVERCOMING *HABITUS*

It is interesting to consider the emphasis placed on military aspects of peacekeeping (seen, for example, in the language surrounding peacekeeping) and compare that to the range of activities peacekeepers are expected to undertake which are explicitly non-military. It is also important to ask the question, given the multiple and complex realities of warzones, are military peacekeepers the most appropriate personnel for the job?

Ironically, much of the impetus to use military personnel for peacekeeping is the undeniable fact that world military organizations are comparatively very wealthy both in terms of cash and in terms of resources such as person-power and equipment. The likelihood is that if peacekeeping continues at its current level, this fact alone will require the use of military personnel. For the future the international community should begin exploring institutional alternatives to military organizations which do have the resource capacity to take on peacekeeping roles. Given the present situation, though, it is vital that potential negative consequences of using military personnel as peacekeepers are recognized and reduced as far as possible. Training could go a long way towards reducing some problems, but troop-contributing countries (as well as the UN) argue that basic military training is still the most appropriate preparation for peacekeeping. In the contexts just outlined this is not the most appropriate preparation for peacekeeping. Rather than basing training on fighting and winning wars, programmes need to be developed within a broader context of the needs of people in warzones.

Peacekeeping has at least as much potential to harm peace processes as it does to facilitate them. Training offers a means of moving beyond traditional conflict management which sets the work of peacekeepers within a mainly military frame. Training is a means of dissemination and inculcation and, therefore, could be used explicitly as a means of overcoming *habitus* rather than reinforcing it. As a precursor to implementation, training could play a key role in the process of bringing about a conceptual (and then actual) shift away from purely traditional conflict management to a broader understanding of the work of peacekeepers as part of a transformative process. Because peacekeepers are the international community's representatives on the ground, they carry the difficult weight of ensuring that the message of non-violent, consensual conflict management gets across in an often overtly violent situation. In effect, this means leading by example. But if peacekeepers themselves are not only unaware of but not trained in alternative possibilities, then there is little chance of that essential message getting across. Considering this, as well as new and more complex demands, the provision of training for peacekeepers should be a priority.

One particularly interesting training programme recently established, which has been supported by the Austrian government, is a training centre at Stadtschlaining, Austria. Here the main training programme is on peacekeeping and peacebuilding and is for civilians. The programme is particularly important because it clearly establishes the link between peacekeeping and peacebuilding activities and in this sense inculcates a broader understanding of conflict management, and trains its participants in a range of contact skills, including communication and cross-cultural skills. This approach could be very usefully expanded to include military peacekeepers.[27]

In general, important lessons can be learned from several areas of training and research work. One is the training that a number of aid agencies provide their field operatives.[28] Another is the experience and training of community and organizational/industrial mediators and negotiators.[29] The field of cross-cultural relations offers a wide-range of training options and research with great potential applicability.[30] Much of the general knowledge which would provide a sound basis for the development of a comprehensive peacekeeping training package exists. It is the collection and application of this information that is missing. Here again, we come back to the lack of conceptualization of the role of peacekeeping within a wider peace process. Without this basic work in thinking about what peacekeepers (and other interveners) do and why they do it, training will continue to be inconsistent and inappropriate. If we only prepare people for war it is far more likely that is what we will get.

TRANSFORMING CULTURES OF VIOLENCE

Left out of both concepts and practices of conflict management are the voices of people who 'own' the problem. At the very least, the extent of structural violence[31] as well as the track record of peace-making and peacekeeping should provide more than adequate warning about focusing the majority of our attention on settlement agreements between the top echelons of particular parties. Rather, given the true scope of warzones, as argued by Nordstrom, Green and others, much more emphasis would usefully be turned toward transforming structures and processes within local communities, since it is these communities who provide the raw material through which war is supported, upon whom war is inflicted and *by whom long-term transformation will be constructed*. If the implications of such arguments were considered in terms of peacekeeping it could – and should, – fundamentally shift the emphasis of the practice of peace-keeping toward peacebuilding and demilitarization. This will require that we overcome *habitus* in thinking about conflict management in the terms and limits of conflict settlement strategies and military security largely adhered to by the international community.

At a minimum training should ensure that peacekeeping does not add to cultures of violence or undermine existing and emergent indigenous activities towards overcoming cultures of violence and in the best case facilitates their activities. Perhaps, as a recent article in the Canadian-based *Peace Magazine* suggests, in rethinking the role of militaries in peacekeeping missions, we may begin to address issues of violence and militarization in our own societies:

> [t]he appropriateness of military action as a contribution to peace and security should be judged in terms of its relation to conversion. Does the contemplated action contribute to redefining the role of the armed forces, that is, to the awareness of war as a moribund institution like chattel slavery, duelling, blood vengeance, or human sacrifice? Or does the contemplated action add to the prestige of the armed forces in their traditional role by adding 'peace-making' to 'war-making' or even by blurring the distinction between the two?[32]

NOTES

1. Aung San Suu Kyi, *Freedom From Fear and Other Writings*, London: Penguin, 1991, p. 181.
2. See A.B. Fetherston, *Towards a Theory of United Nations Peacekeeping*, London: Macmillan/St. Martin's Press, 1994.
3. P. Bourdieu, *Outline of a Theory of Practice*, trans. Richard Nice, Cambridge: Cambridge University Press, 1977, p. 72; see also P. Bourdieu, *The Logic of Practice*, trans. Richard Nice, Oxford: Polity Press, 1990; and P. Bourdieu, *Language and Symbolic Power*, ed. J.B. Thompson, trans. G. Raymond and M. Adamson, Cambridge: Polity Press, 1991.
4. Bourdieu (1977), op. cit., p. 78.
5. SIPRI, *SIPRI Yearbook*, Oxford: Oxford University Press, 1994, p. 81.
6. R.L. Sivard, *World Military and Social Expenditures*, Leesburg, Va.: World Priorities, SIPRI annual 1974 onwards.
7. C. Nordstrom, 'The backyard front', in C. Nordstrom and J. Martin (eds), *The Paths to Domination, Resistance, and Terror*, Berkeley, Calif.: University of California Press, 1992, p. 261.
8. Amnesty International, *Amnesty International Report*, London: Amnesty International Publications, 1994.
9. See C. Nordstrom, *Rape: Politics and Theory in War and Peace*, Working Paper No. 146, Canberra, ANU: Peace Research Centre, The Australian National University, 1994; S. Forbes-Martin, *Refugee Women*,

London: Zed Books, 1992; Amnesty International Newsletter, *Women in the Front Line*, March 1991; UN Doc. S/1994/674, 27 May 1994, Report of the UN Commission of Experts (investigating war crimes) for Former Yugoslavia, and UN Doc. S/25704, 3 May 1993, outlines the establishment and jurisdiction of the Commission of Experts.

10. See Nordstrom and Martin, op. cit.; C. Nordstrom, *Warzones: Cultures of Violence, Militarization and Peace*, Working Paper No. 145, Canberra: Peace Research Centre, The Australian National University, 1994.

11. See, for example, M. Eastmond, L. Ralphsson and B. Alinder, *The Psycho-social Impact of Violence and War: Bosnian Refugee Families and Coping Strategies*, paper prepared for the 4th International Research and Advisory Panel Conference, 5–9 January 1994, Oxford, UK; U. Dolgopol, *Women's Voices, Women's Pain*, Working Paper No. 152, Canberra: Peace Research Centre, The Australian National University, 1994; L.R. Maric, *Coping with Threat: Mental Health Status and Psychosocial Symptoms of Crews Involved in Evacuation of Refugees and the Humanitarian Aid Convoy*, paper presented at the 4th International Research and Advisory Panel Conference, 5–9 January 1994, Oxford, UK; UNRISD, *Rebuilding Wartorn societies*, Report of the workshops on the Challenge of Rebuilding Wartorn Societies and the Social Consequences of the Peace Process in Cambodia, 27–30 April 1993, Geneva, Switzerland; UNHCR, *The State of the World's Refugees: The Challenge of Protection*, New York: Penguin, 1993; A.R. Zolberg, A. Suhrke and S. Aguayo, *Escape From Violence: Conflict and the Refugee Crisis in the Developing World*, Oxford: Oxford University Press, 1989.

12. L. Green, 'Fear as a way of life', *Cultural Anthropology*, vol. 9, No. 2, 1994, p. 227. See also R. Ali and L. Lifschultz (eds), *Why Bosnia? Writings on the Balkan War*, Stony Creek, Conn.: Pamphleteer's Press, 1993; E. Burgos-Debray (ed.), *I, Rigoberta Menchu: An Indian Woman in Guatemala*, trans. A. Wright, London: Verso, 1984 (originally published in Spanish, 1983); R. Gutman, *A Witness to Genocide*, Shaftesbury: Element, 1993; J. Harding, *Small Wars, Small Mercies: Journeys in Africa's Disputed Nations*, 2nd edn, London: Penguin, 1994.

13. E. Arnvig, 'Women, children and returnees', in P. Utting (ed.), *Between Hope and Insecurity: The Social Consequences of the Cambodian Peace Process*, Geneva: United Nations Research Institute for Social Development (UNRISD), 1994, p. 153.

14. Gutman, op. cit., p. 69.

15. UN Doc. S/1994/674, 27 May 1994, and UN Doc. S/25704, 3 May 1993.

16. Gutman, op. cit., p. 68.

17. R.F. Mollica and R.R. Jalbert, *Community of Confinement – The Mental Crisis in Site Two: Displaced Persons Camps on the Thai–Kampuchean Border*, Virginia: Committee on Refugees and Migrants and the World Federation for Mental Health, 1989, quoted in Arnvig, op. cit., p. 155.

18. Ibid., p. 153.

19. Ibid., p. 154.
20. Nordstrom, op. cit., p. 11.
21. Arnvig, op. cit., p. 155.
22. This is a serious problem. See, for example, the recently published UK Ministry of Defence document, *Wider Peacekeeping*. London: HMSO 1995. *Wider Peacekeeping* uses the idea of consent as its conceptual base but at the same time argues that in practice the use of force can legitimately be employed to 'maintain' consent (when is consent consent or consent coercion?).
23. Arnvig, op. cit., pp. 166–7.
24. G. Kirsenbaum and M. Gilbert, 'Who's watching the peacekeepers?', *Ms* magazine, Vol. 4, No. 6, May/June 1994, p. 13.
25. Y. Moser, 'United Nations warriors or peace-keepers: examining the logic of combating war with soldiers', *Nonviolence International Papers*, Bangkok: Nonviolence International, 1992, p. 10.
26. Mozambique: Portuguese UN troops accused of misconduct', Reuter News Service, 8 October 1993.
27. International Civilian Peacekeeping and Peacebuilding Training Programme, Austrian Study Centre for Peace and Conflict Resolution (ASPR), Stadtschlaining, Austria; Training Programme for Civilian Peacekeeping and Peacebuilding Activities, ASPR, Stadtschlaining, Austria.
28. For example, Oxfam in the UK are in the process of developing training programme for their field workers which cover conflict management skills.
29. J.W. Burton and F. Dukes, *Conflict: Practices in Management, Settlement and Resolution Vol. 4*, London: Macmillan, 1990.
30. R. Albert, 'Conceptual framework for the development and evaluation of cross-cultural orientation programs', *International Journal of Intercultural Relations*, Vol. 10, No. 2, 1986, pp. 197–214; R. Brislin, 'A culture general assimilator: preparation for various types of sojourns', *International Journal of Intercultural Relations*, Vol. 10, No. 2, 1986, pp. 215–34; C.L. Grove and I. Torbiorn, A new conceptualization of intercultural adjustment and the goals of training, *International Journal of Intercultural Relations*, Vol. 9, 1985, p. 205–33; T.P. Hannigan, 'Traits, attitudes, and skills that are related to intercultural effectiveness and their implications for cross-cultural training: a review of literature', *International Journal of Intercultural Relations*, Vol. 14, 1990, pp. 89–111; D.J. Kealey, *Cross-cultural Effectiveness: A Study of Canadian Technical Advisers Overseas*, Quebec: Canadian International Development Agency (CIDA), 1990.
31. On structural violence see J. Galtung, *Peace – Research, Education, Action: Essays in Peace Research, Vol. 1*, Copenhagen: Christian Ejlers, 1975, esp. pp. 76–134; J. Galtung, 'A structural theory of imperialism', *Journal of Peace Research*, 81–117; W. Eckhardt, 'Civilian deaths in wartime', *Bulletin of Peace Proposals*, Vol. 20, No. 1, 1989, pp. 89–98.
32. A. Rapoport and L. Johnson, 'Peace-keeping as a conversion opportunity', *Peace Magazine*, Vol. 9, September 1993, p. 14.

8 Gender, Race and the Politics of Peacekeeping*
Sandra Whitworth

Peacekeeping has been a central feature of UN activities for over thirty years, and yet one which has been relatively insulated from any form of critical scrutiny. The general disposition toward peacekeeping has been that it is, at a minimum, a benign use of military force. In part, this assumption depends upon the requirement that peacekeeping forces are brought into a situation with the consent of the parties involved and that they will fire only in self-defence. Those criticisms that exist around peacekeeping tend to focus on the question of whether a particular situation is suitable to peacekeeping efforts (i.e. Bosnia-Hercegovina), and potential 'inefficiencies' in particular elements of peacekeeping exercises, but not on the value and dynamic of peacekeeping itself. Moreover, there has been a renewed interest in peacekeeping, not only at the level of international organizations[1] and national governments, but within the popular media and general public as well. Too much of this attention has adopted uncritically and without careful examination the stance that peacekeeping is a viable and welcome alternative to other forms of military force.

Part of the argument of this chapter is that the favourable image associated with peacekeeping within the international community is not always supported by the events associated with actual missions. This chapter will examine two cases, the United Nations Transitional Authority in Cambodia (UNTAC) and the Commission of Inquiry into the Deployment of Canadian Forces to Somalia, or, as it is more popularly known, the Somalia Inquiry. An examination of these two cases demonstrates that, as in any military mission, the relations of power informing peacekeeping missions are far more complex than a superficial reading of the peaceful and altruistic blue-bereted soldier reveals, and depend at least in part on important gendered and racialized distinctions. Those distinctions sometimes have enormous consequences for the people in countries in which peace-

* I am grateful for the research assistance of Suzanne Baustad, V. Elaine Brown, Leslie Jeffrey and Nicole LaVioletre. I am grateful also for financial support received from the Social Sciences and Humanities Research Council of Canada.

keeping missions are deployed: in the Somalia example, two men were shot by Canadian peacekeepers and a third, Shidane Arone, was tortured and beaten to death; in Cambodia, accusations of sexual harassment, violence and abuse surround public perception of the UNTAC mission there. Under such circumstances, we must ask: if peacekeeping missions result in violence, sexual harassment and abuse, how *peaceful* the peacekeepers?

THE UNITED NATIONS TRANSITIONAL AUTHORITY IN CAMBODIA

The United Nations Transitional Authority in Cambodia – UNTAC – is cited by the UN and regarded by many mainstream observers as something of a success story for the UN. William Shawcross, speaking at the general assembly of the International NGO Forum on Cambodia, called it an 'international triumph'[2] and UN Secretary-General Boutros Boutros-Ghali has written that the 'international community can take satisfaction from the peacekeeping operation it mounted and supported in Cambodia.'[3]

The success, achieved in an 18-month mission in Cambodia, included the reduction of violence, the repatriation of some 370,000 Khmer refugees, and the conduct of a relatively free and fair election in which some four million people, or 85 per cent of Cambodia's registered voters, participated.[4] The UN claimed as well, again in the words of Boutros-Ghali, that the mission 'boosted Cambodia's economy by raising funds internationally for economic rehabilitation and expansion throughout the country.'[5]

The UNTAC effort also achieved some important successes with regard to women within Cambodia. Most notably, the freedom of association which prevailed in many respects during UNTAC and the efforts of UNIFEM to incorporate women's issues into the general election resulted in public education and information campaigns in the printed media and on radio and television. In addition a four-day National Women's Summit brought together Cambodian women from all sectors of society in order to identify and prioritize women's issues in order to lobby political parties contesting the election and then later the government itself.[6] The Women's Summit has been credited with the emergence of an indigenous women's movement within Cambodia as well as a number of indigenous women's NGOs, which in turn have been credited with a very effective lobby of the

Cambodian government such that important equality rights provisions eventually made it into the new Cambodian constitution.[7]

Though UNTAC was considered a success in many respects, there are also some discussions of problems associated with the mission. For example, the UN failed to achieve a situation of political neutrality, as pledged in the 1991 Paris Peace Agreement, in part because the Khmer Rouge withdrew from the demobilization and cantonment process and threatened throughout the mission to disrupt the election campaign.[8] This problem was widely attributed to poor planning in advance of the mission and, in particular, the delayed deployment of the UNTAC mission.[9]

Likewise, the presence of UNTAC may have diminished, but did not stop, political violence, which was aimed at both political party members and ethnic Vietnamese. The massacres and exodus of ethnic Vietnamese, many of whom were second- and third-generation Cambodians, were not sufficiently addressed by the UN according to critics. As Grant Curtis points out, 'no party, including UNTAC, made efforts to protect the rights of Cambodia's ethnic Vietnamese population.'[10] Indeed, the extent of the UNTAC response was to organize the 'Safe Passage' operation, which as Raoul Jennar writes, effectively legitimized the forced departure of the Vietnamese.[11]

These are obviously very serious concerns, but there are also another series of issues which emerged throughout the UNTAC mission, and which are seldom discussed in UN documents or mainstream accounts of the mission.[12] Though credited with helping to create the emergence of a fledgling women's movement as well as a number of women's NGOs, there were also a number of important negative consequences for women within Cambodia as a result of the UNTAC mission. These include the reported exponential increase in prostitution to serve UNTAC personnel, with the Cambodian Women's Development Association estimating that the number of prostitutes in Cambodia grew from about 6,000 in 1992 to more than 25,000 at the height of the mission.[13] Some reports indicated that the majority of prostitutes were young Vietnamese women, though these estimates are more likely a result of anti-Vietnamese sentiment as any reflection of reality.[14]

While the presence of prostitutes was not new, and by many accounts frequenting prostitutes is a regular feature of many Cambodian men's behaviour, Cambodians were nonetheless alarmed by the dramatic increase in prostitution and noted that prior to UNTAC it was quite hidden in Cambodian society but became something which was very prevalent and open.[15] The rise of child prostitution has also been linked in some NGO reports to the arrival of UNTAC.[16] The widespread use of prostitutes was raised by the Khmer Rouge as part of their efforts to undermine the peace process when they accused peacekeepers of being too busy with prostitutes to check on the presence of Vietnamese soldiers.[17] As Judy Ledgerwood wrote: 'Some Cambodians were more inclined to believe Khmer Rouge propaganda that UNTAC was collaborating with the Vietnamese to colonize Cambodia when they saw UNTAC personnel taking Vietnamese "wives".'[18]

The influx of nearly 23,000 UN personnel and the dramatic rise in prostitution also appears to have resulted in a dramatic rise in cases of HIV and AIDS, with the WHO reporting that 75 per cent of people giving blood in Phnom Penh were infected with HIV (though this is considered inflated by some observers) and another report indicating that 20 per cent of soldiers in one French batallion tested positive when they finished their six-month tour of duty.[19] UNTAC's chief medical officer predicted that as many as six times more UN personnel would eventually die of AIDS contracted in Cambodia than had died as a result of hostile action.[20]

As criticism toward UN personnel within Cambodia grew, a number of what Judy Ledgerwood describes as 'telling' actions were announced. Peacekeepers were warned to be more discreet, for example by not parking their distinctive white vehicles outside massage parlours and in red light areas and by not frequenting brothels in uniform.[21] A second response was to ship an additional 800,000 condoms to Cambodia.[22]

In addition to prostitution, charges emerged also of sexual abuse and violence. Raoul Jennar reported that in 1993, 'in the Preah Vihear hospital, there was for a time a majority of injured people who were young kids, the victims of sexual abuse by UN soldiers.'[23] A number of interviewees reported that there were frequent claims of rape and sexual assault brought to women's NGOs during the UNTAC period, but often many days or weeks after the rapes were alleged to have taken place, such that the usual expectations surrounding evidence collection could not be carried out and therefore claims could not be substantiated to the satisfaction of UN officials.[24]

It is also a widely shared view among many Cambodian women and men that the phenomenon of 'fake marriages' was widespread during the UNTAC period. Simply put, a UN soldier would marry a

Cambodian woman, but only for the duration of his posting to Cambodia, at which point he would abandon her. Some women were reported to have been abandoned as far away as Bangkok, and left to their own devices to make their way home. In addition to the emotional trauma of fake marriages, they were enormously 'shameful' for women in a society, which as in most societies, has very strict norms about what is appropriate behaviour in 'good' women.[25]

In part as a response to the sexual harassment which prevailed during UNTAC, an open letter was delivered to the UN Secretary-General's Special Representative in Cambodia, Mr Yasushi Akashi. In the letter, 165 Cambodian and expatriate women and men accused some UNTAC personnel of sexual harassment and assault, violence against women and against prostitutes and of being responsible for the dramatic rise of prostitution and HIV/AIDS.[26] Mr Akashi responded by saying that it was natural for hot-blooded young soldiers who had endured the rigours of the field to want to have a few beers and to chase 'young beautiful beings of the opposite sex'.[27] After an outraged response Akashi pledged to assign a Community Relations officer to hear the complaints of the Cambodian community.[28]

Finally, and in contrast to the claims by Boutros-Ghali about UNTAC contributions to economic development in Cambodia, the UNTAC mission has been blamed instead for economic dislocation. Grant Curtis reports that with skyrocketing inflation the price of a kilogram of high quality rice rose from 450 riels to a high of 3,000 riels, and settled eventually at some 1,800–2,000 riels; the price of fish and meat rose by 80 per cent; housing rental prices increased at least four times and UNTAC personnel often paid Phnom Penh-based rents at the provincial level, resulting in increases there also. UNTAC did contribute somewhat by hiring locals, but also drew most of the few trained or experienced Khmer away from Cambodian administrative structures and into UNTAC, and salary payments to local staff comprised less than one per cent of total local expenditure. Finally, the riel was devalued by 70 per cent during UNTAC.[29] In situations of economic dislocation and inflation, the most vulnerable members of society become even more vulnerable still, and within Cambodia women comprise a large proportion of the vulnerable.

Such an analysis of the mission, while concerned primarily with issues of social justice and security for women in Cambodia, also has implications for those looking for policy-relevant advice. As Kien

Serey Phal notes, there are important lessons to be learned from a mission whose military focus may not have been up to the task of the larger, and more long-term, concerns of community-building, peace-building, human security and development. She writes:

> There is a need for the recognition of the success of the peace process in protecting the political rights of Cambodian people and facilitating the improved political participation of women but also of the relative failure of the process to promote social and economic equality, and in particular, to prevent and mitigate violence against women and ensure the protection of fundamental human rights.[30]

For those of us coming from countries which deploy soldiers on peacekeeping missions, the lessons should be obvious. As Cynthia Enloe notes, 'Everyone who sends troops needs to rethink what kind of soldiering works to keep the peace. Because a peace that involves sexual exploitation and sexual violence is no peace at all.'[31]

THE SOMALIA INQUIRY

Mainstream accounts of the kinds of issues raised above about the UNTAC mission are often attributed, as Janet Heininger writes, to the problems of establishing a 'common standard of behavior' among contributing countries.[32] In other words, the problem is explained by the fact that some contributing countries, usually those with less experience in peacekeeping missions, send troops not well-suited to the expectations associated with peacekeeping. In the Cambodian case, the Bulgarians are cited as the chief offenders. While not to deny that particular contributing country soldiers may have caused specific sets of problems, it is important to note also that such arguments deflect attention away from more general critical concerns and turn such issues into 'technical problems'. Thus rather than ask questions about the value of relying chiefly on *soldiers* as peace-keepers,[33] ethnic arguments are deployed in such a way that the primary concern becomes 'problems of co-ordination'.

One contributor country normally excluded from any concerns about 'coordination' and which has been viewed in general as the peacekeeping country *par excellence* is Canada.[34] The very favour-able image associated with Canadian peacekeeping has been under-mined recently, however, as a result of the shooting of two Somali men and the torture and murder of a Somali teenager, Shidane Abu-kar Arone, by a number of Canadian peacekeepers from the Canadian Airborne Regiment on duty in Somalia in March of 1993. On 4 March of that year two Somali men were shot in the back by Canadian peacekeepers, one of whom died. While an initial investigation concluded that the Airborne members had acted properly, a Canadian military doctor later reported that the dead man had been killed 'execution style' and moreover that he had been pressured to destroy his medical records concerning the murder.[35] On 16 March, at least two Airborne members beat Shidane Arone throughout the evening, abusing him verbally throughout with racist epithets, and by midnight he had died. Arone's murderers also photographed his ordeal, which were released in the course of courts martial proceedings in November of 1994.

The release of the very graphic and horrifying photographs of Arone's murder (the soldiers themselves called them 'trophies'), and the subsequent revelations by the Canadian military doctor that he had been pressured to cover up details of the 4 March shooting led the Canadian Minister of National Defense to call for a public inquiry into the Somalia mission. This was followed two months later by the release of two sets of videos, the first a video from the Somalia mission, portions of which portray Airborne soldiers describing the Somalia mission as 'Operation Snatch Niggers', the second a number of videos depicting the Airborne's hazing rituals which included, among other things, images of Airborne soldiers vomiting or eating vomit, being smeared with faeces, and with the single black soldier in the regiment being forced to walk around on all fours with the phrase 'I love the KKK' written in faeces on his back.[36]

The first reaction by mainstream observers of peacekeeping to the Arone murder was to dismiss it as the act of a few 'bad apples'. The bad apple theory, moreover, was quickly linked by military apologists to problems associated with economic downsizing. As Joseph Jockel argued, the Somalia crisis was the result of a personnel shortage, itself the result of years of underfunding. Under these circumstances, for Jockel, the army 'felt compelled to send to Somalia a unit of the Canadian Airborne Regiment whose fitness for deployment was doubtful.'[37]

The release of the Somalia and hazing videos undermined the 'bad apple' theory and suggested, at least, that the type of behaviour which led to the shootings and Arone's brutal murder was more pervasive within the Airborne Regiment, if not the Canadian military as a whole. And importantly, it was not the shootings or the murder of Shidane Arone, but the release of the hazing video which led the Minister of National Defense to announce on 23 January 1995 that the elite Airborne Regiment would be disbanded.[38] As Romeo St Martin writes:

> Allegations of racism, torture and murder weren't enough to bring down the Canadian Airborne unit. Even a videotape filled with racist comments was dismissed as 'bravado' by the unit's supporters. However, video of the Canadian troops frolicking in a sea of vomit, piss and shit outraged the public and was cause for swift action by Defense Minister David Collenette to disband the regiment.[39]

A concern with a breakdown in the 'chain of command' replaced the assumption that the Somalia murders (usually referred to as 'unfortunate events') were the result of a few bad apples. It is an examination of the chain of command which is the focus of the Somalia Inquiry.

Whether it is a 'few bad apples' or problems in the 'chain of command', what we are *not* likely to see at the inquiry or any of the more traditional analyses made of it is any analysis of the ways in which these events are a product of what many feminists describe as militarized masculinity.[40] What is clear, however, is that there is ample evidence in the shootings, the murder of Arone, the various videotapes and now testimony emerging at the inquiry to support such an analysis. In addition to Arone's torture and murder and the visual evidence from the hazing videos, what has been shown in testimony, questioning and documents submitted thus far to the inquiry is that, in contrast to the notion that the Canadian military by virtue of its participation in peacekeeping missions is a quite benign, altruistic and peaceful institution, in fact, it is one in which the glorification of force, hierarchy, racism and violence against women are, like most militaries, an important part of its culture.

Within the first week of the inquiry's evidentiary hearings, for example, the Canadian public learned that military officials had allowed members of the Airborne who were either known members of racist skinhead organizations or who were under investigation for suspected skinhead and neo-nazi activity to be deployed to Somalia.[41] None of the suspected skinheads were charged in Arone's murder, but considerable concern was raised that knowledge of the racist activity had been clearly documented over a year before the unit was deployed to Somalia. Indeed, those documents indicated that the entire Canadian Forces Base Petawawa (home to the Airborne) 'appear to be one of the several areas where right-wing activities are centered.'[42]

Other revelations followed. In November, lawyers for the Canadian Jewish Congress alleged that members of the Airborne held a celebratory dinner to honour Marc Lepine, the man who massacred 14 women at the Université de Montréal in 1989. A former member of the Airborne confirmed the dinner had taken place and commented, '... it would have been the same as having an Adolf Hitler party on his birthday... It's just the shock value.'[43]

One of the questions which Inquiry Commissioners posed to many witnesses in the first phase of the hearings concerned a number of incidents involving the Airborne prior to its deployment to Somalia. The first was a reported 'torching' of an officer's car at the base and the second was a shooting spree by members of the Airborne within a nearby provincial park. The Commissioners wondered aloud whether officers should have taken these incidents more seriously and as evidence of a real problem of command and control within the regiment.

Retired Major-General Lewis Mackenzie's response to these questions was revealing. He suggested that because the Somalia mission had been upgraded from a Chapter VI (peacekeeping) mission to a Chapter VII (peace enforcement) mission, the soldiers were all 'psyched up', and though he did not want to excuse their behaviour prior to deployment, he thought that excitement might explain these incidents. He pointed out that there had only been three Chapter VII missions in UN history to that point: Korea, the Gulf War and Somalia. Somalia had become 'a non-blue beret fight, as it were', and that while 'some of this is macho stuff', there was 'more prestige' for Airborne soldiers being deployed on a Chapter VII mission than a Chapter VI.[44] There is more prestige, in other words, for soldiers to be involved in a mission of real soldiering, in which they are no longer restricted to firing only in self-defence.

In addition to these various revelations, one of the first documents tabled at the inquiry confirmed what feminists have long argued:[45] the level of violence against women is disproportionately high within militaries, and this is true also of the Canadian military. The Hewson Report was a 1985 inquiry into infractions and antisocial behaviour within the Mobile Command, with particular reference to the Special Service Force and the Canadian Airborne Regiment. Major-General Hewson had been charged with investigating whether there was a higher rate of disciplinary infractions (i.e. criminal behaviour) within the Canadian forces than within Canadian society more generally. The report was initiated after a series of media stories covering crimes by Airborne members, one of which involved the murder of a civilian with a machete.[46]

Hewson reported that there was no higher incidence of crime within the Canadian Forces, and in fact 'there appears to be a lower incidence of serious pathology and violent behaviour in the CF than in the Canadian population at large.'[47] However, two important qualifications were noted, the first was that while there was a lower incidence of violent crime more generally, there was 'a relatively higher frequency of sexual offences which should be further investigated.' The second was that within the Canadian Forces, there was a higher incidence of violent crime within the Canadian Airborne Regiment.

Hewson's explanation for the higher incidence of violent crime within the Airborne relied on explicitly gendered arguments and focused on the 'characteristics' of local residents and the concentration of single soldiers in Petawawa. The Report noted that 'Due to the physical nature of local industry (lumber and agriculture) the local civilian male population is considered robust and tough.'[48] Add to this a concentration of single male soldiers, the report noted, and there resulted the potential for violence, particularly in 'disputes over girls':

> When compared to a relatively small local female population, this high concentration of young single soldiers creates an unbalanced, artificial society which is a source of undue stress to many servicemen. The young single soldier with his new 'sporty' car, regular and higher pay and job security has a tendancy [*sic*] to attract the local female population; this further antagonizes the local male population already frustrated (particularly so in Quebec) by the high level of unemployment. This creates a highly volatile situation; the local civilian police on both sides of the river state that most incidents of violence are over girls.[49]

The report had comparatively less comment to make on the higher incidence of sexual assaults within the Canadian Forces, noting only that it deserved further study. Further studies were not forthcoming, perhaps in part because Hewson never indicated *how much* higher the level of sexual assaults were.[50] In fact, however, an appendix outlining 'crime case synopses' for 1984/85 indicates that the number of sexual offences within the Canadian Forces is staggering. If one includes within the category of sexual assaults all assaults in which the victim is a woman, more than half of the 141 crimes listed were either sexual assaults or physical assaults against women: 76 out of 141 cases, or 54 per cent. It is very telling that not only did these figures not appear in the text of the report but in commenting on these statistics, Hewson noted that the crime case synopsis 'does not, statistically, reveal any significant or alarming trends.'[51] Moreover, the recommendation to study further the 'higher frequency of sexual assaults' did not even make it into the Report's Summary of *Main Recommendations*.[52]

What is being revealed at the Somalia Inquiry is the extent to which even Canada's beloved blue-bereted soldiers rely on the racism, violence and sexism which is inherent in the creation of soldiers and militarized masculinity. In an observation which could serve as a textbook definition of militarism and militarized masculinity (and which could have been read as a prediction of Shidane Arone's murder in Somalia when the Airborne was deployed there almost ten years later), Major R.W.J. Wenek wrote in 1984:

> The defining role of any military force is the management of violence by violence, so that individual aggressiveness is, or should be, a fundamental characteristic of occupational fitness in combat units. This is implicitly recognized in the aggressive norms of behaviour permitted and encouraged in elite units, such as commandos, paratroopers, and special service forces. Particularly in units such as these, but also in other combat units, behaviour which may be considered verging on the sociopathic in peacetime becomes a prerequisite for survival in war. Aggressiveness must be selected for in military organizations and must be reinforced during military training, but it may be extremely difficult to make fine distinctions between those individuals who can be counted on to act in an appropriately aggressive way and those likely at some time to display inappropriate aggression. *To some extent, the risk of erring on the side of excess may be a necessary one in an organization whose existence is premised on the instrumental value of aggression and violence.*[53]

Or, as a paratrooper in the newly recreated Light Infantry Batallion at Petawawa noted: 'People worry we're too aggressive. But that's what soldiers are supposed to be. You don't go out and give the enemy a kiss. You kill them.'[54]

CONCLUSIONS

The observations presented here about the Somalia Inquiry and the peacekeeping mission in Cambodia are intended, first, to call into question the very comfortable assumptions about peacekeeping which prevail in both national and international contexts. They are intended, secondly, to outline some of the ways in which peacekeeping politics – like all politics – depend upon gendered and racialized hierarchies. Soldiers are not born, they are made; and the training of soldiers depends in part upon notions of militarized masculinity which privilege violence, racism and sexism. This is true whether those soldiers are trained for warfare or for peacekeeping, and indeed, many proponents of peacekeeping argue that soldiers *must* be trained in the arts of war in order to be able to perform their peacekeeping duties.[55] The cases presented here, however, suggest that if there *is* a future for peacekeeping, then at a minimum we need to rethink the automatic response found in most quarters that soldiers make the best peacekeepers: for many women in Cambodia and for the Somali men killed by Canadian peacekeepers, it is quite clear that soldiers trained well in the arts of militarized masculinity can by far also make the worst peacekeepers.

NOTES

1. See, for example, Boutros Boutros-Ghali, *An Agenda for Peace*, New York: United Nations, 1992, Ch. V and *passim*; and *Supplement to an Agenda for Peace: Position Paper of the Secretary-General on the Occasion of the Fiftieth Anniversary of the United Nations*, A/50/60, 25 January 1995.
2. Cited from R.M. Jennar, 'UNTAC: "international triumph" in Cambodia?', *Security Dialogue*, Vol. 25, No. 2, 1994, p. 145. See also Judy L. Ledgerwood, 'UN Peacekeeping missions: the lessons from Cambodia', *Analysis from the East–West Center No. 11*, Honolulu: East–West Center, March 1994; Janet E. Heininger, *Peacekeeping in Transition: The United Nations in Cambodia*, New York: The Twentieth Century Fund Press, 1994, pp. 1–8. Peter Utting also notes the way in which 'world opinion has been quick to label the United Nations operation in Cambodia "a success"', and contrasts that view with the research presented in his volume on the social consequences of UNTAC. See Peter Utting, 'Introduction: linking peace and rehabilitation in Cambodia', in Utting, *Between Hope and Insecurity: The Social Consequences of the Cambodian Peace Process*, Geneva: United Nations Research Institute for Social Development, 1994, p. 3 and *passim*.

3. Cited in *The United Nations and Cambodia, 1991–1995*, New York: UN, 1995, p. 55; see also 'What the United Nations learnt in Cambodia', *The Economist*, 19 June 1993, p. 36.

4. Ker Munthit, 'Akashi: election "free and fair"', *Phnom Penh Post*, 6–12 June 1993, p. 3; Nate Thayer and Rodney Tasker, 'Voice of the people', *Far Eastern Economic Review*, 3 June 1993, p. 10. See also Michael W. Doyle, *UN Peacekeeping in Cambodia: UNTAC's Civil Mandate*, Boulder, Colo.: Lynne Rienner, 1995, Ch. 4 and *passim*; Michael W. Doyle and Nishkala Suntharalingam, 'The UN in Cambodia: lessons for complex peacekeeping,' *International Peacekeeping*, Vol. 1, No. 2, Summer 1994, pp. 117–47.

5. *The United Nations and Cambodia, 1991–1995*, op. cit., p. 54; see also Grant Curtis, 'Transition to what? Cambodia, UNTAC and the peace process', in Utting, *Between Hope and Insecurity*, pp. 56–8.

6. *Report from the National Women's Summit*, Phnom Penh, 5–8 March 1993. See also Mang Channo, 'Women's Day highlights gender inequalities', *Phnom Penh Post*, 12–25 March 1993.

7. Interviews, 25 March–1 April 1996. Another way in which UNTAC was cited as having contributed in a positive way to women's lives concerned domestic violence: the Project Against Domestic Violence in Phnom Penh reported that in a context where few cases of domestic violence are ever reported to authorities and fewer still are prosecuted, one provincial judge described the only criminal case of domestic violence she had ever presided over as one in which UNTAC officers had brought in a man caught beating his wife in a marketplace. Cathy Zimmerman, Sar Samen and Men Savorn, *Plates in a Basket Will Rattle: Domestic Violence in Cambodia*, Phnom Penh: Asia Foundation, 1994, p. 140, fn. 99, and pp. 137–42 *passim*.

8. Ramses Amer, 'The United Nations' peacekeeping operation in Cambodia: overview and assessment', *Contemporary Southeast Asia*, Vol. 15, No. 2, September 1993, pp. 211–31; Curtis, 'Transition to What?', p. 59; Doyle, *UNTAC's Civil Mandate*, Ch. 4; Doyle and Suntharalingam, 'Lessons for Complex Peacekeeping', pp. 124–27.

9. In addition to other sources cited above, see also Jarat Chopra, John Mackinlay and Larry Minear, *Report on the Cambodian Peace Process*, Oslo: Norwegian Institute of International Affairs, 1993, Ch. 3 and *passim*; Jarat Chopra, *United Nations Authority in* Cambodia, Occasional Paper No. 15, Providence, RI: Thomas J. Watson Jr. Institute for International Studies, 1994, Part 2 and *passim*; Amitav Acharya, 'Cambodia, the United Nations and the problems of peace', *The Pacific Review*, Vol. 7, No. 3, 1994, pp. 298–308.

10. Curtis, 'Transition to What?', p. 60; Peter Eng, 'Little sympathy for Vietnamese victims', *Phnom Penh Post*, 7 August 1992, p. 4; Kevin Barrington, 'Massacre condemned but...', *Phnom Penh Post*, 26 March–8 April 1993, p. 1.

11. Jennar, 'International Triumph in Cambodia?', p. 148.

12. An important exception here is an excellent collection organized through the United Nations Research Institute for Social Development; see Utting, *Between Hope and Insecurity*.

13.   Mang Channg, 'Sex trade flourishing in capital', *Phnom Penh Post*, 12–25 February 1993, p. 6; 'The problem of prostitution', *Phnom Penh Post*, 12–25 February 1993, p. 6; Andrew Nettie, 'Cambodia: UN Mission cited as sex slavery spreads', *Sunday Age* (Melbourne), 25 June 1995; Eva Arnvig, 'Women, children and returnees', in Utting, *Between Hope and Insecurity*, pp. 166–9; Kien Serey Phal, 'The lessons of the UNTAC experience and the ongoing responsibilities of the international community for peacebuilding and development in Cambodia', *Pacifica Review*, Vol. 7, No. 2, 1995, pp. 129–33; Gayle Kirshenbaum, 'Who's watching the peacekeepers?', *Ms*, May/June 1994, p. 13. Interviews conducted in Phnom Penh from 25 March–1 April 1995 as well as numerous reports by NGOs within Phnom Penh confirm these observations; see, for example, Mona Mehta, *Gender Dimensions of Poverty in Cambodia: A Survey Report*, Phnom Penh: Oxfam, 1993, p. 7.

14.   Jon Swain, 'UN losing battle for Cambodia in the brothels of Phnom Penh', *Sunday Times*, 27 December 1992; *Asian Recorder*, 21–27 May 1993, p. 23144. Indeed, the Cambodian Women's Development Association indicated in 1994 that the majority of prostitutes working in the Toul Kork area of Phnom Penh were likely Cambodian (Cambodian Women's Development Association, 'Prostitution Survey Results', 1994), and interviewees in Phnom Penh indicated to the author that the ethnic origin of prostitutes in Cambodia has always varied, depending on the location of the brothels.

15.   Interviews, Phnom Penh, 25 March–1 April 1996.

16.   UNICEF, *The Trafficking and Prostitution of Children in Cambodia: A Situation Report*, Phnom Penh: UNICEF, 1995, pp. 1–2; Krousar Thmey, 'Child prostitution and trafficking in Cambodia: a new problem', March–October 1995 in Appendix 2 of UNICEF, '*The Trafficking and Prostitution of Children in Cambodia*; Keo Keang and Im Phallay, Human Rights Task Force on Cambodia, 'Notes on the March–April 1995 rapid appraisal of the Human Rights Vigilance of Cambodia on child prostitution and trafficking', in Appendix 2 of UNICEF, *The Trafficking and Prostitution of Children in Cambodia*; Human Rights Vigilance of Cambodia, 'Combating women trafficking and child prostitution', March/April 1995, in Appendix 2 of UNICEF, *The Trafficking and Prostitution of Children in Cambodia*.

17.   Swain, 'UN losing battle for Cambodia in the brothels of Phnom Penh'.

18.   Ledgerwood, 'The Lessons from Cambodia', p. 7.

19.   Swain, 'UN losing battle for Cambodia in the brothels of Phnom Penh', and *Asian Recorder*, 5–11 February 1993, p. 22903. Most observers note that while UNTAC was not responsible for bringing HIV and AIDS to Cambodia, it did contribute to its spread.

20.   Katrina Peach, 'HIV threatens to claim UNTAC's highest casualties', *Phnom Penh Post*, 22 October–4 November 1993, p. 4.

21.   Noted in *Asian Recorder*, 16–22 April 1993, p. 23060. Ledgerwood, 'The Lessons from Cambodia', p. 8, and Arnvig, 'Women, children and returnees', p. 165.

22. The Reuters Library Report, 18 November 1992.

23. Jennar, 'International triumph in Cambodia?', p. 154.

24. Interviews in Phnom Penh, 25 March–1 April 1996. See also Kirshenbaum, 'Who's watching the peacekeepers?', p. 13.

25. Interviews in Phnom Penh, 25 March–1 April 1996.

26. 'An open letter to Yasushi Akashi', *Phnom Penh Post*, 11 October 1992, p. 2; 'Allegations of sexual harassment hit U.N. Peacekeeping forces in Cambodia', *Business Wire*, 11 January 1993.

27. Sara Colm, 'U.N. agrees to address sexual harassment issue', *Phnom Penh Post*, 11 October 1992, p. 1; Swain, 'UN losing battle for Cambodia in the brothels of Phnom Penh'.

28. Colm, 'U.N. agrees to address sexual harassment issue', and 'Akashi responds to community concerns', *Phnom Penh Post*, 20 November–3 December 1992, p. 2.

29. All of this information is from Curtis, 'Transition to what?', pp. 59–65. See also Robin Davies, 'UNTAC and the Cambodian economy: what impact?', *Phnom Penh Post*, 29 January–11 February 1993, pp. 4–5; Gary Klintworth, 'United Nations: a poor job in Cambodia', *International Herald Tribune*, 2 February 1993; and Mats R. Berdal, *Whither UN peacekeeping?*, Adelphi Paper 281 London: IISS, 1993, p. 46.

30. Kien, 'The lessons of the UNTAC experience', p. 132.

31. Cited from Kirshenbaum, 'Who's watching the peacekeepers?', p. 15.

32. Heininger, *Peacekeeping in Transition: The United Nations in Cambodia*, pp. 75–6, 129.

33. A.B. Fetherston makes a similar argument in 'UN Peacekeepers and cultures of violence', *Cultural Survival Quarterly*, Vol. 19, No. 1, 1995, pp. 19–23.

34. Joseph T. Jockel, *Canada and International Peacekeeping*, Washington, DC: Center for Strategic and International Studies, 1994, p. 1.

35. David Pugliese, 'Somalia: what went so wrong?', *The Ottawa Citizen*, 1 October 1995, p. A6.

36. Christopher Dornan, 'Scenes from a scandal', *The Globe and Mail*, 21 January 1995, p. D1, and Corporal Christopher Robin, 'Testimony to the Commission of Inquiry into the Deployment of Canadian Forces to Somalia', 12 October 1995, Ottawa, Canada.

37. Jockel, *Canada and International Peacekeeping*, p. 33.

38. Carol Burke in 'Sex, G.I.'s and videotape', a work in progress, nd, makes the same observation.

39. Romeo St Martin, 'Guilty of conduct unbecoming of an officer on TV', *XPress: The Capital's Newspaper*, 15 February 1995.

40. See, for example, Cynthia Enloe, *The Morning After: Sexual Politics at the End of the Cold War*, Berkeley, Calif.: University of California Press, 1993, especially Chs. 2 and 3; V. Spike Peterson and Anne Sisson Runyan, *Global Gender Issues*, Boulder, Colo.: Westview Press, 1993, pp. 81–91 and *passim*.

41. Commission of Inquiry into the Deployment of Canadian Forces to Somalia, *Document Book No. 8, Racism*, Ottawa: Canada, 1995 (hereinafter *The Racism Document*).

42. David Pugliese, 'Military brass let racist skinheads go to Somalia', *The Ottawa Citizen*, 13 October 1995, p. A1; *The Racism Document*, p. 13.

43. 'Soldier confirms Airborne held massacre party', *The Ottawa Citizen*, 9 November 1995, p. A3; 'Army commander probes report of Lepine dinner', *The Ottawa Citizen*, 10 November 1995, p. A3; 'Racist soldier with criminal past allowed to rejoin the army, inquiry hears', *The Ottawa Citizen*, 3 November 1995, p. A5.

44. Major-General (Retired) Lewis Mackenzie, 'Testimony to the Commission of Inquiry into the Deployment of Canadian Forces to Somalia', 1 February 1996, Ottawa, Canada. It is important to note also that the incidents about which Mackenzie was asked to comment took place some two months *before* the Somalia mission was upgraded to a Chapter VII, making it a thin excuse indeed.

45. For an excellent introduction to this type of feminist work, see Francine D'Amico, *Women as Warriors: Feminist Perspectives*, paper presented at the Annual General Meetings of the International Studies Association, Vancouver, British Columbia, 20–23 March 1992.

46. David Pugliese, 'Almost 20% of '85 Airborne unit had police record, report found', *The Ottawa Citizen*, 4 October 1995, p. A4; Commission of Inquiry into the Deployment of Canadian Forces to Somalia, *Document Book No. 1, Hewson Report* (Ottawa: Canada, 1995, p. 15 (hereinafter *The Hewson Report*).

47. *The Hewson Report*, p. 17.

48. *The Hewson Report*, p. 61.

49. *The Hewson Report*, p. 61 and p. 19.

50. *The Hewson Report*, pp. 27–8.

51. *The Hewson Report*, p. 29.

52. *The Hewson Report*, pp. 20–1.

53. Major R.W.J. Wenek, *The Assessment of Psychological Fitness: Some Options for the Canadian Forces*, Technical Note 1/84, Ottawa: Directorate of Personnel Selection, Research on Second Careers, July 1984, p. 13, cf. *The Hewson Report*, p. 46.

54. David Pugliese, 'Airborne again', *The Ottawa Citizen*, 15 April 1996, p. A1.

55. See, for example, David Bercuson, *Significant Incident: Canada's Army, the Airborne, and the Murder in Somalia*, Toronto: McClelland Stewart, 1996, p. 34 and *passim*.

9 A Future for Peacekeeping?
Edward Moxon-Browne

The question implied in the title of this chapter may seem provocative at a time when peacekeeping operations have been recently, and are currently, deployed around the world on a scale unimaginable before 1990. The question is timely, nonetheless, because the multiplicity of such operations has spawned ever more pressing questions about their conduct, effectiveness, management and impact. Since 1989, opportunities for peacekeeping have increased, partly because the end of the Cold War has made it easier to obtain consent within the United Nations, and partly because public opinion is better informed (the 'CNN effect') about geographically remote conflicts, and less tolerant therefore of inactivity on the part of their own governments. Nevertheless, the nature of conflicts has changed, and so has the required response. The essentially intra-state character of many conflicts raises important questions about sovereignty: in what circumstances is it legitimate for the 'international community' (however defined) to intervene in a situation that is either exclusively, or largely, confined within the borders of a single state? If the situation is perceived as a major humanitarian issue (e.g. ethnic genocide) there may be good grounds for saying that the moral imperative overrides the strictly legal concern for non-interference in the domestic affairs of sovereign states. However, even if such a moral imperative is recognized, there may be reluctance to be involved or disagreement as to how the crisis should best be tackled: opposing factions within one Third World country may be supported, respectively, by separate or overlapping groups of states in the world community. The shift towards these more complex operations, emphasizing the enforcement of peace instead of its maintenance, has drawn the whole question of 'peacekeeping' into more controversial territory. While it is well known that peacekeeping operations have become much more numerous since 1989, it is also true that the risk of failure, and the results of failure, have increased in equal measure. On the one hand, there has been a strong incentive, if not necessity, to veer towards peace enforcement, while, on the other hand, the dangers of straying from the path of classic peacekeeping (the 'thin blue line' ethos) have been only too apparent. At the heart of this conundrum lies the distinction between peacekeeping and peace enforcement.

The definitional differences between peacekeeping and peace enforcement lie at the heart of much of the current debate as to exactly what role should be played by UN forces and other multilateral agencies in conflict situations. So far, the best analysis of the principle of consent as the one which distinguishes between peacekeeping and peace enforcement operations is that contained in the British Army's document *Wider Peacekeeping*. Here it is argued that what distinguishes peacekeeping from peace enforcement is not the level of violence but the level of consent. But even this consent is not ubiquitous or constant: even in the wider peacekeeping scenario it will fluctuate across space and time. The maintenance of consent is achieved by classic techniques of minimum force, impartiality, transparency, legitimacy and mutual respect. In an important passage, the document emphasizes not only that the consent barrier should never be breached, but that if it is breached there is no going back. In other words the transition from peacekeeping should not be casual, unplanned, spasmodic or accidental. It should be:

a deliberate, pre-meditated act, taking account of the risks involved, and matched by appropriate force levels, equipments, and doctrine. It would for instance require substantial force restructuring and redeployment, the evacuation of unarmed monitors and civilian workers, and the probable termination of humanitarian operations.[1]

Even if the conceptual and operational distinctions between peacekeeping and peace enforcement are more clearly defined in the future, there remain numerous organizational and financial problems, some of which are discussed in earlier chapters, and whose solution would greatly enhance the reputation of peacekeeping. Rapidity of response remains a key element in the effective initiation and prosecution of any peace operation; and the relatively tardy and uncoordinated nature of some responses in the past epitomizes the political, financial and administrative bottlenecks that bedevil the world organization. In the summer of 1994, *The Economist* illustrated what it called the 'languor of peacekeeping' by relating the consequences of a Pakistani offer to provide 3,000 unequipped troops for Bosnia: Germany offered tanks to the Pakistanis but, because the tanks were East German, the Pakistanis, accustomed to Western equipment, needed training on the ground. Germany agreed to train them, but then found that this was constitutionally forbidden; so the training was switched to Austria which also discovered that such training would be against its constitution so, finally, a year behind schedule, the training started in Slovakia.[2]

One of the more persistent ideas put forward to improve the efficiency of UN peacekeeping is the idea of a permanent or 'standing' force. This idea is distinct from, but related to, the notion of national 'stand-by' units that have been mooted from time to time, and to which the Canadian and Nordic examples bear the closest resemblance. Diehl[3] identifies four principal advantages of such a force: professionalism, reaction time, efficiency and financial stability. Professionalism results from a common training programme that enables soldiers from a variety of national backgrounds to absorb, and put into practice, a common set of standards, procedures and objectives in peacekeeping operations. Reaction time is significantly less with a permanent force, since the UN does not need to request troop contributing countries to respond to an unfolding situation. Quick response may actually reduce the length and complexity of the operation because interposition of forces can be undertaken in the immediate wake of a ceasefire. Increased efficiency stems from a coherent bureaucratic structure that cuts out delays or difficulties that normally occur either between New York and the peacekeeping operation, or between the force commanders of the participant countries. Financial stability results from predetermined funding, and this obviates bargaining and consequent delays as financial liabilities are argued over. Despite the apparently undeniable advantages of a permanent force, Diehl argues that none of the alleged advantages are foolproof and that national arrangements can be, and often are, superior to the putative benefits of a multinational permanent force. Nevertheless, a sustained argument for a 'rapid reaction capability' has been advanced by a study group established by the Canadian government. The stimulus for this study, and for similar calls elsewhere, was the slowness of the international response to the crisis in Rwanda, and (by contrast) the rapidity of the US response to the invasion of Kuwait. The central theme in the Canadian proposal is the 'vanguard concept' – the ability of the UN to assemble from member-states a multifunctional force of up to 5,000 military and civilian personnel and rapidly deploy it under the control of an operational-level headquarters on authorization of the Security Council.

The most effective way of delineating the contrasting roles of peacekeeping and peace enforcement operations may be to establish two different types of force: one lightly armed and including a multiplicity of civilian units trained for specific functions; and a more heavily-armed force that would have a less prominent civilian component and be more often than not based on a regional organization in which a 'lead-nation' would be more acceptable than in a classic peacekeeping force, the latter being characterized by its multinational and global composition.

Such a dichotomization would provide an opportunity for women to play a greater role than hitherto in peacekeeping operations. One of the clear implications of the chapters by Fetherston and Whitworth is that more women could, and perhaps should, be deployed as peacekeepers. In the past, female participation in peacekeeping has reflected the traditionally male composition of national armed forces. Among around 20,000 military personnel serving in peacekeeping operations between 1957 and 1989, there were only 20 women. Many of these performed military functions. The proportion of women in national defence forces has been increasing, but this is not strongly reflected in the proportions serving as peacekeepers. In 17 UN military peacekeeping missions active in 1993, women accounted for only 1.7 per cent of the total. Now that a few countries (such as Canada, Denmark, France, Norway, Sweden, the United States and Venezuela) allow women to serve in combat roles it will be easier for recruitment of women into peacekeeping forces to take place. Sweden has experimented with direct recruitment of women into peacekeeping forces. Approximately 3.3 per cent of Sweden's UNPROFOR presence consisted of females; and there was one Swedish female police officer serving in ONUMOZ. If an operational distinction were to be maintained between the classic functions of peacekeeping and the newer more 'aggressive' functions of peace enforcement, female participation rates in the former could be dramatically increased.

Among the reasons for encouraging a higher proportion of women to serve in peacekeeping forces, the following may be cited: if a certain proportion of peacekeepers are female it may help local women in a host country to defuse awkward situations without the need for formal peacekeeper intervention; it may also place greater emphasis on 'female' attributes such as non-confrontational approaches in delicate situations, an ability to listen and console, and a willingness to share responsibilities and work cooperatively in teams. Arguably, all these characteristics combined could contribute something of added value to the peacekeeping experience. The presence of women soldiers, in contrast to male soldiers, ought to have a highly salutary effect on the host population: female peacekeepers would underline the essentially pacific and non-force orientation of classic peacekeeping. The fear that male soldiers, armed or otherwise, can arouse in civilians, merely by their presence, would not apply to female peacekeepers. This fact alone suggests that an increased presence of women in traditional peacekeeping (as opposed to peace enforcement) activities would contribute to its greater acceptability. It would also help to draw a distinction between peacekeeping and peace enforcement. In sum, the female role in conflict resolution is predicated on the supposition that women are socially conditioned to be more peaceful and peace-loving than men; that the more pacifist orientation of women is attributable to the biological roles that women play as mothers, responsible for giving birth to and nurturing future generations, as well as acting as conciliators within the family milieu and in their local communities.

As we move into an era of more differentiated conflict situations, the range of responses will similarly become more varied. It will not be in the interest of the United Nations for its peacekeeping machinery to be seen as the 'pill for every ill': along that road lies the slow destruction of UN legitimacy and a dilution of the classic principles of peacekeeping such as impartiality, multinationalism and minimum force. It may be appropriate for regional organizations to shoulder responsibilities in certain circumstances, and for 'great powers' (who traditionally steered clear of direct involvement in peacekeeping) to accept leadership in some operations.

The establishment of an implementation force (IFOR) at the beginning of 1996 offers us a model of what can be achieved when certain helpful factors coalesce. The IFOR took the place of the UN peacekeeping force (UNPROFOR). The principal task of IFOR was to patrol a 700-mile long zone of separation between Serb and Croat/ Muslim forces. Bosnia was divided into three zones: one controlled by the US in the northeast; one controlled by the British in the northwest; and one under French control in the south. Overall command of IFOR has been in the hands of an American admiral. The United States, Britain and France are providing between them 43,000 troops, and a further 23 countries (11 not members of NATO) have been taking part. Germany, for the first time since 1949, has deployed soldiers outside its own territory, and Russia has provided 2,500 troops who have, in effect, been serving alongside American soldiers and under NATO command. Despite different interpretations of what 'peacekeeping' duties involve, the process has gone relatively smoothly. Alongside the military arm of the operation, there has also been a civilian component comprising such tasks as policing, elections and the problems of refugees.

To avoid the dangers of a vaguely worded mandate, the Dayton Agreement was worded in precise language designed to limit IFOR's responsibilities. The emphasis is on traditional peacekeeping – standing between erstwhile combatants, with their consent, to preserve a peace to which they have all agreed. There is more than a little irony in the fact that IFOR is performing exactly the same role as a classic UN peacekeeping force would do, and the irony is further compounded by the fact that UNPROFOR's previous task was closer to a peace enforcement function for which NATO–IFOR might have been more appropriate. IFOR has achieved a multinational composition that the UN might envy – Russian and American soldiers side by side – and rules of engagement that allow for considerable retaliatory flexibility in the event of ceasefire violations. The Dayton Agreement set out a precise timetable for the transition from a ceasefire to the creation of stable political institutions: exchanges of prisoners, transfers of territory and the holding of elections – all these were tied to specific dates for implementation.

What has been most notable about the IFOR experiment has been the extent of American leadership and American military commitment. In weighing up the arguments for and against superpower involvement in peacekeeping, and Somalia notwithstanding, the IFOR framework does suggest that not only can American-led peacekeeping missions work effectively, but in fact that the American presence can be, in some circumstances, indispensable to their success. This runs counter to an increasingly popular argument that a superpower's involvement may not be conducive to the 'legitimacy' of a peacekeeping operation and that this superpower in particular is temperamentally unsuited to the 'long drawn out' commitment that such operations often imply. Needless to say, in this case, American involvement was linked to Clinton's re-election strategy, but the decision of the United States to remain involved after the President's re-election must be interpreted in more favourable terms – even if those terms relate to 'image' in the world, and a concern for stability in Europe. There were a number of other factors that conspired to make IFOR possible and opportune: the receptivity of the Bosnian Serbs to a settlement because of territorial losses; the desire of NATO to define for itself a new security role in Europe; the willingness of France to return to the military side of NATO for the first time since 1960; and the pressures in Russian domestic politics for the government to be seen to be asserting itself more robustly on the world stage alongside the United States.

Despite these special, if not unique, factors, can IFOR provide a model for future peacekeeping operations? In one sense, it is too early to say because the operation is not complete. In another sense, we can already say that IFOR has been a great success. The experience of IFOR runs counter to the record in Somalia where classic examples of 'mission creep' and lack of coordination between national contingents proved disastrous. Another key contrast between UNOSOM and IFOR is that in the former case significant political actors were prepared to defy the UN while, in Bosnia, IFOR's intervention was preceded by a truce signed by all significant political actors. The tightly written mandate and restricted objectives of IFOR are also relevant as examples of good practice for other peacekeeping operations. The inclusion of the USA with Russia and Germany is a potent combination if one is seeking to satisfy a basic criterion for effective peacekeeping, the legitimacy that emanates from the deployment of a truly multinational force.

Having said all that, the increasingly multifunctional character of peacekeeping could well provide a niche for NATO to make a special contribution. NATO has a number of assets that would be (have been) valuable in multifunctional PKOs, such as common operating procedures, interoperable military forces, integrated transport networks and soldiers who have, in many cases, extensive peacekeeping experience. Secondly, NATO has early warning systems and intelligence gathering capabilities that would be invaluable in monitoring ceasefires. Thirdly, especially for the peace enforcement function, NATO can supply forces of a size and quality unavailable elsewhere. Fourthly, within the Partnership for Peace (PFP) framework, NATO has been working with about two dozen countries from Eastern Europe and the former Soviet Union on matters related to peacekeeping and humanitarian assistance. Among other countries to join this Ad Hoc Group on Cooperation in Peacekeeping (AHG) are Sweden, Austria, Finland and Ireland – all with considerable experience in the field.

Finally, looking ahead, what areas of research should now preoccupy scholars interested in the academic study of peacekeeping? Firstly, there is a need to examine the impact of peacekeeping operations on the populations they purport to benefit. This requires fieldwork among people who may be coming to terms with the problems of economic and political reconstruction. Secondly, countries like Japan, Germany and South Africa are new to peacekeeping: but there is a role they can play and research is needed into three issues related to this – the reaction of public opinion in these countries to participation in peacekeeping; the most appropriate role these countries can play; and the reaction of other countries to the entry of these three to the peacekeeping arena. Thirdly, serious consideration needs to be given to the formation and composition of peacekeeping forces themselves. If nothing else emerges from the preceding chapters, it is clear that a distinction needs to be made between peacekeeping and peace enforcement not simply in a conceptual and operational sense, but in the composition, training and equipment of the respective forces involved. Peace enforcement activities are generally handled best by troops trained and equipped to react to ceasefire violations or to enforce the 'will of the international community'. Peacekeepers should in the future be more closely identified with the UN and less with their respective governments. Peacekeepers would be more likely to be constituted into, at least, regional if not global stand-by forces. They would be lightly armed (if at all) and their principal function would be to uphold the 'classic' interpretation of peacekeeping – the maintenance of a ceasefire by impartial interpositioning, with full consent of the erstwhile warring parties. The role of women, police and civilians could be much greater in this strictly interpreted peacekeeping role. Any transition from peacekeeping to peace enforcement would be clearly signalled as such by a new mandate, and new forces where the military–civilian and male–female balance would shift markedly in favour of the former in both cases. Military weaponry would be more apparent, and use of these weapons would be more likely. The distinction between these two types of operation could be further emphasized by the uniforms worn – the UN blue beret and uniform signifying 'traditional' peacekeeping, with more army-type uniforms reflecting the peace enforcement role. Although the UN would play a major role in both types of operation, research needs also to focus on the efficacy of regional organizations such as the OSCE, NATO and the OAS in preparing for, and implementing, operations like IFOR in Bosnia, or the EC mission to Russia in 1992.

The global environment at the end of the twentieth century has been characterized by one American writer as consisting of two worlds: one of growing economic development and integration, and one of increasing ethnic conflict, instability and chaos.[4] These two worlds are not separate or mutually exclusive: on the contrary they overlap and inter-sect in such a way that the forces of economic development and integ-ration actually generate much of the instability, disorder and conflict that feature prominently in what has been rather inappropriately referred to as the 'new world order'. The ending of the Cold War may be seen as the ending of an interlude in world history during which the international order was distracted by transient ideological dichotomies that cut unnaturally across deeper and more durable sources of ident-ity: ethnicity, nationalism and religion. Huntington's celebrated for-mulation of contemporary world politics as a 'clash of civilizations' sees people who were once separated by ideology coming together (as in Germany or Vietnam) while peoples held together by arbitrary cir-cumstance of history or the straitjacket of ideology have either fallen apart (as in the Soviet Union or Yugoslavia) or find themselves embroiled in turmoil (as in Sri Lanka or Kazakhstan). Such conflicts between opposed 'civilizations' contain the seeds of escalation if only because states and groups that share the same civilization as the com-batants rally to support their ethnic and cultural kin.

The implications of such a perspective for the future evolution of peacekeeping are clearly profound, but not entirely negative. On the one hand, the ending of the Cold War has facilitated cooperation between members of the Security Council by the 'decoupling of long-standing regional and internal conflicts from East–West rivalry'[5] while, on the other hand, it has increased both the number and variety of conflict situations in which the United Nations has felt compelled to intervene. Put very simply, the dilemma facing UN peacekeepers today is the choice between either getting involved in conflicts where outdated principles, procedures and practices, accu-mulated in the Cold War era, are patently inadequate, or not getting involved and incurring the wrath that inevitably follows any hesita-tion or inactivity on the part of the UN. The outbreak of savage inter-communal violence in Yugoslavia epitomized this predicament in the starkest terms. As Edith Klein pithily observed:

> [T]he literal and figurative location of this war, in the foothills of Europe and at the crossroads of East and West, and its timing, on the eve of European integration and just after the collapse of East European Communist regimes, aroused intense global concern.[6]

Not for the first time in modern history, the city of Sarajevo and its hinterland opened up a new epoch. It is an epoch in which the chal-lenges to peacekeeping are unlikely to disappear.

NOTES

1. *Wider Peacekeeping*, London: HMSO, 1994, para. 26
2. *The Economist*, 25 June 1994.
3. P.F. Diehl, *International Peacekeeping*, Baltimore, Md.: Johns Hopkins University Press, 1994, pp. 134–42.
4. S. Huntington, 'Clash of civilizations?', *Foreign Affairs*, Summer 1993, pp. 22–49.
5. M. Berdal, *Whither UN peacekeeping?*, Adelphi Papers 281, London: IISS, 1993, p. 3.
6. Edith Klein, 'Obstacles to conflict resolution in the territories of the former Yugoslavia', in D. Charters (ed.), *Peacekeeping and the Challenge of Civil Conflict Resolution*, Fredericton, University of New Brunswick, 1994, p. 149.

Appendix: United Nations Peacekeeping Operations*

This list includes the official United Nations peacekeeping operations, plus some United Nations operations which are often referred to as United Nations peacekeeping operations by other sources. The extra operations included are not considered United Nations peacekeeping operations by the United Nations for one of the following reasons: not under the command of the Secretary-General, no military personnel, or led by a specific UN agency. It has been my intention to broaden the scope, and to incorporate any operation which could be said to include some kind of peacekeeping, as long as they have gone beyond being a mere fact-finding mission. Therefore, UNCC, UNSCOB, ONUVEN and, ONUVEH are included.

Each operation has been listed chronologically (to date of initiation), with its abbreviation and duration in the first line, the full name in the second line. Each operation is then explained through the following headings:

- *Area.* The geographic area in which the peacekeeping operation was/is active.
- *Composition.* The number of personnel involved. For operations already terminated, the maximum strength is indicated, while for the ongoing operations, the current strength (as of November 1996) is indicated. When possible, the number of personnel is also divided into the following subgroups: military observers, troops, CIVPOLs and civilians (if not adjunct to military personnel). It should be noted that almost all operations do have international and local civilian staff attached to the operation, but the exact figures often fluctuate or are not available.
- *Remarks.* Any particular comments about the operation.

UNCC (August 1947–51)
United Nations Consular Commission
Area: Dutch East Indies/Indonesia.
Composition: Max. strength: 63 military observers.
* Compiled by Claus Heje, December 1996.

Remarks: A forerunner to UNTEA/UNSF. Not officially considered a United Nations peacekeeping operation.

UNSCOB (October 1947 – January 1952)
United Nations Special Commission on the Balkans
Area: Greek side of Greek borders.
Composition: Max. strength: 36 military observers.

UNTSO (June 1948 – Present)
United Nations Truce Supervision Organization
Area: Middle East.
Composition: Currently: 163 military observers.
Remarks: UNTSO has become sort of a 'training camp' for military observers. UNTSO military observers have assisted in setting up ONUC, UNYOM, UNGOMAP, UNIMOG, UNIKOM, UNPROFOR, ONUMOZ. Assists currently UNDOF and UNIFIL.

UNMOGIP (January 1949 – Present)
United Nations Military Observer Group in India and Pakistan
Area: Jammu/Kashmir.
Composition: Currently: 46 military observers.

UNEF I (November 1956 – June 1967)
United Nations Emergency Force
Area: Suez Canal, Sinai, Gaza.
Composition: Max. strength: 6,073 military troops.
Remarks: UNEF I ended due to Egypt's withdrawal of its consent.

UNOGIL (June 1958 – December 1958)
United Nations Observation Group in Lebanon
Area: Lebanon and Lebanese–Syrian border.
Composition: Max. strength: 591 military observers.

ONUC (July 1960 – June 1964)
United Nations Operations in the Congo
Area: Republic of Congo (later Zaire).
Composition: Max. strength: 19,828 military troops and 2,000 civilians.

Remarks: ONUC was more heavily armed than other peace-keeping forces and is sometimes referred to as a forerunner of peace enforcement operations.

UNTEA/UNSF (October 1962 – April 1963)
United Nations Temporary Executive Authority/United Nations Security Force
Area: West New Guinea (West Irian).
Composition: Max. strength: 1,576 military troops.
Remarks: UNSF was a rather unique case in the period, acting as a transitory authority in a sort of administrative 'vacuum'.

UNYOM (July 1963 – September 1964)
United Nations Yemen Observation Mission
Area: Yemen.
Composition: Max. strength: 25 military observers, 164 military troops.

UNFICYP (March 1964 – Present)
United Nations Force in Cyprus
Area: Cyprus.
Composition: Currently: 1,197 military troops and CIVPOLs.
Remarks: First operation with CIVPOLs.

DOMREP (May 1965 – October 1966)
Representative of the Secretary-General in the Dominican Republic
Area: Dominican Republic.
Composition: Max. strength: 2 military observers.

UNIPOM (September 1965 – March 1966)
United Nations India–Pakistan Observer Mission
Area: Along the Indian/Pakistan border outside the state of Jammu and Kashmir.
Composition: Max. strength: 96 military observers.

UNEF II (October 1973 – July 1979)
Second United Nations Emergency Force
Area: Suez Canal, Sinai.
Composition: Max. strength: 6,973 military troops.

Remarks: The so-called 'UNEF II rules' are often referred to as the principles of traditional peacekeeping.

UNDOF (June 1974 – Present)
United Nations Disengagement Observer Force
Area: Syrian Golan Heights.
Composition: Currently: 1,053 military troops.
Remarks: Approximately 80 military observers from UNTSO assist the operation.

UNIFIL (March 1978 – Present)
United Nations Interim Force in Lebanon
Area: Southern Lebanon
Composition: Currently: 4,526 military troops.
Remarks: Approximately 60 military observers from UNTSO assist the operation.

UNGOMAP (April 1988 – March 1990)
United Nations Good Offices Mission in Afghanistan
Area: Afghanistan, Pakistan.
Composition: Max. strength: 50 military observers.
Remarks: Not always seen as 'real' peacekeeping, but as the Secretary-General's Good Offices.

UNIMOG (August 1988 – February 1991)
United Nations Iran–Iraq Military Observer Group
Area: Iran and Iraq.
Composition: Max. strength: 400 military observers and troops.

UNAVEM I (January 1989 – June 1992)
United Nations Angola Verification Group
Area: Angola.
Composition: Max. strength: 70 military observers.

UNTAG (April 1989 – March 1990)
United Nations Transition Assistance Group
Area: Namibia, Angola.
Composition: Max. strength: 4,500 military troops, 1,500 CIV-POLs, 2,000 civilians.
Remarks: The first multi-component peacekeeping operation.

ONUVEN (August 1989 – February 1990)
United Nations Observation Mission for the Verification of Elections in Nicaragua

Area:	Nicaragua.
Composition:	Max. strength: 120 civilian observers.
Remarks:	Not officially considered peacekeeping by the UN because there were no military personnel involved in the operation.

ONUCA (November 1989 – January 1992)
United Nations Observer Group in Central America

Area:	Costa Rica, El Salvador, Guatemala, Honduras, Nicaragua.
Composition:	Max. strength: 1,098 military troops.

ONUVEH (1990–91)
United Nations Observer Group for the Verification of Elections in Haiti

Area:	Haiti.
Composition:	Max. strength: 265 civilians
Remarks:	Like ONUVEN, not officially considered peacekeeping by the UN because there were no military personnel involved in the operation.

UNIKOM (April 1991 – Present)
United Nations Iraq–Kuwait Observation Mission

Area:	Demilitarized zone (DMZ) along the border between Iraq and Kuwait.
Composition:	Currently: 1,112 military observers and troops.

UNAVEM II (June 1991 – February 1995)
United Nations Angola Verification Mission II

Area:	Angola.
Composition:	Max. strength: 350 military observers, 126 CIV-POLs, 400 electoral monitors.
Remarks:	Replaced by UNAVEM III.

ONUSAL (July 1991 – April 1995)
United Nations Observer Mission in El Salvador

Area:	El Salvador.

Composition: Max. strength: 380 military observers, 631 CIV-POLs, 900 electoral monitors.

MINURSO (September 1991 – Present)
United Nations Mission for the Referendum in Western Sahara
Area: Western Sahara.
Composition: Currently: 230 military observers and CIVPOLs.

UNAMIC (October 1991 – March 1992)
United Nations Advance Mission in Cambodia
Area: Cambodia.
Composition: Max. strength: 1,504 military and civilian personnel.
Remarks: Replaced by UNTAC.

UNTAC (March 1992 – September 1993)
United Nations Transitional Authority in Cambodia
Area: Cambodia.
Composition: Max. strength: 22,000 military and civilian staff.
Remarks: UNTAC absorbed at its start UNAMIC.

UNPROFOR (March 1992 – December 1995)
United Nations Protection Force
Area: I Crotia. II: Bosnia-Hercegovina. III: Macedonia.
Composition: Max. strength: 38,614 military troops, 637 military observers, 671 CIVPOLs.
Remarks: UNPROFOR is the largest UN peacekeeping operation ever. The mandate and objectives of the three areas varied and changed during the operation. In March 1995 UNPROFOR was restructured and divided into three operations: UNCRO in Croatia, UNPROFOR in Bosnia-Hercegovina, and UNPREDEP in Macedonia. The three operations were, until January 1996, interlinked, and under the command and control of UNPF (United Nations Peace Forces), which was also responsible for liaison with NATO. The NATO-led IFOR (Implementation Force) took over from UNPROFOR in December 1996.

UNOSOM (April 1992 – April 1993)
United Nations Operation in Somalia

Area: Somalia.
Composition: Max. strength: 4,219 military troops.
Remarks: In November 1992, UNOSOM was allowed to use
                 force. From December 1992 UNOSOM worked in
                 conjunction with UNITAF (Unified Task Force)
                 which, spearheaded by the United States, consisted
                 of approximately 37,000 troops. UNOSOM was
                 replaced by UNOSOM II.

ONUMOZ (December 1992 – December 1994)
United Nations Operation in Mozambique
Area: Mozambique.
Composition: Max. strength: 6,625 military troops, 354 military
                 observers, 1,144 CIVPOLs, 900 electoral monitors.

UNOSOM II (May 1993 – March 1995)
United Nations Operation in Somalia II
Area: Somalia.
Composition: Max. strength: 25,945 military troops.

UNOMUR (June 1993 – September 1994)
United Nations Observer Mission Uganda–Rwanda
Area: Ugandan side of the Uganda–Rwanda border.
Composition: Max. strength: 81 military observers.
Remarks: Integrated into UNAMIR.

UNOMIG (August 1993 – Present)
United Nations Observer Mission in Georgia
Area: Georgia.
Composition: Currently: 124 military observers.

UNOMIL (September 1993 – Present)
United Nations Observer Mission in Liberia
Area: Liberia.
Composition: Currently: 60 military observers.
Remarks: Operates in cooperation with ECOMOG, a mono-
                 toring group established by ECOWAS.

UNMIH (September 1993 – June 1996)
United Nations Mission in Haiti
Area: Haiti.

Composition: Max. strength: 1,200 military troops, 300 CIVPOLs.

UNAMIR (October 1993 – March 1996)
United Nations Assistance Mission for Rwanda
Area: Rwanda.
Composition: Max. strength: 5,500 military troops, 320 military
                 observers, 120 CIVPOLs.

UNASOG (May 1994 – June 1994)
United Nations Aouzou Strip Observer Group
Area: Aouzou Strip between Chad and Libya.
Composition: Max. strength: 9 military observers.

UNMOT (December 1994 – Present)
United Nations Mission of Observers in Tadjikistan
Area: Tadjikistan.
Composition: Currently: 44 military observers.

UNAVEM III (February 1995 – Present)
United Nations Angola Verification Group III
Area: Angola.
Composition: Currently: 7,138 military observers, troops and CIV-
                 POLs.

UNCRO (March 1995 – January 1996)
United Nations Confidence Restoration Operation in Croatia
Area: Croatia.
Composition: Max. strength: 14,663 military troops, 328 military
                 observers and 531 CIVPOLs.
Remarks: Detached from UNPROFOR. Command and con-
                 trol by UNPF.

UNPREDEP (March 1995 – Present)
United Nations Preventive Deployment Force
Area: Macedonia.
Composition: Currently: 1,087 military observers, troops and CIV-
                 POLs.
Remarks: Detached from UNPROFOR. March 1995 – Janu-
                 ary 1996: command and control by UNPF. Since
                 then, independent operation. Only example of a pre-
                 ventive deployment until present.

UNMIBH (December 1995 – Present)
United Nations Mission in Bosnia and Hercegovina.
Area: Bosnia and Hercegovina.
Composition: Currently: 1,707 CIVPOLs.
Remarks: Cooperates with the NATO deployment in Bosnia-
                   Hercegovina (in 1996 IFOR, and in 1997 SFOR
                   (Stability Force). Only CIVPOLs.

UNTAES (January 1996 – Present)
United Nations Transitional Administration for Eastern Slavonia,
Baranja and Western Sirmium
Area: Provinces in Croatia.
Composition: Currently: 5,405 military troops, observers and CIV-
                   POLs.

UNMOP (January 1996 – Present)
United Nations Mission of Observers in Prevlaka
Area: Prevlaka peninsula, Croatia.
Composition: Currently: 27 military observers.
Remarks: Replacing functions of UNCRO in Prevlaka.

UNSMIH (July 1996 – Present)
United Nations Support Mission in Haiti
Area: Haiti.
Composition: 1,588 military observers and troops.

Index